BOOKS & LIFE

Books & Life

Jan Clausen

Ohio State University Press • Columbus

The lines from "My Goodbyes," "Toward the Jurassic Age," "We Were Three," and "Santa Ana in the Dark" are reprinted from *Flowers from the Volcano* by Claribel Alegría, translated by Carolyn Forché, by permission of the University of Pittsburgh Press. © 1982 by Claribel Alegría and Carolyn Forché.

The lines from "Artemis" are reprinted from *Beginning with O* by Olga Broumas, by permission of Yale University Press. © 1977 by Olga Broumas.

Excerpts from Joy Harjo's *She Had Some Horses* are reprinted by permission of Thunder's Mouth Press.

The lines from June Jordan's "Gettin Down to Get Over" are reprinted by permission of the author.

The lines from "School Note" and "A Litany for Survival" are reprinted from *The Black Unicorn*, poems by Audre Lorde, by permission of W. W. Norton & Company, Inc. Copyright © 1978 by Audre Lorde.

Excerpts from Nancy Morejón's *Where the Island Sleeps Like a Wing* are reprinted by permission of The Black Scholar Press.

The lines from "Tradition," "Lake Superior," "Paean to Place," "Old Mother," "In the great snowfall," and "Wintergreen Ridge" are reprinted from *The Granite Pail*, copyright © 1985 by Lorine Niedecker, edited by Cid Corman. Published by North Point Press and reprinted by permission.

Excerpts from Grace Paley's *Leaning Forward* are reprinted by permission of Granite Press.

Library of Congress Cataloging-in-Publication Data

Clausen, Jan, 1950–
  Books & life.

  Bibliography: p.
  1. Books—Reviews.   2. Feminism—Book reviews.
3. Poetry—Book reviews.   4. Women—Book reviews.
I. Title.   II. Title: Book and life.
PS3553.L348B6   1989   814'.54   88-17975
ISBN 0-8142-0465-1
ISBN 0-8142-0470-8 (pbk.)

Printed in the U.S.A.

Books & Life is for Rima Shore,
long-time companion in my experience of both.

ACKNOWLEDGMENTS

"A Movement of Poets: Thoughts on Poetry and Feminism" originally appeared in *The New Women's Times Feminist Review* in three installments, #18 (November/December 1981); #19 (January/February 1982); and #20 (March/April 1982). The essay was reprinted as a Long Haul Press pamphlet in 1982.

The six "Books & Life" columns appeared as follows: "Books & Life" in *The New Women's Times Feminist Review* 31 (January/February 1984); "If We're Allowed to Live" in *The New Women's Times Feminist Review* 32 (March/April 1984); "On Reading Men" in *The New Women's Times Feminist Review* 33 (May/June 1984); " 'A Revolution of Poets': The Impact of Nicaragua" in *The New Women's Times Feminist Review* 36 (November/December 1984); "The Political Morality of Fiction, Part I" in *off our backs* XV 6 (June 1985); "The Political Morality of Fiction, Part II" in *off our backs* XV 7 (July 1985).

The review of *Women on the Breadlines, Harvest, Song for My Time*, and *Rites of Ancient Ripening* by Meridel LeSueur appeared in *Conditions: Three* (1978). The review of *Shikasta* by Doris Lessing appeared in *The New Women's Times Feminist Review*, April 25–May 8, 1980. The review of *This Bridge Called My Back: Writings by Radical Women of Color*, edited by Cherrie Moraga and Gloria Anzaldúa, appeared in *Conditions: Eight* (1982). The review of *Right-Wing Women* by Andrea Dworkin appeared in *Womanews* IV 5 (May 1983). The review of *Woman's Worth: Sexual Economics and the World of Women* appeared in *The New Women's Times Feminist Review* 27 (May/June 1983). The review of *Flowers from the Volcano* by Claribel Alegría and *She Had Some Horses* by Joy Harjo appeared in *The Women's Review of Books* II 1 (October 1984). The review of *The Granite Pail* by Lorine Niedecker, *Leaning Forward* by Grace Paley, and *Where the Island Sleeps Like a Wing* by Nancy Morejón appeared in *The Women's Review of Books* III 10 (July 1986). The review of *Letters from Nicaragua* by Rebecca Gordon appeared in slightly different form in *The*

Village Voice, December 16, 1986; reprinted with permission of the author and *The Village Voice*, © 1986.

"Women and Militarism: Some Questions for Feminists" originally appeared in *off our backs* XI 1 (January 1981), and was reprinted in *WIN Magazine*, March 1981, under the title "Is Militarism a Feminist Issue? (And Other Pertinent Questions . . .)." "To Live Outside the Law You Must Be Honest: A Flommy Looks at Lesbian Parenting" was delivered as the keynote address at a conference entitled "Mother's Courage: Lesbians Creating a Parenting Community," Albany, New York, April 5, 1986. First published in *off our backs* XVI 8 (August–September 1986), it was reprinted in *Politics of the Heart, a Lesbian Parenting Anthology*, edited by Sandra Pollack and Jeanne Vaughn (Firebrand Books, 1987).

"Mending the Silences" was delivered at the St. Mark's Poetry Project, New York City, February 25, 1987.

CONTENTS

INTRODUCTION

Ever since I can remember I've enjoyed using language. In a sense it's also been the path of least resistance. As a child I quickly learned the advantages of being able to impress grownups with my large vocabulary, to slip through the escape hatch a library book offered. Now the attempt to tame experience by writing it down almost always seems to come naturally, if not without effort. In the realm of action, on the other hand— whether it's pounding a nail, rearing a daughter, or planning a political demonstration—I usually feel like a clumsy if assiduous amateur. How much simpler life would be if I could only be persuaded, as so many writers (including some feminists) conveniently are, that language can be *enough*, that naked syllables have power to change reality, or to compensate for the planet's harrowing shortcomings. Instead, I perch on the cusp of art and activism. A central theme of this collection is expressed in my introduction to the "Books & Life" columns which provide the book's title: "passionate involvement with the written word" tempered by "sober consciousness" of all that language cannot do.

"Remember, the trees are real/remember this, in your city": these lines from a poem I wrote some years ago suggest a second theme, a certain resolute off-centeredness, an insistence—from New York, the Belly of the Beast—on the values of the periphery. I grew up in the far Northwestern corner of the country, impressed by the power of forests, mountains, ocean; on that cool foggy edge, everything made by people, language included, was clearly secondary. My parents were upwardly mobile Minnesota natives, farm life and Europe not far behind them, who'd gone to college (majoring in forestry and home economics) but knew how to work with their hands, expected practical results. We were sturdy provincials, proud of "our" land, like most white North Americans culpably indifferent to the habit of genocide that had given it to us—but at least we nursed a healthy disrespect for the authority of the East, that remote grey power center where history was made, which beamed us grainy images of presidents and armies. I would go on explicitly to reject that history, that power: first as a disaffected high school girl on the fringes of hippiedom, then as a college dropout whose initial exposure to radical politics had come through a Black Student Union sit-in and anti-war protests on my campus.

Apparently this provincial education somehow produced in me an appetite for unpopular pursuits, questionable companionship, and truth invisible to the naked "mainstream" eye. That appetite both fostered and is honed by my feminism. Undoubtedly I was able to get involved with the movement for women's liberation in the early 1970s partly because I was already attuned to injustice that slips through the cracks of the network news reports, and solutions undreamed of by two-party-system thinking. On the other hand, living as a feminist and lesbian has placed me on an edge that continues to sharpen what might be termed a sort of social "peripheral vision," prompting me to look for allies and explanations in out-of-the-way corners. A small but significant instance of this is the fact that the bulk of the poetry, fiction, and theory discussed here was published by small presses, many of them feminist. The alternative / women's press movement has been one of the key provincial settings of my adult life, invaluable for its championing of books that would never have seen print in the metropolis of commercial publishing.

If I locate myself in the margins (which after all is only to say that I embrace the culture's estimation of my rebellious womanhood), certainly this is not a matter of resignation or modesty. Rather, it flows from a conviction, shared by those I count teachers and peers, that the hinterlands of empire, the "back yards" and back alleys, the colonies and kitchens, are in the process of emerging as our capitals and heartlands, diffused pulse-points of the life we dream of building on the ruins of dead cities. I aspire to membership in that motley throng of outsiders who intend to remake reality in our own multitudinous image—that is, with all the discounted, disrespected, historically "disappeared" experience of oppression and desire, sorrow and triumph—*our own stories*—given voice and weight at last. What engages me is an insurgent literature and practice— whether labeled as lesbian or Third World feminist, Marxist or pacifist or Sandinista.

My reflections on that literature and practice are organized here into five sections. "A Movement of Poets: Thoughts on Poetry and Feminism," published in 1981, opens the collection; the closing piece, "Mending the Silences: New Directions for Feminist Poetry," from a talk delivered in 1987, recapitulates and then develops further some of my ideas about the possibilities and limitations of an art form shaped in the heart of an activist movement. These two extended examinations of poetry and politics combine to form a sort of parenthesis enclosing three sections arranged internally in the chronological order in which the individual pieces appeared: "Books & Life (columns written for the *New Women's Times Feminist Review* in 1984 and 1985); "Reviews" (eight reviews of fiction, theory, and poetry which appeared between 1978 and 1986); and "Struggle" (an essay on women and militarism from 1981, a speech on lesbian parenting from 1986, and another essay, completed specifically for this volume, on feminism in the Central America solidarity movement).

Among the ambitious periphery dwellers at the heart of this collection are the guerrilla poets of the early years of feminism's Second Wave whom I discuss in "A Movement of Poets." These women, many of them lesbians, dared to hope that their blunt, even harsh commentary on the female condition would find an audience of sisters; they sought that audience through the most direct means possible, the roughly printed broadsides and chapbooks, the underground newspapers, and the open readings that strongly influenced emerging feminist consciousness. In the "Books & Life" section I consider theory by a range of guerrilla thinkers who focus on the relationship between female experience and the chronic states of war (frequently disguised, in Cynthia Enloe's phrase, as "militarised peacetime") in which most contemporary societies are enmeshed. This anti-militarist theory is little known and incomplete, but richly suggestive of a range of crucial questions bearing on women's oppression, U.S. imperialism, and the nuclear threat.

In the "Reviews" section a few rebel voices particularly stand out for me. One is that of Meridel LeSueur, who, working in the context of Communist Party organizing in the 1930s, produced in fiction and journalism a lasting, unique vision of Midwestern working people. She survived the living burial of the McCarthy years to emerge, a "Lady Lazarus" as she wryly calls herself, something of a national figure in her old age. The contributors to *This Bridge Called My Back: Writings by Radical Women of Color* dare to insist on what co-editor Cherríe Moraga calls "the specificity of the oppression," as well as the specificity of their cultural strengths. As I think back now on the impact and implications of this classic anthology, I'm enormously moved by its courageous depth, its sheer, undated *relevance*. Lorine Niedecker's is a quiet but tenacious dissidence: loyal throughout her life to her provincial birthplace, Lake Koshkonong, Wisconsin, she clung to two unfashionable passions, nature and poetry. An unsentimental celebrator of Midwestern working-class life, for me she makes a piquant counterbalance to the exuberant, ideological LeSueur, her elder by three years and temperamental opposite.

The article "Women and Militarism: Some Questions for Feminists" in the section "Struggle" was prompted by the Women's Pentagon Action, a group of feminists who organized to demonstrate against the war machine in the fall of 1980, well before the nuclear nightmare became (so briefly you missed it if you blinked) a cover story in newsmagazines. "Premature anti-militarists," we might have been called, after the "premature anti-fascists" who provoked right-wing suspicion by risking their necks in Spain trying to stop Franco at a point when fighting Nazis had not yet become an acceptably all-American crusade. (That's another hallmark of the upstarts who attract me: a lousy sense of timing.) In another arena of insurgency, personal and private yet politically charged, the lesbian parents to whom I addressed "To Live Outside the Law You Must be Honest: A Flommy Looks at Lesbian Parenting" reject the fetish of blood kinship and conventional family structure, insisting instead on the positive potential (for adults and children both) of a range of variations on the theme of motherhood.

Each one of these examples, I believe, constitutes a radical challenge to the cultural and political hegemony that white / bourgeois / heteropatriarchy currently enjoys in the "United States of North America" (Sandino's name for us). Yet to be a radical in North America is often a shifty, ambiguous business. It's hard to find a footing in the Empire's soggy center; in fact, it sometimes feels like struggling in the bowels of a marshmallow. Not that the powers that be don't intend to bury us; it's just that, with rare exceptions, we're unlikely to be directly targeted in a manner commensurate with the threat we'd like to represent. Sometimes the price of escaping dramatic martyrdom is being absorbed, shrugged off, worn down, ignored, co-opted. Or consigned to a safe past tense: "the protests of the sixties." For those of us whom skin or economic privilege has shielded from the offhand, everyday brutality which the land of opportunity showers on its second-class citizens, these conditions can generate a false sense of invulnerability, making it very difficult to set priorities. Contact with other realities, other struggles both grimmer and more sharply delineated than our own, can hold invaluable lessons.

Over the past few years the region-wide liberation effort in Central America and the Caribbean has often played that role for me. I discuss its impact in the essay "In Pieces: A Feminist in the Central America Solidarity Movement" and in several columns and reviews which focus on the Nicaraguan revolution, that much mythologized yet achingly concrete, contradictory, floundering, authentically heroic instance of the periphery's challenge to a rigid center. Self-determination also emerges as a theme in reviews of poetry by Salvadoran Claribel Alegría and Afro-Cuban Nancy Morejón who, writing out of a rich tradition of politically engaged poetry (or should I say poetically charged politics?), affirm the autonomous life of *their* America and resolve to recast its thus far bitter destiny.

I find I've been speaking of *my* affinities and *my* preoccupations, almost as though the contents of this book could be separated from the community of women within and to which it was written. But of course my concerns have been profoundly shaped by my residence in a busy, ever-changing "neighborhood" of literate dissidents. This is not the place to name names or trace in detail the convoluted story of attraction and dissension, love and rivalry and enmity, that is the history of my generation of feminist writers—that will have to wait for tell-all memoirs, or oral histories finally recorded in the mythic tranquility of the Lesbian Old Age Home. Suffice it to say that I've been incredibly fortunate that not only the nationwide community of writers and activists which feminism created, but also my literal, local neighborhood of Park Slope, Brooklyn, have placed me in the center of a web of accomplices, teachers, critics.

Most of these comrades have been, like me, preoccupied by a mix of art and politics; most have been, like me, intellectuals without being academics; most have been lesbians; most have been involved at some time or other with the feminist small press publishing movement—since for the dissident writer control over the means of reproduction of the work is often the one sure guarantee of free expression. Unlike me, a majority come from backgrounds that distance them from the self-anointed "center" of the white, middle-class, Christian: they are Jewish, Black, Latina,

working-class. Their daringly nuanced versions of identity politics, their
courage, their language, their stories have influenced every piece of writing in this book. A few of them figure in it even more directly, since on
occasion I've reviewed work by personal friends, which puts an end right
there to the masquerade of critical "objectivity"—though not, I believe,
to honest criticism, an endeavor that's almost never emotionally neutral.

Among various small press projects and other shoestring institutions
which for years helped give this network an informal but indispensable
cohesiveness, *Conditions* magazine, of which I was a co-founder, deserves
special mention. The four of us who started *Conditions* in 1976 all saw it, I
believe, as an effort to create, virtually from scratch, a context for what
we then perceived to be our unprecedentedly woman-identified lives and
writing. We were discovering as much as attempting to define the pa-
rameters and possibilities of a new poetry and fiction, coming to grips
with what might constitute a truly feminist criticism. For me, work on
the magazine was not only a major source of a sense of literary and political community throughout the latter half of the 1970s, but a central
influence on my thinking about art and politics. Though my editorial
stint ended in 1981 before the majority of the pieces included here were
written, lessons it taught me permeate this book.

Perversely yet predictably enough, when at last I succeed in finding a
longed-for community I sometimes discover that its embrace results in
claustrophobia. "For the embattled / there is no place / that cannot be /
home / nor is" (Lorde, "School Note," 55). The beleaguered communities of the periphery, self-defined in opposition to the dominant
culture, too often resort to a defensive orthodoxy. Or they simply become inbred, self-satisfied, boring. For me the critical impulse, the need
to make distinctions, to analyze my attractions and reservations, has always tempered my keenest enthusiasms.

Threaded throughout this collection are two major critical themes.
The first is my objection to the tendency, common to many political
movements, to apply dogmatic ideological yardsticks to poetry and fiction; "A Movement of Poets: Thoughts on Poetry and Feminism" and
"The Political Morality of Fiction," completed in 1981 and 1985 respectively, represent two different stages of my wrestling with that subject.
The second, less explicitly developed here, is my response to a specific
branch of feminist theory, radical feminism, which regards women's op-

pression as the primary contradiction, the single underlying flaw, in the vast scheme of global inequities. Both "The Political Morality of Fiction" and my review of *Woman's Worth: Sexual Economics and the World of Women* contain brief discussions of my problems with this approach.

Though a number of Third World feminists, socialist feminists, and others have taken strong exception to some of radical feminism's tenets, very little has been attempted in the way of overall critique,* with the result that popular books by radical feminists (for instance, Mary Daly, Andrea Dworkin, and Susan Griffin) are too often perceived by readers both sympathetic and hostile to women's liberation as defining the undisputed outlines of contemporary feminist thought. At one time I was sufficiently disturbed by the impact of radical feminist assumptions on a range of feminist writing and political practice to plan an essay on the subject. I wanted to object to a "ranking of oppressions" which seemed to me grossly inadequate to account for the complex causes of human suffering worldwide; I also wanted to analyze the way in which some radical feminist theory has, ironically enough, simply turned traditional philosophy "on its head," reversing classic Western patriarchal dualism in a crude equation of everything female with what is good and life-affirming, everything male with what is bad and destructive.

I intended to argue for a less Euro-American centered and ahistorical view, and one that conformed more closely to my own experience of women's knack for competition as well as nurturance. I felt we needed to get back to the earlier feminist insight that both "male" and "female" values and roles were parts of a problematic whole that needed drastic alteration. Further, I found inadequate an idealist approach which seemed fixated on changing language and consciousness—not material factors in our lives—as the single key to ending women's oppression. I thought of titling this essay "After the Fall: Radical Feminism and the Earthly Predicament" by way of calling attention to radical feminism's basic moralism, its thinly disguised reworking of old myths of sin and redemption.

---

*See, however, Alice Echols's "The Taming of the Id: Feminist Sexual Politics, 1968–83," in Vance: 50–72. Echols analyzes what she calls "cultural feminism" (to distinguish it from the approach of earlier "radical feminists" such as the Redstockings, Shulamith Firestone, etc.) in terms of problems with its approach to female sexuality. She identifies, among the major texts of cultural feminism, books published in the second half of the 1970s by Adrienne Rich, Mary Daly, Janice Raymond, Kathleen Barry, and Susan Griffin.

Other projects intervened, and "After the Fall" stayed in the note stage. It nevertheless constitutes a sort of ghostly presence here, given that the critical perspective I've just sketched underlies so much in these essays and reviews. That perspective might be stated in positive terms as a quest for a balanced materialist feminism, one determined to engage with a gorgeous as well as corrupt universe, and which scants neither the spirit nor the imagination. I find foreshadowings and fragments of such theory in some of the books discussed here; *This Bridge Called My Back* and Rebecca Gordon's *Letters from Nicaragua* spring to mind immediately, as well as some of the poetry and fiction. I want to see that theory developed further, in more concrete terms, to enable feminists to tackle the world (as we're doing increasingly in a range of coalitions) in a way that doesn't risk neglecting earlier insights about women's specific and diverse experience.

I write this in a time of uncertainty and change. I began, in fact, in a pessimistic mood, attuned to a history of failure as well as of achievement, rather sharply missing the familiar, too-insular "women's community" I restlessly inhabited five or ten years ago, its narrowness balanced by intensity and a sense of common purpose. In that frame of mind, the past looked littered with losses, with might-have-beens: the collectives that dissolved, presses and bookstores that went under, political groups that self-destructed, lesbian couples that broke up. The eighties have been rough on North American progressives. Feminists *are* some of "the embattled," and we've paid a heavy price for our victories, one that needs to be acknowledged. That realization, that sense of fragility, may have something to do with my interest in "Mending the Silences." Contemplation balances activity—though our political schemes so seldom make room for it.

Yet, as I continue to mull over not only the recent past but a much lengthier sweep of feminist agitation, I feel a renewal of ambition, a surge of energy. The fact that my life these days takes me to many places where my feminism seems an alien concept (a village in Nicaragua's war zone, a class of first-year college students, a Central America solidarity group with roots in the "male left") begins to sound like more of an opportunity, less some shameful badge of failure. What can I learn in these settings, what can I teach? An offhand phrase in "To Live Outside the Law You Must Be Honest" catches my eye, a reference to "complicated efforts to figure out some tolerable way of living as a woman." This—in a collective, not merely personal, sense—is after all what feminism means: our struggle to invent (not just imagine, but create the preconditions for) some ways of being female that we can stand, that don't kill us off before our time or stunt our growth. And that project isn't going out of style anytime soon.

Have I written too much about life, not enough about books? If so, what follows will redress the balance. For if as an activist I'm aware of all those places and situations in which language falls short, that doesn't change the fact that words are what I do best. For me, in the end books and life are not opposites or enemies—that view yet another figment of Western patriarchal dualism!—but lovers, comingled, interpenetrating. In the face of dense, chaotic, almighty experience, I turn to my flimsy craft. In protest. In celebration.

I

A MOVEMENT OF POETS: THOUGHTS ON POETRY AND FEMINISM

In January 1974, then 23 years old, I came to Brooklyn in search of feminism. I took the GG train from Queens, where in the weeks since my arrival from Portland, Oregon, I'd been living in Flushing with a male lover. My destination was the New York Women's School, an ambitious new outpost of the Women's Liberation Movement housed in a decrepit brownstone on Ninth Street in Park Slope, which at that time was still a comfortably blowsy neighborhood years away from its more recent incarnation as a free-fire zone for developers and real estate brokers.

Several of the Women's School's peer-taught courses attracted me. One was the class on lesbianism; however, though I'd had one affair with a woman and badly wanted to have another, I was afraid to risk the criticism I thought my current lifestyle might occasion. I ended up joining a women's literature class instead, and there met several women who would figure in my life throughout the next decade and beyond.

Many of the School's principal organizers had previously been involved with the anti-war movement and student protests, so its feminism had a leftish tinge which suited my own (somewhat formless) political sympathies. The "anti-imperialist" perspective of a group associated with the Prairie Fire Organizing Committee would affect my thinking significantly, though I was turned off by an ideological rigidity which swiftly destroyed the School's potential as a gathering place for radical women with a range of views. Still, it was through the Women's School that I would enter an atmosphere in which feminist poetry and activism intersected on an almost daily basis.

What I recall from that time in the mid-seventies is a unique and fertile eclecticism. Along with other members of the women's literature class, I attended several poetry readings, including one in the studios of radio station WBAI which featured Adrienne Rich and Robin Morgan, then often publicly paired as the authors of two sensational volumes of radical feminist poetry, *Diving into the Wreck* and *Monster.* I read Margaret Randall's *Part of the Solution* and *Cuban Women Now.* I went to poetry benefits to raise money for the legal expenses of Joann Little and Inez Garcia, two women who'd "fought back" against rape and faced criminal charges for it. Later I was introduced to the prison poetry of Assata Shakur, and with some of the Women's School "anti-imperialists" demonstrated in front of the courthouse during her New Jersey trial.

Through a contact made in the literature class, I was invited to join a group which named itself Seven Women Poets and functioned as a sort of combination poetry workshop, coming out C-R group, dating service, and booking agency for reading gigs. I left Queens and my male lover— who was coming out himself—and moved to Park Slope. During this time I was writing the poems that would make up *After Touch,* my first book. Working cooperatively with three other lesbians who had manuscripts they wanted to self-publish, I issued *After Touch* under the imprint of Out & Out Books and got my first taste of alternative publishing.

It was in part the flavor of this remarkable time that I was trying to recapture when in 1981 I sat down to write "A Movement of Poets." As the essay itself makes clear, by then I'd begun to have a strong sense of the historical character of Second Wave feminism, which had already gone through several developmental phases and one day would belong to history altogether. Rereading my words now in what feels like a much later stage, I'm glad that I made the effort to call attention to the circumstances under which modern feminist poetry first flourished and the central facts of its development, facts which are so easily forgotten as fragile artifacts disappear (when, for instance, small press books go out of print) and fragile memories fade.

At the same time, I can now see that in 1981 I was writing in the shadow of troublesome questions about ideology and art that would become more pressing for me as the 1980s wore on. It startles me to read my own statement that I sometimes "fled the typewriter in tears," since the challenge to feminist orthodoxy mounted by "A Movement of Poets" now seems rather mild and tentative to me. What, I wonder, seemed so threatening? Yet I must have sensed I was asking questions that would only lead to other questions.

A Movement of Poets: Thoughts on Poetry and Feminism

From a world where my poems were as necessary as bread I came into a
world where no one needs poems, neither my poems nor any poems, where
poems are needed like—dessert: if anyone—needs—dessert . . .
    —Marina Tsvetaeva, 1936

The relationship of poets to the American feminist movement has been, in the decade and more since the inception of the still-unfolding "Second Wave," remarkable, crucial, and in one sense at least thoroughly astounding. Not that there is by now anything particularly surprising in the assertion that feminism has made possible the recent notable development of women's poetry (what term is, by the way, adequately descriptive of this phenomenon: renaissance? flowering? earthquake? volcanic eruption?); that this tremendous release of poetic energy cannot be understood without reference to the catalytic role of feminism as ideology, political movement, and cultural/material support network. For if we are feminists, so much of what we do has in some sense been made possible by the movement; it seems quite natural that the force which has everywhere in our lives produced transformative bursts of insight, extraordinary and unanticipated displays of creative activism, should have had its impact on our literature as well. More startling—for poets can rarely expect to exert much social influence—is the evident merit of the reverse proposition: that any serious investigation of the development of contemporary feminism must take into account the catalytic role of poets and poetry; that there is some sense in which it can be said that poets have made possible the movement.

It might even be claimed, at the risk of some exaggeration, that poets *are* the movement. Certainly poets are some of feminism's most influential activists, theorists, and spokeswomen; at the same time, poetry has become a favorite means of self-expression, consciousness-raising, and communication among large numbers of women not publicly known as poets. This article represents my effort to grasp the significance of this

3

singular conjunction of a literary form and a political movement—in particular, its implications for the contemporary feminist poet and her work.

It seems to me high time that we attempted such an analysis. The feminist poetry movement has come of age, having been around long enough to have produced a substantial and diverse body of work created by a loosely knit but vitally interdependent nationwide community of writers. We might even be said to have an historical tradition: the words "feminist poetry" themselves suggest a substantially different phenomenon from the one they might have suggested a decade ago, and it will, I think, be instructive to examine how we got here from there, and to inquire in what direction we may be headed.

However, my *need* to undertake this project really had little to do with such well-reasoned considerations. In fact, I began it in an effort to come to grips with my own situation as a feminist poet; to account for a sense— ill-defined, half-conscious, and ignored for months or perhaps years—of dissatisfaction, blockage, of being somehow hampered in my movements, not only as a writer of my own poems, but as a reader of the poetry of others.

To begin to take this uneasiness seriously has not been a simple matter. I have found it easy enough to blame my inattention to poetry on my involvement with fiction, without really exploring the factors that have made one form more attractive than the other. In part, I have been discouraged from admitting my dissatisfaction by the very success of the feminist poetry movement. The feminist press resounds with the good news of our triumphs: the supportiveness of our networks, the strength of our positive, woman-centered vision, the power of burgeoning consciousness released into speech. What sort of ingrate am I, a published and in many ways privileged feminist poet, to be feeling isolated, at odds with what I perceive as the "mainstream" of feminist poetry? Whatever ails me is probably a private, personal, rather embarrassing affliction best not talked about.

Such, at any rate, has been the counsel of a nagging internal voice I have had to ignore in order to attempt this article, the writing of which has proven extraordinarily difficult. At times, neither my personal perspective nor any generalizations I might attempt have seemed to me likely to interest anyone; at times I've fled the typewriter in tears, feeling quite irrationally that somehow not only the success of this article but the validity of my own identity as a poet, perhaps even as a feminist, was at stake. And yet I have clung to the suspicion that my difficulties and doubts have everything to do with the dilemmas of being a feminist poet, from the basic material level on which I have trouble justifying an investment of time in writing an article on poetry (guaranteed to appeal to a very limited audience and to produce no income whatsoever) to the intellectual and moral level on which I find myself repeatedly hobbled by the fear of saying the wrong thing, of being "politically incorrect" (as we laughingly term it, implying we're far too sophisticated to *believe* in such a concept, much less allow it to determine what we write, or don't). I have clung to the hope of uncovering those tensions or contradictions endemic to a literature embedded in a political movement, a politics largely shaped by literature, which might help to explain my dissatisfactions and uncertainties.

Throughout this writing, one of my major difficulties has been that relationship between the individual "I" and the collective "we" which concerns and to some extent plagues all politically involved writers. To what degree, I have had to ask myself, is my perspective legitimately representative of that of "feminist poets"? Despite our supposed emphasis on the subjective, I've noticed that the familiar feminist "we" is often used in place of the discredited patriarchal-academic "objectivity" as a means of legitimizing our private perceptions, sometimes even of concealing our vested interests. My awareness of the potential for falsification inherent in this usage has been heightened by those women of color who have vehemently protested the false inclusivity of the white feminist "we";[1] their experience also suggests the dangers of other exclusions and falsifications. And yet, as I soon enough discovered, to write this article without saying "we" was quite impossible, for it is not only as an individual but very much as a member of a political and literary community that I experience my poet self.

Who, then, is this "we" I have in mind when I speak of "feminist poets"? It comprises poets who not only call themselves feminists, but who confirm that identification through the radicalism of their vision, and frequently of their activism. Many are lesbians of color, non-lesbian women of color, white lesbians; a few are straight white women, though it appears only slightly less difficult for these to cling both to their straightness and to their radicalism than it is for the camel to negotiate the needle's eye. Few are academics; fewer still are academically respectable.

Though they share political commitment, they do not share a single feminist ideology: they are socialist feminists, radical feminists, dyke separatists, and all the unnamed shades between and around. Some have important political commitments outside the feminist movement.

I view this motley collection of feminist poets through the lens of who I am: a poet, a lesbian poet, a white self-published lesbian poet slightly over thirty, of middle-class Protestant background, negligible academic credentialing, intense ambition and uncertain reputation, whose poems have been written and whose literary identity has evolved primarily within the womb/crucible of seventies feminism, a woman-identified radical American poet attempting to face, poetically and otherwise, the vague promises and vivid threats of the second-to-the-last decade of this unprecedented and terrifying century. I am highly conscious that the concerns reflected here are symptomatic of a particular historical moment in the development of feminist poetry—a moment I view, moreover, with the specific geographical bias of a New York City–based feminist and writer. This article, in other words, is but one phase of a process, one facet of a multi-sided conversation. I hope for an answer in the form of assessments from other angles of issues I have raised and others I may not even have considered.

Among the questions I want to explore here are these: What has been the development of feminist poetry over the last decade, and where does it leave us? Why was it poetry and not some other form which came to occupy such a central role within feminism, and what are the implications of that seemingly privileged position? Why has a movement which has generated such an extraordinary and compelling body of work produced so little in the way of critical reflection on that work? In the absence of explicit critical standards, what implicit assumptions and preconceptions about the form and function of feminist poetry, and the role of the poet, may be inferred? How do these assumptions affect the poems we write? What is the relationship between the role of poet and that of political spokeswoman? What are the implications, positive and negative, of the intellectual and artistic "ghettoization" which characterizes a functionally separatist literary community? What is the future of an essentially exploratory literary movement—one dedicated to taboo-breaking, to investigating the hitherto unspeakable—once the initial explosive power of self-affirmation in the face of oppression has been tapped? In what ways have we instituted new taboos to replace the old?

What do we, as a movement, as readers, and as writers, want out of poetry? What can poetry properly be expected to give us?

The Awakening

The history of participation by poets in American social and political movements of this century has been important to the feminist poetry movement. For one thing it has proven, in the face of the artificial separation between poetry and politics which the literary establishment has generally taken such pains to enforce, that there *is* such a thing as political poetry, and has influenced our ideas of what that poetry should look like. For another, it has provided examples of women poets, some of them early feminists, to whom we have been able to look for inspiration and encouragement. The Harlem Renaissance, a chapter of the Black struggle that was a social as well as cultural movement, was led by poets.[2] Muriel Rukeyser was active in Left movements from the 1930s on. Gwendolyn Brooks, Nikki Giovanni, and Sonia Sanchez were closely identified with the Black Power movement. Denise Levertov, widely read by feminists in the early seventies, was prominent in opposition to the Vietnam War. Alice Walker has written extensively of her work in the Civil Rights movement; Robin Morgan and Marge Piercy of their roots in, and disillusionment with, the New Left.

Yet important as these precedents are in understanding the emergence of the feminist poetry movement, what is perhaps most important and—from a 1980s perspective—most difficult to grasp about the situation of the pre-feminist woman poet is the profound isolation in which she worked. A rereading of Adrienne Rich's 1971 essay "When We Dead Awaken: Writing as Re-Vision" has provided me with a salutary reminder of the consequences of that isolation, one in which a great number of non-feminist women writers are of course still immersed. It is simply impossible for the woman poet working in a male literary tradition to speak in a natural voice of her natural concerns—incessantly aware as she must be, whether or not on a conscious level, of men's judgment of her words, her very being. That woman can be the center of the poetic universe, can be *assumed* as author, subject, and audience of the poem—that is the staggering achievement of the past ten years or so of the feminist poetry movement.

I have my own painful if mercifully abbreviated memories of The Bad

Old Days: going through three years of college as a philosophy major, utterly terrified of my school's male literary establishment for whom Gary Snyder was the great poet-guru (how his lines about the girlfriend he once beat up, "drunk, stung with weeks of torment," the two women in the Japanese whorehouse who "dyked each other for a show" still echo in my head; how his career in the merchant marine intimidated me); sitting across from Elana Dykewomon (then Nachman) in "Yeats and Eliot," the one English literature course I took, never dreaming the two of us might have even writing—let alone feminism or lesbianism—in common; soliciting advice on study and reading matter from a male poet with whom I had undergone a humiliating sexual experience; dropping out of school in a desperate, and what then felt quite dangerous, determination to find my own direction; ignoring, at first, the work of Adrienne Rich because it came to me through a suspicious source, my Freudian-oriented shrink who in 1972 handed me a copy of *The Saturday Review* containing some poems from the forthcoming *Diving into the Wreck.*

But why, in my determination to become a "writer," and in my groping, semi-conscious attempts to understand my situation as a woman, did I turn to poetry? And why did poetry come to occupy a similar role in the lives of so many feminists emerging from the social ferment of the 1960s?

Certainly poetry has not always been the genre women have found most accessible. In nineteenth century England it was the novel, a relatively new, popular, and less prestigious form, which was seen as appropriate to women.[3] Poetry was upheld as the highest and purest of the literary arts, most difficult because of its rigid formal requirements—the province, hence, of aristocrats by birth, education, and/or "genius" (read: white men of the middle and upper classes). But American women struggling into feminist consciousness were the beneficiaries of a populist literary tradition, stretching back into the nineteenth century, which had established the possibility of a poetry close to everyday speech.[4] Fiction—The Novel—had come to be perceived as the major literary form; poetry now appeared less intimidating, at least to most would-be *writers.* (Ironically, the "poetry anxiety" traditionally instilled in high school English classes seems to persist in many feminist *readers*, resulting in the twin axioms familiar to feminist poets that "women don't read poetry" and "poetry doesn't sell.")

Important material considerations favor poetry as a "woman's" form.

Poetry seems the easiest thing to write under conditions of interruption or limited time—though, interestingly, Virginia Woolf argued the opposite in *A Room of One's Own*: "Less concentration is required," she says of fiction (70). Poetry is cheaper to self-publish than fiction; more easily fitted into such public contexts as the anthology, the newspaper, or the open reading; and probably offers the beginning writer a surer bet for acceptance in periodicals.

I know I began with poetry because it seemed the easiest thing to write—which is to say, at least remotely possible. It was blessedly short, for one thing, and therefore meant less of an investment of time and energy than a story, which would obviously have to go on for several pages. But perhaps even more important was the fact that I didn't think of poetry as "made up" in the same sense as fiction. A poem, it seemed to me, would be an authentic and therefore unchallengeable record of my feelings, perceptions, and experiences—whereas if I "faked it," fictionalized, I felt I somehow became more vulnerable to external, probably male, standards. I now see these issues very differently, recognizing the "fictional" possibilities of poetry and the way that an author's personal experience is central to all prose fiction, whether or not literally autobiographical. But the point is that I had to learn to speak in poetry: it seemed, initially, the only way for me to be certain of owning my own voice.

I think that for many feminists, as for me, poetry represented the clearest opportunity for the direct statement of women's experience; it was the literary counterpart of the C-R groups' attempt at breaking down the distinction between the personal and the political. In the beginning, we had an enormous appetite for *the evidence*, for anything that could provide testimony concerning the conditions of women's lives. Every woman's story was to be told and listened to, and poetry was one way of accomplishing this. Almost anything a woman wrote seemed important, simply because a woman had written it. (But that statement is both true and false; many of us, white and well educated, were comfortably naive in our assumptions about the universality of our exploration, arrogant in our attempt to construct, from a very limited perspective, what we thought of as the total picture.)

The connection between poetry and feminism was intense and immediate. Fran Winant said of her activity during this period:

> I wrote many of my poems specifically for the open poetry readings that were considered important at the start of the women's

movement. The knowledge that there was a place for my work to go, and an all-women's audience to listen to it, immediately made me able to write about my personal experiences and feelings as I never could before. (62)

(Note that she implies open readings were no longer popular by 1975, when this statement appeared.) The early, influential commercial press anthology on women's liberation *Sisterhood Is Powerful*, edited by poet Robin Morgan, included as a matter of course a section entitled "Poetry as Protest."

Initial feminist interest in poetry took two forms: an intensive reading and gathering together of previously published poetry by women from Sappho to Sylvia Plath, and an outpouring of new poetry, much of it shared through open readings, via the pages of small and "underground" periodicals, or in the form of hastily assembled books and pamphlets issued by the first feminist publishing efforts. In either case, "I am a woman" was the core revelation sought or expressed. Anger, as Adrienne Rich noted, was omnipresent, for the focus was frequently on the circumstances of women's oppression within patriarchy ("When We Dead," 48–49).

The selection of commercially available contemporary poetry embraced on political grounds during this phase might strike us today as startlingly eclectic. Often it was enough that the poet be a woman; she need not necessarily be a feminist, and she was highly unlikely to be a lesbian, or at least not openly so. Possibilities included work by June Jordan (*Some Changes*, E. P. Dutton, 1971); Denise Levertov; Marge Piercy (then published by a university press); Muriel Rukeyser; Sylvia Plath and Anne Sexton, those enormously influential poets of female anger and victimization; early Erica Jong; middle Diane Wakoski; Nikki Giovanni's extremely male-identified *Black Feeling, Black Talk, Black Judgement* (William Morrow and Company, 1970); and Diane diPrima's equally male-identified *Revolutionary Letters* (City Lights Books, 1971). I remember seeing selections from the last volume, in particular, admiringly reprinted in feminist newspapers.

It is interesting to note how many of these poets (not, of course, all) have lapsed from feminist fashion, or met with feminist wrath. A friend of mine reports, for instance, that by the mid-seventies she felt considerable chagrin at having to admit she was writing a dissertation on the once-idolized but now "non-feminist" Plath. As late as 1974 I jumped at the opportunity to take a workshop with Jong, a distinction I had become reluctant even to mention only a year or two later. And it is a sobering experience to note the virulent homophobia and anti-Semitism in Giovanni's early seventies work (as it is, for that matter, to read early "underground" heroine Rita Mae Brown's musings on the joys of owning a Rolls Royce in a recent issue of *Savvy*).[5]

Though it lacked commercial distribution advantages, the grassroots, "underground" poetry scene enjoyed those of ad hoc immediacy: a poet could publish new work in a pamphlet or newspaper days or weeks after writing it. Such poetry satisfied a demand for poems explicitly feminist in their perspective, flourishing in the gap between the explosion of feminist consciousness and the commercial publication of feminist poetry anthologies and individual volumes.

Much "underground" publishing was then, as it is today, in fact self-publishing. Many of the poets involved were lesbians, and a number wrote out of their experience as working-class and / or Black women, as well.[6] The Women's Press Collective published Judy Grahn's *Edward the Dyke and Other Poems* in 1971 and Pat Parker's *Child of Myself*—originally issued by Shameless Hussy Press—in 1972. Alta, founder of Shameless Hussy, also published her own work and early work by Susan Griffin. Rita Mae Brown's *The Hand That Cradles the Rock* was issued by a university press in 1971 (and reissued by Diana Press in 1974). Fran Winant self-published her *Looking at Women* (Violet Press, 1971) and subsequently compiled *We Are All Lesbians* (Violet Press, 1973), the first lesbian poetry anthology. Audre Lorde published four small press poetry volumes before her first commercially published book appeard in 1976. In her capacity as poetry editor of *Amazon Quarterly*, the influential lesbian magazine founded in 1972, she became one of the very few women of color to have exercised editorial control over even a portion of a nationally distributed feminist periodical in the past decade.

A transition to increased commercial publication of explicitly feminist poetry began in 1972, the year in which Robin Morgan published *Monster*. Adrienne Rich's *Diving into the Wreck* appeared the following year. These books by white women, one by a new poet already known for her feminist activism, the other by a well-established poet for whom it marked a turning to explicitly feminist concerns, enjoyed the advantages of commercial promotion and distribution. The two volumes were in a position to exert enormous influence on a large feminist audience, shaping its idea of "feminist poetry" and of the poet as activist and theorist. Also in 1973, Alice Walker's second book of poems, *Revolutionary Petunias*, was published commercially, and Broadside, a small Black press, issued Audre Lorde's *From a Land Where Other People Live*. The Lorde, Walker, and Rich volumes were nominated for the National Book Award in the following year. Rich accepted the award, given for *Diving into the Wreck*, on behalf of all three poets, reading a collective statement which rejected the divisiveness and tokenizing implicit in the awards process.

The years 1973 and 1974 also saw the commercial publication of three widely distributed, influential poetry anthologies edited from a white, mainly heterosexual feminist perspective: *Rising Tides* and *No More Masks* (1973) and *The World Split Open* (1974). *We Become New* followed in 1975. Along with the National Book Award nominations, these publications apparently constituted the high water mark of establishment and commercial press interest in feminist poetry; other such mass market anthologies have not been forthcoming. They made a significant contribution to the widespread availability of "women's poetry"— predominantly that of white heterosexual women. The volumes, however, do include significant selections by a few Black poets, and Louise Bernikow's introduction to *The World Split Open*, which acknowledges the historical correlation between women's poetry and woman-loving, was of particular significance in the development of lesbian poetry. Poets of color who are not Black are strikingly absent from these volumes, as they have been from my discussion so far: at this point white feminists, to the extent that we transcended white solipsism at all, still thought overwhelmingly in terms of a Black/white dichotomy.

Mid to Late Decade: The Cultural Separatist Alternative

Two major and interconnected developments of the mid-seventies helped to modify the omnivorous early emphasis on "women's" poetry. The first of these was the increasing prominence of openly lesbian poets, a phenomenon largely reflective of the emergence of lesbian-feminism as an influential tendency within the women's movement. The second was the growth of the lesbian-led feminist press movement with its encouragement of a functional cultural separatism. As a result of these trends, what appear in retrospect to have been two parallel feminist poetry movements—a largely lesbian underground of insurgent small press poets, and a largely heterosexual "mainstream" of commercially published poets—fused into what might be characterized as a lesbian-feminist poetry movement with non-lesbian adherents.[7] This was a movement focused less on examining the conditions of women's subjection than on moving out, as Adrienne Rich had forecast in 1971, toward "the boundaries of patriarchy" ("When We Dead," 49).

During the mid-seventies, for instance, establishment-certified Adrienne Rich and Marilyn Hacker came out publicly as lesbians; small press-published Audre Lorde and Susan Griffin began to publish commercially; and Olga Broumas received the Yale Younger Poets award for her explicitly lesbian first collection. Despite the visibility resulting from commercial publication of lesbian poetry, however, the feminist press movement remained the mainstay of lesbian literature, and such lesbian poets as Ellen Marie Bissert, Karen Brodine, Alison Colbert, Willyce Kim, Irena Klepfisz, Jackie Lapidus, Joan Larkin, Susan Sherman, Lorraine Sutton, and I published small press first volumes.

Several of these lesbian writers are Third World (Willyce Kim, Asian-American, and Lorraine Sutton, Puerto Rican). Important work by other women of color was also introduced by a few feminist small presses at this time: Shameless Hussy Press published first volumes by Black poet Ntozake Shange and Japanese-American poet Mitsuye Yamada in 1975, for instance. *Sunbury* magazine and press presented the poetry of a number of women of color, including that of Sutton in 1975, and volumes by Jodi Braxton and Rikki Lights (who are Black) in 1977; Kelsey Street Press published Chinese-American Nellie Wong's first collection in the same year.

By the mid-seventies, Diana Press and Daughters had emerged as relatively powerful, well-organized lesbian-controlled publishing efforts. Out & Out Books issued its first titles in 1975, among them *Amazon Poetry: An Anthology*, the largest collection of lesbian poetry then available, and the most comprehensive through the end of the decade. *Amazon Quarterly* ceased publication in that year, but Audre Lorde subsequently became poetry editor of *Chrysalis*, begun in 1976—as was the more explicitly lesbian-focused *Sinister Wisdom*. *Azalea*, a magazine by and for Third World lesbians, and *Conditions*, a magazine of women's writing with an emphasis on writing by lesbians, began publication in 1977. Throughout the mid-seventies, most feminist presses and periodicals published substantial amounts of poetry; the major exceptions, Diana Press and Daughters, were nevertheless extremely important to lesbian poets because of their role in the development of a specifically lesbian-feminist literary culture and community.

Interesting evidence of this emerging culture is to be found in *Margins* 23 (1975) and *Sinister Wisdom* 2 (1976), both edited by Beth Hodges, both with a focus on lesbian writing and publishing. The latter included my article "The Politics of Publishing and the Lesbian Community," which discussed the results of a questionnaire survey I had conducted among lesbian-feminist writers. Responses suggested that a number of lesbian writers had at that point become rather defensive about their publishing choices. The article—and the defensiveness—were in part occasioned by a vociferous campaign conducted by June Arnold and Parke Bowman of Daughters and Coletta Reid of Diana, who maintained that it was the duty of feminist writers to publish their work with feminist presses.

Now that the dust of that old debate has settled, it is easier to see that, couched in radical-sounding rhetoric, what Arnold, Bowman, and Reid offered that was attractive to feminist writers was a middle ground between the uneven production, poor distribution, and nonexistent royalties of the early feminist press efforts, and the exploitation, insensitivity, and undependability of the male-controlled commercial presses. Feminist writers, they promised, could have it both ways: they could sustain their radicalism *and* reap professional rewards, be both politically correct *and* paid. Lesbian-feminist literature need not subsist on patriarchal crumbs. It should emerge proudly from its "underground," peripheral status and, declaring itself "major," expect to succeed on its own terms— through the creation of feminist institutions which (if enough feminists supported them) could hope to compete with "the boys."

The lack of realism inherent in this ambitious program is perhaps suggested by the fact that both Daughters and Diana ceased publishing activities shortly after formulating it. And certainly not all lesbian-feminist writers (let alone heterosexual feminists!) were comfortable with the implications of narrowness and rigid definition lurking in the air of the time and manifested also, for instance, in the phenomenon of doctrinaire lesbian separatism. However, the impulse towards an autonomous feminist culture has continued into the present, as has the trend towards increased professionalization of publishing efforts and writing careers, at least by contrast with the poetry "underground" of the early 1970s.

If "I am a woman" had been the central proposition focusing the poetic explorations of early-seventies feminists, then "I am a lesbian" was by mid-decade the resounding theme. Certainly I recall feeling it was the message the poetry audiences I encountered at that time overwhelmingly wanted and expected to hear. I suspect that this expectation influenced perception of (and perhaps self-presentation by) poets like Irena Klepfisz, Audre Lorde, and Susan Sherman, for whom lesbianism was, though important, not necessarily their primary subject. For other poets—the Olga Broumas of *Beginning with O*, the Susan Griffin of the newer poems appearing in *Like the Iris of an Eye*, and the Adrienne Rich of "From an Old House in America" and *The Dream of a Common Language*—the declaration "I am a lesbian," interpreted not merely in a sexual sense but as self-affirmation, proclamation of independence from patriarchy, and assertion of the primacy of emotional bonding among women, was indeed at the heart of their work.

"The Assumptions in Which We Are Drenched"

"Until we can understand the assumptions in which we are drenched we cannot know ourselves," Adrienne Rich wrote in 1971 ("When We Dead," 35). She was thinking then of the need for feminists to examine the assumptions of patriarchal literature, but it seems to me that the observation is equally applicable to the anti-patriarchal poetry which feminists have since striven to create. So far as I am able to identify them, I want to investigate the nature and implications of the assumptions which have influenced the creation of feminist poetry. I will do so before going on to discuss recent developments, partly because these assumptions seem to me largely the product of the two phases of feminist poetry I have so far discussed, partly because I think that an understanding of them helps to illuminate the shifts and transformations of the current period.

My task here is made more difficult by the absence of much in the way of written theory or analysis of feminist poetry as a general phenomenon. To the extent that we have produced it at all, our "criticism" has generally been limited to reviewing, or at the most to articles focusing on the work of a single poet; with a few exceptions, several of which are discussed below, feminists have not written about what feminist poetry is or ought to be. Symptomatic of this situation is, for example, the fact that although poetry has certainly been at least as prominent a form of literary endeavor among lesbians as fiction, almost all theoretical discussion contained in the *Margins* and *Sinister Wisdom* issues on lesbian literature and publishing focuses on the latter form; even an article comprehensively entitled "Lesbian Literature: Random Thoughts" by Cathy Cruikshank ignores poetry. Similarly, the discussion of contemporary lesbian writing in Lillian Faderman's recent *Surpassing the Love of Men* is concerned almost exclusively with fiction.

What does this dearth of criticism say about the feminist view of poetry? Do we believe, as some of us were once taught about sex, that poetry is supposed to "just happen," that talking about it will ruin the romance? Or do feminists share the contemporary American prejudice that fiction is the major form, the one worthy of serious attention? Whatever the case may be, I do not believe that the absence of articulated criticism signals a corresponding absence of assumptions about how a feminist poem should look (or sound) and what it ought to do. Instead, I think that we must often look to the poems themselves, or to comments poets and readers make in extra-poetic contexts, to identify implicit assumptions. Precisely because they are unstated, such assumptions may at times function more tyrannically than would explicit "standards," particularly for the younger or less experienced feminist poet.

A poet friend told me this: at a point when her style had changed in the direction of a longer, looser poetic line, someone remarked of her earlier work that perhaps she'd been trying too hard to write "feminist poetry." When I asked what that meant, she explained that initially she'd been heavily influenced by the work of Pat Parker, Judy Grahn, and Robin Morgan, with the result that she set out to write poems which she saw as communicating very directly with audiences of women in the way those poets' work has done. She also expected a concentration on "women's issues" (e.g., rape) and use of traditional "women's forms" (e.g., a folk song form) to offer the ideal poetic embodiment of her feminism. Eventually she discovered she could more satisfactorily explore her feminist concerns in a style she felt was influenced by Tennyson and other male poets she'd read in earlier years.

Though the feminist poets of the early 1970s must frequently have felt almost intoxicated by their sense of feminist poetry as a clean slate, an open field, the truth was that feminist poetry was not being created in a vacuum. It was from the start "anti-patriarchal," almost bound to be defined, negatively, in contrast to what was perceived as the male poetry tradition.[8] Much, I think, has been either self-imposed or self-excused on the grounds that it is as unlike what "the boys" do as possible. Consider, for instance, one woman's reply to my objection to a review in which she had, among other things, badly misquoted my poetry: that she "wasn't like the *New York Times*" and "tried to be as creative as possible with her reviewing."

But almost anything can be shown to be unlike what some male poet or critic has done. Just what are these assumptions with which a beginning poet may have to grapple—and against which, I suspect, a more experienced poet may continue to measure her work, even while heeding the imperative of her own voice? I am about to sketch what amounts to a caricature of feminist poetic practice; happily, it does not constitute a standard to which we universally adhere—otherwise our poetry would be flat, stuffy, and boring, which, at its best, it certainly is not. Nor are these assumptions unchanging: the ideal feminist poem of 1971 might have looked somewhat different from its 1981 counterpart.

Feminist poetry is useful. Usefulness seems to be one of the most universal expectations of feminist poetry, as it has been, historically, of political art in general. (For example, "Art is a weapon" was a characteristic Communist slogan of the 1930s and later.) Here is a passage from Karen Brodine's "Politics of Women Writing," one of the very few discussions of the practice of feminist poetry to appear over the past decade:

> I have yet to know the use of a poem the way I know the use of a hammer. Yet I feel a poem is surely a tool. My friend who works as a gardener says that only after months of learning to work with tools, did she realize they are not foreign objects, but simple extensions of the hand. So our writing should not be some awkward object or product, but an extension of our feeling/dream/belief. . . .
>
> Part of the use of art is its ability to express the ideas of the movement. The strongest writing today expresses the contradictions of this society.[9]

Judy Grahn makes a strikingly similar statement in "Murdering the King's English," the introduction to *True to Life Adventure Stories*; her remarks seem applicable to poetry as well as prose:

Art, in my terms, is like a basket, and a basket is useful. . . .
Women's art, feminist writing, has a definition which I have used
in this anthology: it must be useful to women, must work in our
interest. Must not work to divide us further, must not lie about us to
each other, must not give false information which would fall apart
when people try to make use of it. (12–13)

Note the slipperiness of these "definitions." A tool implies the existence of some specific, consciously held objective in the service of which
it is employed, an analogy inconsistent with the amorphous "extension
of our feeling/dream/belief" toward which Brodine's passage shifts,
while Grahn avoids specifying *how* she gauges art's usefulness, detailing
instead what art must *not* do. (How, I wonder, can we be sure that the
telling of a hard truth will not "work to divide us further"? How can we
be certain in advance that the information we give will not "fall apart
when people try to make use of it"?)

I see prescriptions of this sort as dangerous because they seem to call
for a conscious control which I believe poets do not, or should not, always have. In our efforts to "express the ideas of the movement," or
"work in [women's] interests," we are too likely to go over old, safe
territory, rather than undertaking explorations whose usefulness is not,
and may never be, readily apparent.

I am troubled by the defensiveness about art which the insistence on
poetry as tool or utensil seems to reveal—as though feminists will be
unwilling to keep art around unless it can be shown to pay its own way.
Defensiveness is similarly reflected in that leftist euphemism, sometimes
heard in feminist circles, "cultural worker"—the implication being that
art has to be justified by the pretence that its creation resembles standing
on an assembly line eight hours a day.

A study of earlier political-literary movements—the various Communist ones, for instance—reveals striking parallels to these utilitarian analogies, suggesting the commonality of certain issues and concerns to artists working within seemingly divergent political contexts.[10] But the
mesh of poetry and politics within feminism appears at first glance to go
far beyond the historically familiar scenario according to which writers
have served as appendages to political groups, flimsy cultural "super-
structure" tacked onto the solid political "base." And yet some feminist
poets, in their sincere desire to be politically effective, have adopted a
view of art which betrays a fundamental suspicion of its workings, re-

quiring that it justify its existence on the basis of what it can be demonstrated to *do*.

A seemingly very different expression of feminist desire for a useful poetry is seen in the stress certain poets place on the transformation of language as a key to the transformation of reality itself. Olga Broumas writes:

> I am a woman committed to
> a politics
> of transliteration, the methodology
> of a mind
> stunned at the suddenly
> possible shifts of meaning—for which
> like amnesiacs
>
> in a ward on fire, we must
> find words
> or burn. (24)

"It was an old theme even for me: / Language cannot do everything," Adrienne Rich remarks, yet goes on to admit that "what in fact I keep choosing / are these words. . . ." ("Cartographies," 19–20). The "dream of a common language" is for her far more than metaphor for connection—as the "politics of transliteration" would appear to be for Broumas. "Language is as real, as tangible in our lives as streets, pipelines, telephone switchboards, microwaves, radioactivity, cloning laboratories, nuclear power stations," Rich reminds us elsewhere ("Power and Danger," 247). Judith McDaniel, appearing at the 1977 Modern Language Association convention on a panel entitled "The Transformation of Silence into Language and Action," said:

> . . . I can't talk about language and action in separate modes. Language for me is action. To speak words that have been unspoken, to imagine that which is unimaginable, is to create the place in which change (action) occurs. I do believe our acts are limited—ultimately—only by what we fail or succeed in conceptualizing. To imagine a changed universe will not cause it to come into being, that is a more complex affair; but to fail to imagine it, the consequences of that are clear.
>
> If feminism is the final cause—and I believe it is—then language is the first necessity. (17)

These poets, far from being apologetic about the possibilities of their chosen medium, make rather grandiose claims for it. Despite their disclaimers ("language cannot do everything"; "to imagine a changed universe will not cause it to come into being"), it is hard to come away from a reading of the works in which the passages I have quoted appear without feeling that for these writers the politics of language actually take precedence over other politics.

Perhaps such an emphasis is quite natural for a poet; after all, it is because of our intense involvement with the power of language that we *are* poets. But feminist poets tend also to take on roles as theoreticians and political spokeswomen. And the blurring of distinctions between literary prominence and political leadership has meant that sometimes feminist theory and practice have been skewed in the direction of too much stress on the transformation of language, too little emphasis on the other sorts of transformations which a political movement that hopes to succeed in the material world must undertake.

Or perhaps the causal relationship goes the other way; perhaps it is in part precisely because of what a Marxist would call an idealist bent in our movement, a weakness for mind-over-matter approaches, that poets have emerged as leaders. This would help to account for the popularity of such feminist thinkers as Mary Daly, who has focused almost exclusively on language as a vehicle for feminist transformation.[11]

It seems to me that this inflated expectation of language may ultimately lead to the same predicament invited by those who would have us see poetry as tool or utensil: the placing of an intolerable burden on poetry. Apparently feminist poets have in common with other political writers a tendency to require of our poems feats which elude us in real life. We expect our poems to offer, if not a comprehensive solution, at least a clear direction, an optimistic program which in fact may amount to not much more than a ringing declamation of "the people united will never be defeated" against the evidence.[12]

I have struggled with my own expectations along these lines. Particularly in trying to conclude long poems that I felt represented "major statements," I have racked my brains for a suitably positive note, feeling that my failure to find it would somehow constitute a *political failure.* And how could I read my poem from the platform to the audience at the benefit, rally, or cultural event if I could not match Judy Grahn's promise, "death, ho death / you shall be poor" ("A Woman," 131); if I could not echo June Jordan's threat, ". . . from now on my resistance/my simple and daily and nightly self-determination/may very well cost you your life!" ("Poem About My Rights," 88); or affirm, with Susan Sherman, that "Your enemies are endless Amerika/. . . By our life we will finally/destroy you/Even as you try to level us/with your death" (59)? In fact, the three poems which end with these lines are strong and moving, but their impact seems to rest more on our *desire* to believe their closing assertions than on the intrinsic credibility these assertions possess based on what we know of the world or the evidence the poems themselves present. A little of this technique goes a very long way; the danger it poses is of the slide into rhetoric, the rote chanting of slogans we are unable to make real, the temptation to dish up to the audience what it wants or has learned to expect in the way of exhortation and uplift.

In her essay "Poetry Is Not a Luxury," Audre Lorde suggests a view of poetry as neither mundane tool nor instrument of quasi-magical transformation, but as closely akin to dream in its functioning in our lives. (I find interesting, by the way, the defensive implications of her title—evidently she perceives a danger that poems *will* be seen as luxuries.) For her, poetry is "illumination," "the quality of light by which we scrutinize our lives":

> When we view living, in the european mode, only as a problem to be solved, we rely solely upon our ideas to make us free, for these were what the white fathers told us were precious.
>
> But as we become more in touch with our own ancient, Black, non-european view of living as a situation to be experienced and interacted with, we learn more and more to cherish our feelings, and to respect those hidden sources of our power from where true knowledge and therefore lasting action comes.
>
> At this point in time, I believe that women carry within ourselves the possibility for fusion of these two approaches as keystones for survival, and we come closest to this combination in our poetry. I speak here of poetry as the revelation or distillation of experience, not the sterile word play that, too often, the white fathers distorted the word poetry to mean—in order to cover their desperate wish for imagination without insight. (36)

I find Lorde's questioning of the view of life "only as a problem to be solved" particularly suggestive. I am swayed by her belief in the possibilities of a poetry which can be of use, not in a narrowly utilitarian sense nor one which undervalues the place of action in the world, but as "the revelation or distillation of experience."

Yet I would like to request feminists to entertain at least briefly the seemingly perverse and heretical notion that it may be poetry's stubborn quality of rockbottom, intrinsic *uselessness* which—despite all the useful things it is sometimes observed to do, from eliciting that "CLICK" of feminist recognition that *Ms.* magazine is so keen on, to drawing crowds at the latest fundraiser—constitutes the guarantee of its integrity, and hence of its ultimate value to us. No matter how we seek to disguise the unpleasant fact, a poet remains a person whose life is essentially unjustified and justifiable: her most basic task, her "calling" (of course she will have many other occupations) is simply to *be*, to experience, and to metabolize that experience through the process we call poetry. This view of the poet is reflected in the following engagingly defiant passage by the Russian poet Osip Mandelstam, whose bad attitude was his ticket to the Stalinist labor camp where he died:

> No matter how hard I work, whether I carry a horse slung across my shoulders, whether I turn millstones, I shall never become a worker. My work, regardless of the form, is considered mischief, lawlessness, mere accident. But I like it that way, and I agree to my calling. I'll even sign my name with both hands. ("Fourth Prose," 324)

The very success of feminist poetry, accustoming poets to expect relatively enthusiastic audiences and a relative degree of prestige or acclaim, requires us, I believe, to remind ourselves that a poet's work may or may not connect directly and immediately with hearers; may or may not produce some tangible material result or some far-reaching transformation in consciousness—in the here-and-now, or ever. These factors are often beyond a poet's control, and they should not be taken as a measure of feminist commitment or political responsibility.

If it's results you're after, hire an organizer.

Feminist poetry is accessible. This assumption surely has its origins at least in part in feminist poetry's antipatriarchal premises: men's poetry is inaccessible, therefore ours will be accessible. (In fact, there is a tradition of male political poetry which also values accessibility; Pablo Neruda changed his style drastically in an effort to make his work less obscure, for example.) However, the concept of accessibility is seldom examined critically, and in the absence of such evaluation, one unfortunate connotation seems to be *easiness*, instant comprehensibility. Adrienne Parks, in her 1975 essay "The Lesbian Feminist as Writer as Lesbian Feminist," asserts:

> Lf audiences tend to understand lf writings, song, art, etc. without any difficulty. Their expectations of what is being offered coincide both with what is actually offered and with what their own experience tells them is "true to" the lf experience. (69)

In fact, the poetry which is most clearly *not* inaccessible is that which draws a predictable laugh at the reading, elicits the response, "Hey, I can relate to that"—the poetry which makes a direct, unambiguous statement. All of us have enjoyed such poetry, but is it really what we want exclusively to cultivate? What about poetry's ability to mean several or many or even contradictory things all at once, its trick of defying translation and synopsis? What about its musical qualities, and the *listening* with the whole being—not just the rational part of the brain—that this calls for? Is accessibility merely a matter of employing short, commonly used words? Of renouncing traditional forms? Does it imply the necessity of making use of concepts, feelings, subject-matter which will threaten no one, because they are comfortably familiar to all? Stereotypes and clichés are, by this standard, eminently accessible.

I think the feminist obsession with accessibility reflects, in part, the process of intimidation that begins early in school, where we learn to be afraid of feeling stupid when we are not sure what literature, and particularly poetry, mean. What we are almost never told then is that even people with lifetimes of practice often have a hard time deciding "what a poem means." What if, instead of trying to resolve things by demanding that every poem state its business as efficiently as though coughing up name, rank, and serial number, we affirmed each reader's right to approach poetry in her own way?

We do need to examine seriously the class functions of language and literary forms, and to reject the tyranny of standard English, which has functioned so effectively to hush and to exclude. Judy Grahn's "Murdering the King's English" is an important, and courageously forthright, step in this direction. So is June Jordan's "White English/Black English: The Politics of Translation."[13] I do not, however, believe that those of us who are most comfortable with standard English should renounce our use of it—or that the solution to problems of class and literature is likely to be found in what Michelle Cliff, discussing a Third World woman's criticism of parts of *Claiming an Identity They Taught Me to Despise* as written in "inaccessible language," characterizes as literary downward mobility:

> The one thing that saved me all these years coming out as a lesbian, being a woman of color, was the ability to read and to write. . . .
>
> . . . I think we, Black women specifically, have an enormous literary tradition and have knowledge of it and there is this pretense that we should be downwardly mobile to reach everybody which I don't think is necessary. I find it very much like economic downward mobility which I don't particularly care for either. Once you have the privilege, if you want to reject it that's fine, but if you've worked hard for your education it doesn't make much sense. (Hammonds, 6, 28)

Unfortunately, feminist discussions of privilege and language are seldom so direct and public. Instead the subject is surrounded by an intimidating silence that has its parallels in other art fields. I am thinking, for instance, of a composer who discovered her work was being scorned as unfeminist because her influences were classical western ones. Not that she was told so directly—her friends let her know what was being said behind her back.

Feminist poetry is "about" specific subject-matter: oppression, woman-identification, identity. It avoids both traditional forms and distancing techniques such as persona and third-person narration. It is a statement of personal experience or feeling, with the poet a first-person presence in the poem. These assumptions have their origins in the initial impulse of many feminist poets to reclaim their own experience, and to express that experience in ways they could be sure had not been imposed from without. For feminists deeply immersed in the consciousness-raising process, it was the authenticity of fact, the truth of each woman's direct testimony—not that of the imagination, or of observed experience—which was central to poetry.[14]

Certainly the past ten years have produced an impressive body of work which meets these criteria. Certainly, too, some feminist poets have consistently written other sorts of poetry—I think, for instance, of Irena Klepfisz' frequent use of persona, Marilyn Hacker's fondness for rhymed forms—but to the extent that they have done so, they tend to seem somewhat anomalous. (My own experience suggests that this sort of "deviation" frequently makes it extremely difficult to decide what to read to feminist audiences.) Again, the danger is that of adopting a knee-jerk anti-patriarchal stance, and thereby limiting the possibilities of feminist poetry.

Sometimes narrow expectations of the feminist poem can constitute a particularly outrageous violation of the poet's being and vision, as happened several years ago following a reading (by someone other than the poet) of Audre Lorde's "Power," her reaction to the murder of a young Black boy by a white policeman: a white woman remarked that Lorde "was focusing too much on racism and not enough on sexism." Aside from the fact that racism *is* a feminist issue, Lorde's poem is an unmistakably female and, I think, deeply feminist statement about racism; it is as inconceivable to me that a Black man could have written that poem as it is that a white woman could have done so.

Women are affected by absolutely everything that goes on in the world, and it is the right and necessity of the feminist poet to explore whatever occupies the center of her field of vision. Even that poetry which is most directly based in the poet's real life is something more than raw experience; art always selects and shapes. Recognition of these facts can perhaps free us to consider possibilities of subject matter and form which have so far not been typical of feminist poetry.

Feminist poetry is a collective product or process; the individual ego plays a minimal role in its creation. This assumption (or perhaps "aspiration" would be more accurate?) evokes the tension between the "I" and the "we" which I discussed at the beginning of this article as chronic for political writers, who have sometimes been asked to submerge the "I" altogether. An extreme example of a piously correct position on this issue was exhibited by a poet with whom I read at a recent political event. She had, she announced, requested to be introduced by name only, without mention of any publications or affiliations, because she regarded her work as a simple and direct expression of the voice of The People. I'm not sure whether this particular leftist poet calls herself a feminist, but she certainly got an enthusiastic response from a largely feminist audience.

In her essay "Thinking About My Poetry," June Jordan gives an interesting and perhaps useful account of her own changing approach to this issue, based on her activism in the Black community:

> Toward the close of the sixties, I . . . decided that I wanted to aim for the achievement of a collective voice, that I wanted to speak as a community to a community, that to do otherwise was not easily defensible, nor useful, and would be, in any case, at variance with clarified political values I held as my own, by then. . . .

But a few years into the seventies, and I reconsidered again; aspiration toward a collective voice seemed to me conceitful, at least. . . . it did seem to me . . . that if I could truthfully attend to my own perpetual birth, if I could trace the provocations for my own voice and then trace its reverberations through love, Alaska, whatever, that then I could hope to count upon myself to be serving a positive and collective function, without pretending to be more than the one Black woman poet I am, as a matter of fact. (125–26)

More prevalent among feminists than insistence on a collective voice is our emphasis on the collective process of feminist poetry, its emergence from a network of mutual influence and support without which our work would, for most of us, be inconceivable. Melanie Kaye, in her essay "On Being a Lesbian-Feminist Artist," enthusiastically expresses this spirit of interdependence:

I have passed around my copies of Wittig's *Les Guérillères*, Toni Morrison's *Sula*, Arnold's *Sister Gin*, until pages fall out. My sister in New York, I in Oregon, discover on the phone that we have each been profoundly shaken by Adrienne Rich's piece on lying. I gather with sister poets to celebrate Gertrude Stein's birthday by reading her work on the radio. This is a circulatory system that shows me we are one body: the network is literally vital. (7)

One of our tasks as feminist writers is to preserve and expand the identity we have labored to record and create.

As women, we need this identity to survive. As writers, these connections enlarge what we can say. They enable us to speak less personally, without lying or distance but because we are seeing and feeling less personally; that is, less separately. . . . I pass on to women not only what I have to say, but what has been said to me. *In every sense, we do not work alone.* (8)

We are seeing in this decade a gathering of demands on artists to tell the truth(s) about female experience. I write for an audience who requires responsible work, an audience who shares to an extent unprecedented in twentieth century poetry a sense of common concerns. We grow together or not at all: this we know. (9)

I am in sympathy with much of this, but am disturbed by what is missing, the other side of the picture that is typically slighted in discussions of this sort. What happens when we sense that what we are experiencing is *not* echoed in the work of other women, when we feel isolated despite the existence of the community, when we find ourselves at odds with or bored by much of what feminists write? These discordant sensations are all the more difficult to cope with when we are busy telling each other that artistic alienation and isolation are diseases confined to privileged male poets.

Poems like Adrienne Rich's "Transcendental Etude" have told us what our creativity ought to be:

> Such a composition has nothing to do with eternity,
> the striving for greatness, brilliance—
> only with the musing of a mind
> one with her body, experienced fingers quietly pushing
> dark against bright, silk against roughness,
> pulling the tenets of a life together
> with no mere will to mastery. . . . (77)

But what happens when we fall short of this ideal, when we detect in ourselves motives akin to the ambition and competitiveness of the virtuoso, that male creator with whom this poem suggests we should have nothing in common? Generally, our response is denial: ambition and competition are simply not considered topics suitable for mention in public, certainly not in print—which means that we forego the chance to investigate them calmly and honestly. I am afraid that this failure may condemn us to repeat the lesson suggested by Rich's grim vision of Marie Curie, who

> . . . died   a famous woman   denying
> her wounds
> denying
> her wounds   came   from the same source as her power ("Power," 3)

What we have going for us as women, I believe, are not "better" emotions and motives than men, but the chance, if we will take it, to be truthful with ourselves and each other about them.

Where feminist poetry is concerned, criticism is politically suspect—or irrelevant. In a mid-seventies interview first published in *Big Mama Rag*, Pat Parker remarked:

> All standards seem to exist to obscure meaning. I just want to *say*
> what I mean. Poetry has been controlled by men for so long. They've
> set the standards, the criteria for what's a good poem. It's all a bunch
> of shit, academic wanderings. (Woodwoman, 61)

Her statement reveals a good deal about the origins of an anti-critical attitude which has been quite common among feminist writers in general,

perhaps particularly those whose identities—race, class, or uncompro-
mising public lesbianism—have rendered them especially vulnerable to
damaging establishment prescriptions for the writing of "literature."[15]
Too, criticism has understandably not been a priority for women who
often enough have had their hands full just getting the organizing done
and the poems written. And, as I remarked earlier, for some mysterious
reason poetry seems to receive less of what meager critical attention *is*
accorded to feminist work than does fiction.

Our criticism is further held back by the familiar confusion as to just
what is an authentically feminist criticism—which translates roughly as:
how honest can a critic be about negative reactions and still be considered
feminist? Some reviewers who have tested this out have generated public
controversies; most prefer to play it safe with positive or nonevaluative
reviews. Marge Piercy, in a letter published in *Sinister Wisdom*, sums up
her own perspective on this issue in refreshingly trenchant fashion; her
evident anger says something significant, I think, about the extent and
consequences of public pressure on feminists not to be critical:

> If we cannot tell the truth as we see it, if we cannot be honest in
> women's publications for our own audiences, when do we tell the
> truth? Never? Then let's cash it all in now. If reviewing means patting
> on the head and on the fanny in mindless approbation whether we
> think what is being done is worth the price of admission or not, then
> it's patronizing mush. Traditional feminine behavior. "Oh, darling,
> you look fantastic in that dress." Then afterward, "Where did she
> get it? That's the sort of thing your maid gives you when she wears it
> out." Class example intentional, because we're discussing, after all,
> ladylike behavior. Be nice in public. Say something nice no matter
> what you think. After all, you can say in private what you like later
> on.[16]

As a poet, I know that I want and need to think analytically about other
poets' work, and that I benefit from external perspectives on my own. I
am grateful for the serious considerations of feminist poetry which occasionally appear in print, for the periodicals which make space for reviews
and criticism. Too often, however, I find myself enraged by yet another
narrowly academic article (typically, one which either focuses, in a
manner utterly compatible with the pursuit of tenure, on some dead
white straight poet, or discusses Adrienne Rich's work without recogniz-

ing she's a lesbian)—or by some three-paragraph review which turns out to be sloppily disrespectful even on the minimal level of plot summary. Unless more feminists who care for poetry adopt careful criticism as a conscious, publicly espoused priority, I do not see how this state of affairs can be expected to change.

The world of feminist literature is sufficient unto itself; the feminist poet need look no further for inspiration, audience, or support. "Admit it," a writer friend said to me one evening (we were, it so happens, discussing fiction, but it might as well have been poetry), "you want them to have to take you seriously." She didn't have to tell me who them meant—I who every week read the New York Times Book Review from cover to cover, groaning and cursing throughout. Her remark was not an accusation. We were enjoying one of those small private gatherings in which heresies may safely be aired, and she was simply acknowledging our common—and highly "incorrect"—ambition.

I sometimes have the sense that I live my life as a writer with my nose pressed against the wide, shiny plate glass window of the mainstream culture. The world seems full of straight, large-circulation, slick periodicals which wouldn't think of reviewing my work and bookstores which will never order it, because small press stuff doesn't plug into the nexus of commercial publication which proclaims an author worthy of serious notice, and because even the cover reveals that I'm focused on the "narrow concerns" (to use the code phrase I've been encountering lately) of the lesbian-feminist.

It doesn't help much to remind myself that all "minority" writers encounter this business about narrowness (while we are flooded with books exploring the broad concerns of white straight upper-middle-class professionals), or that the literary establishment is riddled with corruption, homophobia, myopia, sexism, racism, and just plain stupidity. It doesn't help because, unlike Adrienne Parks, I don't experience an automatic fit between my "lesbian-feminist art" and the "lesbian-feminist audience." In fact, I'm not so sure that a randomly picked lesbian-feminist would be any more likely to have a positive response to my poetry than a randomly picked anybody else female, except perhaps that she'd be less likely to be frightened off by the dyke label. And if there are a couple of men out there somewhere who are interested in what I have to say, I'm not too proud to have them for readers, either. But the existence of this nonlesbian audience remains largely hypothetical; I am after all a self-published lesbian-feminist poet, and there are too many places my books simply cannot go.

I sometimes find myself thinking of life in the feminist literary community—even in bustling New York—as "life in the provinces." This is my private, rueful phrase for a feminist literary existence which, both for reasons of our choosing and ones not of our choosing, tends to be extremely isolated from other literary communities, the work they produce, and the resources and opportunities they offer at least some writers some of the time. (This is not just a matter of our distance from the literary establishment, but from other dissident literary groupings: Black literature which is not explicitly feminist, for example, or the less reactionary facets of the white-male-controlled small press movement.) The problem involves not only audience, but also the ingrown nature of our publishing networks, the underdevelopment of criticism, and our narrow—and narrowing—assumptions about what a feminist poet ought to read, what influences she should permit herself.

What is the meaning of my secret relief at learning that a poet I like and respect has dared to be influenced by Tennyson? What about my astonishment at June Jordan's celebration of Whitman's influence on American literature (a *Black feminist* poet recommending a *white male nineteenth century* one?)—followed by pleasure at the thought that I'd been given "permission" to reread *Leaves of Grass?* What does it mean to label *any* writer incorrect or off limits (as June Jordan does Emily Dickinson in that same essay)?[17] Why is this such a necessary exercise for us, the division of the world into the permitted and the forbidden? I find it significant that, following an extended period of boredom with poetry, it was my reading of work by Bertolt Brecht and Osip Mandelstam which rekindled my enthusiasm, and eventually prompted the writing of this article—leading me, in turn, to an appreciative rereading of much feminist poetry.

To say that I believe the assumptions outlined above have sometimes unhealthily constrained feminist poets is by no means to belittle our immense achievements. The fact that many of the issues discussed here have preoccupied writers connected with other political movements suggests that they are basic matters which could neither have been avoided nor easily resolved. But I have thought it important to suggest that our poetry has hardly been the medium totally lacking in standards and prescribed forms which we have sometimes proclaimed it to be. I also think it important to make explicit "the assumptions in which we are drenched," rather than adding to their power over us by adhering to positions of public correctness, airing our doubts and deviations, if at all, only in private. Finally, I think that this discussion suggests one possible reason for the perceptible flagging of feminist interest (specifically *white* feminist interest) in poetry in the period following the lesbian poetry renaissance of the mid-seventies: what had begun as an anti-traditional movement had to a certain extent developed its own dogmas, conventions, cautions, clichés, taboos.

Seventies into Eighties

> Do I dare speak of the boredom setting in among the white sector of the feminist movement? What was once a cutting edge, growing dull in the too easy solution to our problems of hunger of soul and stomach. The lesbian separatist utopia? No thank you, sisters. I can't prepare myself a revolutionary packet that makes no sense when I leave the white suburbs of Watertown, Massachusetts and take the T-line to Black Roxbury.
> —*Cherríe Moraga, Introduction to* This Bridge Called My Back

The most significant development for feminist poetry in the past few years has been, so far as I can see, the emergence into public voice of a large group of feminist poets of color—Native American, Asian-American, or Latina as well as Black. Many of them are lesbians; most have managed, with considerable difficulty, to get their work published by the white feminist or male-controlled small presses, or have resorted to self-publication. (Ntozake Shange and Alexis DeVeaux are the commercially published exceptions I am aware of.) These poets join with the prominent Black feminist poets so frequently isolated and tokenized by white feminists, thereby creating a movement-within-a-movement of great power and vitality.

For example, in addition to feminist poets of color mentioned in my earlier discussion of mid-seventies feminist publishing, recent years have seen the appearance of volumes by Indian / Native American poets Paula Gunn Allen (*The Blind Lion*, Thorp Springs Press, 1975 and *Coyote's Daylight Trip*, La Confluencia, 1978), Joy Harjo (*The Last Song*, Puerto del Sol Press, 1975 and *What Moon Drove Me to This*, I. Reed

Books, 1979), and Linda Hogan (*Calling Myself Home*, Greenfield Review Press, 1978); Chinese-American poet Fay Chiang (*In the City of Contradictions*, Sunbury Press, 1979); Japanese-American poet Barbara Noda (*Strawberries*, Shameless Hussy Press, 1980); Black poets Joan Gibbs (*Between a Rock and a Hard Place*, February 3rd Press, 1979) and Michelle Cliff (*Claiming an Identity They Taught Me to Despise*, Persephone Press, 1980); and Chicana poet Alma Villanueva (*Mother, May I?*, Motheroot Publications, 1978). Meanwhile, Chicana poets Gloria Anzaldúa and Cherríe Moraga have edited *This Bridge Called My Back: Writings by Radical Women of Color* (Persephone Press, 1981), an important collection including poetry and a number of essays expressing "an uncompromised definition of feminism by women of color." Some other significant sources for poetry by feminists of color include the multiethnic *Ordinary Women* (1978); *Conditions: Five*, The Black Women's Issue (guest-edited by Lorraine Bethel and Barbara Smith, 1979); and *Lesbian Poetry: An Anthology* (compiled by white editors Elly Bulkin and Joan Larkin, Persephone Press, 1981). The ongoing publication of *Azalea: A Magazine by and for Third World Lesbians*, and the recent founding of Kitchen Table / Women of Color Press, offer hope for the development of this poetry independent of the control of white editors and publishers.

In certain ways the emergence of this body of work recalls the emergence of early white feminist poetry: these poets are exploring oppressions and drawing on reserves of experience and tradition which have hitherto seldom entered literature. Theirs is the power of anger released when growing consciousness hits the flashpoint of precise articulation (and this includes much anger at white feminist racism); the discovery of anciently rooted strengths; the radiant energy of new forms of female connection. In this sense, the poetry of women of color belongs specifically to them: it is a literature white feminists can learn from, enjoy, support—but from the sidelines. In another sense, however, I think that much of this work points a direction for the entire feminist poetry movement—toward a complexity of vision, away from "too easy solutions." This is a journey that requires of us a courageous scrutiny of what is most frightening and destructive in ourselves as well as in the world outside us.

Feminists of color, and particularly lesbians, have rarely found in women's communities or in feminist ideology the refuge from painful complexity which has been available there, albeit at great cost, to some white women. Black feminist poets have been saying this loud and clear all along: Audre Lorde in much of her poetry and prose; June Jordan in her "Declaration of an Independence I Would Just as Soon Not Have";[18] Pat Parker in this description of her rebellion against labeling of her poetry: ". . . I'm advertised as lesbian poems, fuck poems, kill the whites poems. Sometimes I feel I'm not angry enough to be billed this way. . . . If I'm advertised as a black poet, I'll read dyke poems" (Woodwoman, 61). Their insistence on complexity now resonates with the work of such poets as Cherríe Moraga and Gloria Anzaldúa (see their essays, and Moraga's poetry and introductory remarks, in *This Bridge Called My Back*); Jamaican-born Michelle Cliff, for whom "claiming an identity" has meant investigating and coming to terms with the intersection of Blackness and whiteness in her own heritage; Native American Chrystos, whose extraordinary pieces in *This Bridge Called My Back* range from an expression of rage at white feminist racism ("I Don't Understand Those Who Have Turned Away From Me") to self-questioning regarding her own complicity in the destruction of the planet ("No Rock Scorns Me as Whore").

Similar issues of identity and responsibility are alive for some recently published white feminist poets as well. Melanie Kaye (*We Speak in Code*, Motheroot Publications, 1980) writes out of her Jewish working-class background, lesbian reality, and activist consciousness. Minnie Bruce Pratt's *The Sound of One Fork* (Night Heron Press, 1981) expresses both love for her southern rural environment and her efforts to understand and reverse the patterns of racism in her life.

I referred earlier to the trend toward increased professionalization of feminist poetry which began to be apparent in the mid-seventies. This has continued, with a move from small press to commercial publication (only for a few well-known poets, however); increasing sophistication about production and distribution methods on the part of small press and self-publishers; and the proliferation of feminist writers' conferences and privately run poetry workshops. In 1978 Melanie Kaye offered the following perspective on this trend:

> What I see now in most places is a regrouping of hierarchy, of *women* writers this time: poetry as performance rather than dialogue.

Important women, women with book or books, read longer, get paid more, are flown in to places like Portland, and to some extent get treated as stars. I say this without accusation. I myself have profited from this formation. . . . And I think this evolution occurred for reasons. More women began writing, open poetry readings got longer and more chaotic, our unwillingness to apply alien standards of criticism made us chary of applying any standards at all (beyond the occasional not very useful one of "how right-on is this?"); and we got bored with what sometimes seemed repetitive.

The danger is that the space which allowed me and many of us to become writers has been enclosed, filled, and made inaccessible to new women, except through an old-girls network of workshops and who-one-knows. We all have stories, they should be told. (10)

In addition to the reasons Kaye lists, certainly economic pressures on poets have encouraged this process. Early in the movement, the writing, reading, and publishing of feminist poetry were often taken for granted as volunteer efforts—as they generally continue to be for poets whose work is little known. Few of us imagined that writing could ever become a source of income; in fact, the necessity for time-consuming, energy-draining jobs was one reason to write poetry rather than novels or books of feminist theory. But volunteerism becomes increasingly exhausting as the years go by, and poets' efforts to parlay writing into an income source inevitably lead to at least some degree of professionalization. Poetry readings become job opportunities of a sort; the teaching of workshops may provide a supplemental income making it possible to squeeze by on unemployment, an adjunct lectureship, or a half-time clerical job rather than a full-time one.

Ironically, though material circumstances may originally dictate the writing of feminist poetry, they may end by discouraging it. For once income from writing is seen as a real possibility, it becomes evident that any significant sum is far more likely to come from prose. Besides, readers are so clear in their preference for prose! I have had some first-hand experience of these pressures myself recently: earning about a thousand dollars from my fiction collection over the past year certainly hasn't supported me, but it *has* begun to make fiction seem more like legitimate work, and poems (or this article) like self-indulgence. Meanwhile, after years of peddling poetry to a largely reluctant public, having fiction received graciously and often with thanks feels like a dangerously addictive pleasure.

Whatever the reasons, though most of the feminist poets of the early-to mid-seventies have continued to publish new poetry, a number have become heavily involved with other forms as well. (It is interesting to note that the reverse process—writers known for their prose turning to poetry—almost never occurs.) Adrienne Rich and Susan Griffin have published influential works of feminist theory; Judy Grahn has edited several volumes of "True to Life Adventure Stories" and is at work on a book of prose; Audre Lorde's most recent book publication is *The Cancer Journals* (Spinsters, Ink, 1980), and her "biomythography" is forthcoming from Persephone Press; Marge Piercy and Alice Walker, both of whom have been ambidextrous in poetry and fiction over the past decade, are now probably far more widely known as fiction writers than as poets.

Contemporary feminist poetry is marked by a broadening of focus which characterizes the feminist movement in general; we are perhaps somewhat less intense and concentrated than we were five years ago. For poets this may mean, for instance, more room for sonnets and sestinas as well as for resolutely anti-formal poetry; for publishing options all the way from separatist volumes put out for lesbians only (such as Elana Dykewomon's *fragments from lesbos*, Diaspora Distribution, 1981) to commercial press collections. I find these developments generally encouraging, though it isn't always clear to me to what extent they indicate a true pluralism, rather than a drifting apart, a slackening of once-taut bonds which permits mere uneasy, even grudging, coexistence. Certainly I am exhilarated by the extraordinary range of themes and styles to be encountered in *Lesbian Poetry: An Anthology*, which contains the work of sixty-four living American lesbian poets, and whose 1981 publication to an enthusiastic reception is in itself encouraging evidence of the continuing vitality of feminist poetry.

But the phase of initial exploration, of poems written, often enough, in the creative heat of the feminist "conversion experience," and necessarily in symbiosis with a dynamic, expanding political movement—that phase seems definitely over. *I am a woman; I am a lesbian:* for so many white feminists, especially, these bald, obvious sentences stand for tremendous revelations which, during the early and mid-seventies, formed the core of our lives and poetry in a simpler way than they could (we may now see) have been expected to do indefinitely. Yet for many who lived through it, feminist poetry's "heroic age" will, I think, be hard to let go of, move away from both in expectation and in practice. What, we may uneasily inquire, can we do for an encore?

The Possibilities of Poetry

In considering the future of feminist poetry, we cannot very well avoid the dismal material realities and political conditions which will inevitably affect its creation. Grants to the arts, especially those with any sort of progressive political content, are seriously jeopardized. (While I was working on this article, an attempt was made in Congress to excise the *entire* Literature Program from the budget of the National Endowment for the Arts.) Women's studies becomes an increasingly narrow, often reactionary area of academic concentration. Librarians are being given every reason to exercise caution in their acquisition of feminist—and certainly lesbian—materials. Any book with serious feminist content is now more likely than ever to be shunned by commercial publishers. Marginal enterprises like feminist newspapers, magazines, presses, and bookstores—upon which the development of feminist poetry has been so heavily dependent—are ill-situated to withstand the combination of severe economic and political pressures increasingly likely to be exerted against them. The issues, of course, extend far beyond the realm of the arts. As the organizers of the October 1981 Women in Print conference stated with chilling brevity: "The rationale for the conference is survival. The survival of the women's movement, as of any revolutionary movement, depends directly on that of our communications network."

It may be argued that feminist poetry, never having been heavily subsidized by government or other institutions, is in a relatively good position to withstand these onslaughts. After all, even those of us who've forgotten how to crank a mimeograph machine can easily refresh our memories. But self-publishing, too, becomes increasingly difficult in hard times, and we're likely to be surprised at what a difference even small grants and occasional gigs make, once they are gone.

Still, these factors seem to me no more important than the negative effects the ominous political climate is likely to have on our own view of ourselves as feminist—as female—poets. The fragility of the public context which has enabled us to place women at the center of the poetic universe—to do so *as a matter of course*—cannot be overemphasized. The erosion of that context in a period of reaction will inevitably mark our work. And it will even more certainly and stringently constrict the efforts of the next generation of women poets (and affect how our own work is remembered, or forgotten)—if, indeed, human society is so fortunate as to survive into the next century, and at a level of organization which permits ongoing literary endeavor.

We have no choice about these extremely unpleasant facts, apart from whatever we are able to do in the political realm to stem them. But we do have a choice of responses. An obvious temptation seems to be the retreat into a new feminist literary orthodoxy, a withdrawal further into an insular, functionally separatist literary community. As a defensive measure, such a response seems to me understandable, but also a serious mistake, likely to result in claustrophobia, boredom, and both political and literary sterility.

One thing we can and should do instead, I believe, is to start taking poetry more seriously. For as a movement, we are far too used to the assumption that poetry and poets will be *there* when we want them, no matter how long they have been ignored, taken for granted, misused. After all, isn't poetry a form of prophecy, and aren't prophets known for their talent for flourishing in inhospitable deserts and other bleak surroundings?

Maybe. But maybe not indefinitely.

What do I mean by "misuse"? By "taking poetry seriously"?

I think, first of all, that the attempt to control poetry, to subordinate it to extra-poetic ends, constitutes misuse. And, as I suggested earlier, I think we have often made this attempt—not even necessarily conscious that we were doing so. I am not, of course, advocating "art for art's sake": poetic values are ultimately life-values, deeply political values. But those values must emerge from the poetry, not be imposed on it. And it is particularly difficult for the feminist writer dependent upon a small, relatively homogeneous community for her support and audience to ignore narrow political expectations about poetry. Poetry will always be found to have uses, and we will want to evaluate the relationship between our consciously espoused *ideas* and our literature. But the most difficult thing to remember from within the context of a political movement, with its emphasis on ideology and on results, is the need to be open to the unconscious, the unforeseen, the unplanned.

I believe we might benefit from what I think of as an increased "separation of powers"—those of the poet and those of the political leader. The blurring of the roles of poet and political spokeswoman has given feminist poetry a range of influence it might otherwise not have enjoyed, and has to some extent infused feminist organizing with poetic values, but it has also sometimes led to an overemphasis on words, language, and the ideas they embody—and to the placing of an impossible burden upon poetry. Feminism desperately needs actions as well as words. And while I firmly believe that poets should be activists, that is not to say that they are necessarily best suited to provide practical, tactical leadership.

I think we further misuse poetry when we present it in such a way as to make of it a spectacle, an entertainment extravaganza, or a branch of political speechifying. Again, this is a matter of degree, of emphasis. There is a place for the marathon poetry reading with its circus atmosphere, the obligatory cultural event at the political rally. But when these become the main or the only settings in which feminist poetry gets heard, there is a serious problem, an inevitable distortion of what gets read and what the audience is able to absorb. Such contexts are bound to encourage in poets the impulse to court easy laughter and easy applause; they are simply not conducive to the serious listening which poetry requires and deserves. Poets themselves are going to have to insist on better reading/ listening conditions, if these are to materialize.

In other ways, too, we need to make more of an effort to provide access to feminist poetry. The understandable reluctance of most feminist small presses to publish it (a great deal of the feminist small press poetry in circulation is *self*-published) on the grounds that it doesn't sell, and the reluctance of feminist bookstores to stock it (except for a few well-known, commercially published titles) on the same grounds, or because "there's so much feminist poetry around," may in the long run have serious consequences—like the channeling of poets into the writing of prose.[19]

Ironically, I suspect that poetry as a genre has lost prestige within the women's movement for the same reason that fiction lacked it in nineteenth-century patriarchal England—because it is perceived as something almost anyone can do. That is the hidden meaning of a code phrase like "there's so much feminist poetry," and it points to the hypocrisy of the general feminist rejection of critical standards: rather than apply them, we have sometimes simply stopped paying attention to poetry at all. This seems to suggest that the development of feminist criticism may be more vital to the health of feminist poetry than we have realized.

But suppose we make an effort to do all these things, to provide a context which takes feminist poetry seriously. What about the essential task, the poetry itself?

While preparing to write this article, I read the following in Adrienne Rich's 1975 essay "Vesuvius at Home: The Power of Emily Dickinson":

> It seems likely that the nineteenth-century woman poet, especially, felt the medium of poetry as dangerous, in ways that the woman novelist did not feel the medium of fiction to be. . . . Poetry is too much rooted in the unconscious; it presses too close against the barriers of repression; and the nineteenth-century woman had much to repress. (174–75)

Later I discovered these lines, written in the early 1950s by self-exiled Polish poet Czeslaw Milosz:

> The objective conditions necessary to the realization of a work of art are, as we know, a highly complex phenomenon, involving one's public, the possibility of contact with it, the general atmosphere, and above all freedom from involuntary subjective control. "I can't write as I would like to," a young Polish poet admitted to me. . . . "I get halfway through a phrase, and already I submit it to Marxist criticism. I imagine what X or Y will say about it, and I change the ending."[20]

I have since been haunted by the implications of these passages for contemporary feminist poets and poetry. "What do *we* have to repress?" my notes inquire. I expect that our own corsetings and evasions will appear (*if*, again, the human community survives) quite as sadly obvious to poets of a hundred years hence as those of nineteenth-century women poets or twentieth-century poets bound by the strictures of doctrinaire Marxism appear to us.

One vast area of uneasiness which suggests the workings of repression has been that of questions surrounding whatever privilege we may ourselves possess, whatever processes of oppression and destruction we participate in. In my own work I notice, and am increasingly disturbed by, the enormous difficulty I experience, not only in *mentioning* certain topics (particularly, for me, race and class oppression) but in approaching them honestly and directly, avoiding the sterility of carefully manicured "correctness." Some recent work (for instance, poetry by Minnie Bruce

Pratt and much of the material in *This Bridge Called My Back*) demon-strates encouraging evidence of attempts to breach this "barrier of repression."

Though issues of female anger (particularly anger at men) and female sexuality may have become somewhat less tabooed for us recently, the problem of our own power often remains, I think, as thornily central as it was for Emily Dickinson—and is therefore another significant area of repression, one closely related to questions of privilege. Given our his-tory as women and that of the world at large, there is no way for us to avoid the negative connotations the concept of power inevitably suggests—though many feminists have tried to solve the problem by that act of repression which involves positing female power as inherently good, constructive, non-competitive, nurturing. I think of Audre Lorde's work, particularly the poem "Power," as an unusually coura-geous, head-on confrontation with this issue, remarkable in its refusal of easy, unconvincing resolutions.

Finally, I am struck by our determined repression of the magnitude of the destruction which stares us in the face: not just piecemeal, sniping attrition or agonizingly slow starvation—these have been commonplace throughout what we know of history—but the definitive end of the hu-man experiment, the "*No* of no degrees" (Rich, "Phantasia," 4). Nuclear war threatens to obliterate all of us. So does the only slightly more nebu-lous spectre of irreversible ecological imbalance. Yet feminist poetry (and theory) usually mention these terrors only obliquely, or as some kind of metaphor for generalized patriarchal destructiveness. (Chrystos's wrenchingly moving "No Rock Scorns Me as Whore" in *This Bridge Called My Back* is an important recent exception.) Increasingly, I find myself turning to the work of Eastern European writers for their serious attempts to undestand the nature of a machinery which is capable of this level of destruction.

Privilege, power, destruction: insofar as these are areas of tension, un-easiness, repression, they are also—as Rich's comment on Dickinson seems to suggest—extremely important areas for poetic exploration, if we are prepared to undergo the risk that exploration entails. Recently women of color have frequently taken the lead in these areas, perhaps because they have had far less opportunity to indulge in illusions of safety. But the challenge is there for all of us.

When I was on the verge of coming out, I remember picturing the lesbian-feminist community as a narrow, cloistered preserve separated from me by a high wall over which I would have to leap—a society both attractive and frightening in its purity. I imagined, I suppose, that the choice to undertake that leap would define, and simplify, the remainder of my life. Not to mention my poetry.

But there are no guarantees. Seven years later, I find myself very much alive in the world, confronted by all its choices and perplexities—companioned, yes; but equally alone. Aware that in creating a feminist context for women's poetry, we have created possibilities only, not certainties.

And convinced that the risk of poetry, the mingled danger and promise, is inseparable from the risk of life itself. Or, as Audre Lorde has written:

> And when the sun rises we are afraid
> it might not remain
> when the sun sets we are afraid
> it might not rise in the morning
> when our stomachs are full we are afraid
> of indigestion
> when our stomachs are empty we are afraid
> we may never eat again
> when we are loved we are afraid
> love will vanish
> when we are alone we are afraid
> love will never return
> and when we speak we are afraid
> our words will not be heard
> nor welcomed
> but when we are silent
> we are still afraid.
>
> So it is better to speak
> remembering
> we were never meant to survive. ("A Litany," 31–32)

NOTES

1. See, for example, Lorraine Bethel's "What Chou Mean *We*, White Girl?" *Conditions:Five* (1979): 86–92.

2. Gloria T. Hull discusses the (hitherto undervalued) role of women poets

in the Harlem Renaissance in her "Afro-American Women Poets: A Bio-Critical Survey," in Gilbert and Gubar: 165–82.

3. For an interesting discussion of the politics of genre as they affected nineteenth-century British female novelists, see Gaye Tuchman and Nina Fortin, "Edging Women Out: Some Suggestions about the Structure of Opportunities and the Victorian Novel," *Signs*, VI 2 (Winter 1980): 308–25.

4. See, for instance, June Jordan's fascinating and opinionated discussion of Whitman as the "father" of an anti-elitist "New World poetry" in "For the Sake of a People's Poetry: Walt Whitman and the Rest of Us."

5. "The only car I now own is a 1964 Rolls-Royce Silver Cloud. . . . You can wear a skirt wherever you go and not suffer embarrassment when you step out of the Cloud. . . ." (*Savvy*, April 1981, 56). "I have my doubts about the Industrial Age and about the future of cars but never about my Rolls. . . . Like any work of art, she is proof that humankind, in the midst of chaos, war and personal catastrophe, can still create something of enduring beauty" (57).

6. Elly Bulkin's introduction to *Lesbian Poetry* gives a good picture of the early "underground" feminist poets as outsiders in multiple senses.

7. See Elly Bulkin's introduction to *Lesbian Poetry* for a discussion of the origins of the lesbian poetry movement. Also interesting in terms of this historical shift and the consciousness surrounding it is Adrienne Rich's dicussion in *On Lies, Secrets, and Silence* of the controversy aroused by remarks she originally read at the Modern Language Association in December 1976, published here as "It Is the Lesbian in Us . . . " (199–202). I was present at that event and vividly recall the alarm evinced by several feminist poets at her suggestion that "It is the lesbian in us who is creative" (201).

8. See Elly Bulkin: "[Lesbian poets] sought to create a tradition that was . . . anti-hierarchical. . . . The work of these early lesbian writers seems to be deliberately, perhaps even defiantly, 'anti-poetic' " (*Lesbian Poetry* xxvi–xxvii). For an extreme statement of an anti-patriarchal aesthetic, see Adrienne Parks, "The Lesbian Feminist as Writer as Lesbian Feminist," *Margins* 23 (August 1975): 69.

9. *The Second Wave* V 3 (1979): 9. See subsequent issues for correspondence discussing the ideas expressed in this article.

10. For revealing discussions of the experiences of creative writers within several revolutionary/Communist movements, I have found the following books particularly valuable: Daniel Aaron, *Writers on the Left* (New York: Avon, 1969); Czeslaw Milosz, *The Captive Mind* (New York: Vintage, 1981); Jonathan D. Spence, *The Gate of Heavenly Peace: The Chinese and Their Revolution, 1895–1980* (New York: Viking, 1981). The last volume contains extensive material on feminist/Communist writer of fiction Ding Ling. Notable for its sensitive treatment of both positive influences and negative constraints on a young American Com-

munist writer is Deborah Rosenfelt's "From the Thirties: Tillie Olsen and the Radical Tradition," *Feminist Studies* VII 3 (1981): 371–406.

11. See, for example, Daly's remarks in "The Transformation of Silence into Language and Action" (5–11) and *Gyn/Ecology: The Meta-ethics of Radical Feminism* (Boston: Beacon, 1978). See also Julia Penelope Stanley's remarks as the chair of that panel, and Marilyn Frye's "To Be and Be Seen: Metaphysical Misogyny," *Sinister Wisdom* 17 (1981): 57–70.

12. Negativity and pessimism have been charges frequently leveled against male poets by feminists. "To the eye of a feminist, the work of Western male poets now writing reveals a deep, fatalistic pessimism as to the possibilities of change. . . . " (Rich, "When We Dead," 49). For an interesting parallel, compare Czeslaw Milosz. "[Polish Communist] critics upbraided him for his chief sins. They proclaimed that his work resembled depraved, or American, literature; that it was pessimistic; and that it lacked the element of 'conscious struggle,' i.e. struggle in the name of Communism" (127). Milosz comments further on, "To approve convincingly is difficult, not because 'positive' values are incompatible with the nature of literature, but because approbation, in order to be effective, must be based on truth. The split between words and reality takes its revenge, even though the author be of good faith" (237).

13. In *Civil Wars* (Boston: Beacon, 1981): 59–73. See also "The Voice of the Children" in the same volume; Hope Landrine's "Culture, Feminist Racism & Feminist Classism: Blaming the Victim," *off our backs* (November 1979): 2; and the numerous discussions of class, race, and language in *This Bridge Called My Back: Writings by Radical Women of Color*, eds. Cherríe Moraga and Gloria Anzaldúa.

14. See Elly Bulkin's introduction to *Lesbian Fiction* for a discussion of feminist perceptions of the possibilities for directly expressing personal experience in poetry, and the ways in which this may have influenced writers' choice of genre.

15. See Becky Birtha's "Toward a Truly Feminist Criticism," *Sojourner*, VI 2 (October 1980): 4, for a practicing feminist critic's discussion of the destructive influence of traditional criticism upon attempts to develop feminist criticism.

16. Marge Piercy, letter printed in "Responses" section, *Sinister Wisdom* 17 (1981): 105. For one example of forthright feminist criticism and the ensuing controversy, see Elly Bulkin, "Racism and Writing: Some Implications for White Lesbian Critics," *Sinister Wisdom* 13 (1980): 3–22; and subsequent issues.

17. June Jordan, "For the Sake of a People's Poetry: Walt Whitman and the Rest of Us."

18. Reprinted in *Civil Wars*.

19. Feminist periodicals, traditionally the mainstay of feminist poetry publication, have also begun to exhibit a disdain for poetry in some cases. *Quest* recently announced its decision to cease publication of any poetry. The editors of

the new quarterly *Common Lives / Lesbian Lives*, after soliciting submissions in sixteen categories of verbal and graphic forms not including poetry, and encouraging women to develop new forms, state, "Although CL / LL will be publishing poetry, the emphasis of the magazine will be on prose forms."

20. Czeslaw Milosz, 14–15.

II

BOOKS & LIFE

By 1983, when I got the idea for a column I would call "Books & Life," my frame of mind had changed considerably from the relatively optimistic one in which I'd written "A Movement of Poets." One reason for the gloom was undoubtedly the fact that the country was now firmly in the grip of the Reagan right wing. The survival issues I'd mentioned at the conclusion of the essay on poetry loomed ever more ominous, with both feminist institutions and individuals feeling the pinch.

On top of this, I was reeling from a recent personal / political trauma, the trashing of my then-unfinished novel *Sinking, Stealing* on the grounds that its depiction of an unscrupulous Jewish father in conflict with a non-Jewish lesbian co-parent was anti-Semitic. This episode, which I allude to in the final column of the series, Part II of "The Political Morality of Fiction," was baroque in its details and still mystifies most nonparticipants to whom I attempt to explain it. Probably both the rarefied atmosphere of political moralism which encouraged it and the degree of psychological pain it caused are incomprehensible to anyone who hasn't spent a few years on Planet Lesbian Feminism, or inhabited a comparable, ideologically bounded village like the CPUSA.

At any rate, the combination of diminishing publishing outlets for all radical literature and my private sense—however temporary—of being a feminist pariah made me worry that I'd soon be writing for the drawer. Doing a column seemed like a healthy alternative, so I approached the *Feminist Review* with the idea. This was a nationally known review of books by women which appeared as a bimonthly supplement to the Rochester *New Women's Times* and had published "A Movement of Poets" as well as several of my reviews. The editors welcomed my proposal and I began "Books & Life," this time abandoning the qualified "we" of the poetry essay for an "I" voice that at times approached the perspective of the "dissident-within-a-dissident-movement," in a phrase I used to describe Richard Wright.

Over the year and a half beginning in January 1984, I would publish six columns at irregular intervals. Susan Jordan, my editor, provided consistent and much-appreciated support. Sadly, by the time I'd decided to stop writing the column in order to devote more time to fiction, the *New Women's Times* had become yet another casualty of the pressures that beset alternative feminist institutions; it succumbed to a combination of staff exhaustion and financial troubles. An even more venerable feminist periodical, *off our backs*, picked up material which had been accepted but not yet printed by the Rochester paper at the time of its demise; "The Political Morality of Fiction" appeared there in two installments in 1985.

Books & Life: A Column

The first installment of "Books & Life" appeared in the January/February 1984 Feminist Review, *introduced by the following paragraph:*

"Books & Life" is planned not as a review column but rather a regular feature devoted to a feminist's reflections on political, literary, psychological and philosophical questions raised by what she reads. As such, it may include discussion of books reviewed elsewhere in this paper. It is rooted in passionate involvement with the written word—but also, I hope, in the sober consciousness that "language cannot do everything."* The opinions expressed here are mine alone.

Several recent anthologies have been important to the American women's movement not only for their specific contents, but because their publication has generated widespread discussion of the issues they address. *Reweaving the Web of Life: Feminism and Non-Violence* (Pam McAllister, ed., Philadelphia: New Society Publishers, 1982) is such a collection. Despite serious flaws, it is highly significant as the first widely distributed anthology to explore connections between feminist and non-violent/pacifist approaches to social change—and, beyond that, to reflect growing feminist involvement in anti-militarist organizing.

Reweaving sat on my shelf for months before I began to read it. I was perfectly well aware that my procrastination had to do, in part, with resistance to facing once again the searing truth that we're playing for keeps this time, this century, and we simply may not make it, maybe not any of us, despite all our love and hope and honest work. (Not that the grief and terror associated with that thought were unfamiliar to me. But denial and numbing recur like bouts of sleeping sickness; they require, I find, continual warding off.) Partly, though, I was skeptical about non-violence as a comprehensive theory of politics and morality. Although I've been arrested several times in anti-militarist civil disobedience protests (including one at the 1980 Women's Pentagon Action), I did not consider myself a pacifist.

Nevertheless, I valued what I knew of the spirit as well as the tactics of

---

*"It was an old theme even for me:/Language cannot do everything—/chalk it on the walls where the dead poets/lie in their mausoleums. . . ." (Rich, "Cartographies" 19).

traditional nonviolent struggle. When I finally opened *Reweaving* I hoped to find a sourcebook for feminists on nonviolence. And I did encounter valuable historical information (on Lucretia Mott's Quaker pacifism, for example; on women—Black and white—in the Civil Rights Movement; on Gandhi), but it seemed to be delivered up more or less at random. I missed an overview which might have traced the development of pacifism from a feminist perspective. This lack seemed especially important with respect to the Civil Rights Movement, where an examination of how non-violence worked and why later Black struggles moved in different directions might have uncovered important lessons for feminists. The basic question I wanted answered, and which the book consistently skirts, was: is nonviolence equally appropriate—equally possible—to all kinds of people in all kinds of movements at all times?[1]

In fact, the Civil Rights Movement was one short though crucial chapter in a long history of resistance, some of it violent, much of it peaceful but not philosophically "nonviolent." The distinction is imporant, as McAllister points out: "the word 'nonviolence' . . . is often used incorrectly . . . to mean any event or time when physical violence is not employed." Yet *Reweaving* includes a piece by Rosemarie Freeney-Harding on Ida B. Wells's founding role in the Black anti-lynching movement, even though an introductory statement mentions that Wells "probably" did not consider herself a pacifist and even carried a pistol for protection. This is tokenistic. It sweeps a powerful Black figure into the confines of what, in context, is essentially white-defined theory, without examining how that theory might have to change if it took into account Wells's political and ethical reality.

A number of *Reweaving*'s contributors assert an inherent connection between feminism and nonviolence, one they apparently regard as so self-evident that it requires a minimum of reasoned demonstration. In arguing for the moral necessity of their position, they typically resort to a "straw woman" approach, writing as though mindless mayhem were the sole alternative to nonviolence. McAllister contrasts a visit to feminist pacifists with a stay in a collective where a militant feminist compliments her by calling her a "natural killer" when she performs well in a target practice session. Margaret Bishop implies that feminists who reject nonviolence will soon be calling on their sisters to slaughter "fathers, brothers, husbands and sons." The suggestions that *any* violence inevitably leads to *total* violence holds no more water than the "right-to-life" claim that abortion rights today will mean enforced euthanasia next week.

What, in fact, does it mean to feminists that Ida B. Wells, who "spent a lifetime involved in what was essentially courageous, persistent, nonviolent struggle," found carrying a gun consistent with her life-affirming goals? By analogy, are the Sandinistas justified in their "arms to the people" campaign of defense against U.S.-backed destruction of the Nicaraguan revolution—or should they be holding C.D. training sessions? Should or could Jewish resisters to the Holocaust, partisan fighters against the Nazi armies, have renounced violent struggle on philosophical grounds?

Some traditional pacifists have wrestled with such questions. Perhaps the nearest *Reweaving* comes to addressing them, however, is in two articles which discuss the possibility of nonviolent self-defense for women. Here the stakes are at least clear: you could get killed. Aside from these pieces and the articles on Black resistance, there's little recognition that the conditions of struggle in most communities are considerably less genteel than those commonly prevailing at North American Take Back the Night marches and anti-nuclear rallies.

Let me be quite clear that many male radicals (and a few female ones) have done tremendous damage through their glorification of violence. And that I worry that even the reluctant violence of true revolutionaries like members of South Africa's African National Congress may end by corrupting those who resort to it.[2] But to imply that pacifists have the last word on constructive change the world over, or that those who would take up arms to defend themselves or their people are equivalent to the Reagans, Andropovs, and Thatchers who "project" their hideous death wishes around the globe, seems to me as arrogant as it is illogical.

On one level *Reweaving* can be read as an encounter between radical feminists, many of whom blame all violence on that conveniently vague scapegoat, "patriarchy," and women who have come recently to a more moderate feminism out of their involvement in the traditional peace movement. Interestingly, even when the latter group's feminism struck me as undeveloped, I was frequently moved by contributions written out of long-term personal experience of activism. With a few exceptions, the radical feminists were far more abstract, given to metaphorical pronouncements whose application to concrete political work seemed unclear at best. (Barbara Zanotti enthusiastically repeats Mary Daly's soothing but empty proposition that "female energy is essentially bio-philic," while Sally Miller Gearhart proposes that men voluntarily [!] reduce themselves to 10 percent of the population.)

Different as the two groups of feminists are, one thing they have in common is an idealist approach—each relies heavily on the power of ideas, symbols, language, morality. I feel two ways about this: on one hand, a "spiritual" emphasis might help to counterbalance the lopsided, often downright superstitious rationalism of traditional left politics. On the other, too much of American feminism is already top-heavy with idealist assumptions, "vision" standing in for activism.

Idealism that loses touch with reality often represents a complicated intersection of privilege and oppression, of struggle and retreat. I have sensed that idealism in some of the most popular recent works of white feminist theory, and I sense it in places in this book. Anything is possible on paper. How easy to identify, out of limited experience, problems and solutions which we assume to be universal—especially when we possess that thin margin of privilege which can make it seem possible to avoid tarnishing our shining theories in the mundane arena of practice.

Most American upper- and middle-class women (and probably many working-class ones as well) are socialized to avoid violent behavior. Despite the ideology, we of course fall victim to men's violence—but we're certainly not supposed to participate. How many middle-class women know how to load and fire a gun; have seriously considered join-ing the police force; have executed calisthenics to the cheerful, chilling refrain, "I wanna kill me an Eye-ranian," as the women recruits do in the film *Soldier Girls?* How, then, can we separate what in our rejection of violent methods is genuine principle, what is simply instilled disdain for behavior we have been taught to perceive as "unfeminine," "low-er-class"?

I see a connection between the questions about power, violence, female conditioning, and change which are implicit in *Reweaving* and aspects of the feminist sexuality debate. Commentators on that controversy have noted a "good girl / bad girl" split, a conflict between feminists who in-ternalized early lessons about keeping skirts down and legs crossed, and those who rebelliously adopted the values, symbolized by pornography, of the sexual revolution. Well, there are "bad girls" in politics as well as in bed, and I'm sure that some of my mistrust of nonviolence theory is born of a pre-rational revolt against prescribed feminine behavior. I am also convinced, however, that many recent radical feminist pronouncements spring from the "good girl" impulse I have come to call "the quest for innocent power," the hope of eluding our chains while remaining as pure and blameless as women are in romanticized images of female victimization.

Donna Warnock has this to say about power:

> Both feminism and non-violence see that power, in its healthy form
> . . . leads naturally to the cooperative and nurturing behavior necessary for harmonious existence. Both feminism and nonviolence oppose power which is exploitive or manipulative. Competition and dehumanizing objectifications of individuals are seen as forms of domination and aggression and precursors or components of physical violence. (29)

Now, for me this has the ring of advertising copy. I measure it against what I know of the frequently unlovely workings of the feminist movement itself, against my sneaking suspicion that real power, while it is by no means *synonymous* with violence and coercion, can also never be entirely or permanently separated from them—and I see an analogy between my alienation and that of women who've complained that their actual sexuality is seriously at odds with public prescriptions for "feminist" desire.

On the other hand, when *Reweaving* works for me, it's often as a kind of running dialogue—or respectful argument—with women who raise more questions than they have answers for. One such speculative piece is the conversation among Barbara Deming, Minnie Bruce Pratt, and Mab Segrest. Another is radical feminist Jane Meyerding's "Reclaiming Nonviolence," in which she considers how we might integrate "specific ideas from nonviolence theory into feminist theory and practice." I come away unsure of how the "nonviolent empowerment of individuals" she advocates can be effective without simultaneous structural transformations which she connects to "violent methods of social change which tend to concentrate and centralize power"—yet convinced that "personal power" is quite real, and with heightened awareness of my own uneasiness at the perils of institutionalized control. Then I feel how much our work is not a matter of either / or, of "spirituality" *versus* "politics," "idealism" *ver-*

sus "materialism"—but that we have got to become, all at once, both more wisely materialist and more authentically in touch with the spirit-sources of faith, love, will.[3]

For me, then, *Reweaving* only begins to raise issues about power, change, and violence which require more extensive exploration. Meanwhile I see an even more urgent need for a broad feminist discussion of militarism, one which will include pacifists and non-pacifists alike. Like everyone concerned with the inseparable issues of justice and survival, we have got to find more effective means of *un*-weaving the web of death which becomes increasingly entangled with everyday existence in this country while it strangles the lives and hopes of our sisters—and brothers—the world over. (As I write the third draft of this piece, American marines are landing in Grenada.) We have got as a movement to deepen our commitment, not to self-congratulatory "visions" of the perfect world we could have had without the patriarchs, but to rescuing the inhabitants of this real and tortured planet.

The requirement that we do so falls upon us first of all as human beings. It underscores what connects, not what separates. But that isn't to say that as feminists (and feminists are so different from one another!) we won't have our own concerns, our own struggles to pursue even within the context of a "larger" movement—larger not because other groups or issues are more important than ours, but because it has got to be greater than the sum of its many parts. No single approach can solve this mess we're in.

In my next column I'll consider some recent writing on what militarism means to women in general and feminists in particular.

NOTES

1. *Reweaving* contains a number of valuable creative contributions which relate to the issue of feminism and nonviolence but do not explicitly argue for a nonviolent approach. They fall outside the scope of this piece, the purpose of which is to examine specific implications of feminist nonviolence theory.

2. An article by Joseph Lelyveld in the *New York Times* of May 25, 1983, "Blacks Seem to Applaud Bomb Attack in Pretoria," outlines the development of the African National Congress. At its founding in 1912, the group sought change through legal channels; it evolved to espouse nonviolent civil disobedience (1949). In the face of the most murderous repressive violence, including the 1960 Sharpeville Massacre, it resorted to guerrilla tactics and sabotage while

avoiding "indiscriminate violence." The article suggests that the ANC may now be prepared to embrace "indiscriminate violence"—a contention I would like to see examined from a more credible political perspective.

3. A number of Third World feminists, in particular, have written and worked out of what Cherríe Moraga has called (in her introduction to *This Bridge Called My Back*) "the faith of activists," a consciousness which transcends the false division between material and spiritual which is so deeply embedded in European thinking. This is one important theme of Toni Cade Bambara's novel *The Salt Eaters*, as it is of Alice Walker's "Only Justice Can Stop a Curse"— which, though it is reprinted in *Reweaving*, does not appear to be a specifically pacifist appeal. Barbara Smith discusses the confluence of material and spiritual values as they relate to the nuclear issue in her " 'Fractious, Kicking, Messy, Free': Feminist Writers Confront the Nuclear Abyss," *New England Review and Bread Loaf Quarterly*, V 4 (1983): 581–92.

If We're Allowed to Live

Why is this age worse than earlier ages?
In a stupor of grief and dread
Have we not fingered the foulest wounds
And left them unhealed by our hands?
  —Anna Akhmatova

. . . *what is distinctive about the era in which we are currently living is that militarisation is no longer conceived of as a war-time, short-term anomaly; it is the new normality.* The present post-war era is a militarised peacetime.
  —Cynthia Enloe

Oh, my God. They have turned the guns against the people.
  —last reported words of Maurice Bishop

"A stupor of grief and dread" is a pretty fair description of my state of mind during the waning months of 1983. Despite my rational under-standing that global emergency is ongoing, despite my suspicion that the three-ring-circus atmosphere of international crisis serves the interests of the powers that be by keeping us narcotized in front of our TV screens,

I remain one of those people (sweetly dubbed "nervous nellies" in the fifties) who gets all worked up over wars and rumors thereof. I jump when the prim *New York Times* stretches a banner headline, even get taken in by the opportunist *Post*, whose sleazy bulletins cause my head to swivel as I pass midtown newsstands. I was once a Cold War child secretly convinced she was living through the Final Days, and am not terrifically impressed by the fact that ultimate disaster has seen fit to hold off for another quarter century or so.

Autumn, of course, brought a bumper crop of horrors, fittingly deployed against the Tuesday night backdrop of "Vietnam: A Television History." In a way, the Grenada invasion seemed the worst of all, so graphically did it illustrate the general public's lust to be manipulated, its criminal taste for patriotic thrills. Four more years, I thought. How will the world survive this? Yes, I was enraged and sorrowful on behalf of the Grenadians, the Cuban construction workers, the American Black people for whom, I tardily learned, the Bishop revolution had meant so much. At the same time, I was fighting down the sensations of *global* claustrophobia, of disembodiment and divorce from reality, that I recognize as symptoms of nuclear panic.

The public events were reflected in private encounters. There was the conversation with a woman in her seventies, someone for whom I care a good deal, one of those tough-minded, politically savvy elders on whom I long to rely for a comforting sense that there are grownups in the world who know how to handle things, in which she confessed (speaking of the *planet*), "You find yourself thinking, well, it'll probably last my time, but what about my children's, and my grandchildren's?" The obligatory discussion of nuclear war with a 13-year-old daughter who assured me, in a striking non-sequitur, that she wouldn't be scared to watch "The Day After" because, "It's really the truth, or almost the truth." The talk with a Latina who'd been in Mexico City during the Grenada invasion: when I said I'd have liked to be there, could have gotten behind the flag burnings she described, the furious crowds shouting A-SE-SI-NOS in front of the U.S. Embassy, she quietly pointed out how unnerving I might have found it to be thus forcefully confronted with the implications of my American identity.

There were the encounters with several white feminists I used to work with in the Women's Pentagon Action: one, active as recently as last summer's Seneca Peace Encampment, said she just couldn't muster the energy for political work lately—if we're all going to die, why not party and have fun? Another explained she'd become more spiritual, planned to move out of the city and conserve her time during "these final years." And there was the conversation with a Black lesbian friend in a D.C.-bound car on the eve of yet another demonstration. When, somewhere near the Molly Pitcher Service Area on the Jersey Turnpike, I alluded to my terror, she reminded me that "if we're allowed to live" the things we'll have to face are minor compared to what others have contended with in the past; I replied that sometimes that *if*, that hideous *if*, seems the one condition I simply cannot bear.

Such was the climate in which I read Joanna Rogers Macy's *Despair and Personal Power in the Nuclear Age*.[1] This book makes a more powerful statement than anything I've yet come across on the emotional and spiritual effects of fear for our human and planetary survival. It is simply written, direct; I found it enormously healing in its matter-of-fact insistence that despair is a natural response to the future we're up against, and one which, moreover, cannot usefully be repressed or denied. Indeed, Macy strongly believes, acknowledging despair can be a beginning point for commitment and activism. She devotes much of her book to describing workshop exercises developed by Inter-help, a group involved in "despair and empowerment work," and relating the experiences and comments of workshop participants.

I was intrigued by Macy's contention (supported by some moving anecdotes) that simply allowing people to talk about their feelings—providing a space in which grief and dread can be acknowledged—is an effective way of facilitating change. Not that this is so novel an idea: after all, something very much like it is the basis of most psychotherapies. Yet how foreign it is to the time-honored tactics of political movements with their traditional assumption that, at least in the public arena, one side's right and one side's wrong and the way to mobilize people is through rational argument, maybe combined with some sort of moral harangue. Even within feminism, where the personal / political connection should have laid the foundation for a more integrated approach, therapists and politicos often seem to have carved out separate spheres of influence: private and public, feeling- and policy-oriented. As I read Macy's descriptions of calm conversations with people whose reactionary attitudes would have driven me up a wall, it occurred to me to wonder what it is I'm protecting when I angrily dismiss all those I can't convince.

Yet I'm not prepared to abandon the political worldview. Sides do have to be taken. Righteous indignation has its place. Beyond a certain point I rebel against the notion that we're all of us human beings, including Cap Weinberger. That point came for me in this book when Macy appeared to suggest that there is something inappropriate about "the angers that some in the peace movement vent on the political and military establishment."

Macy excels at expressing one half of the truth about the global fix we're in: that we *are* in it together, that the collective nature of our jeopardy potentially unites us on a psychological/spiritual plane the species has never before experienced. The other half, mostly neglected here, is that all human experience short of apocalypse continues to be richly varied, contradictory, poorly suited to generalization. Macy never discusses what factors shape our perceptions of and reactions to our peril, and this weakens her book. She doesn't even consider whether there are gender-linked differences in people's responses (are women more easily able than men to express doubt and fear?)—let alone explore what impact being Black or WASP or gay or Jewish or Indian or Asian or middle-class or poor might have. She does list "the unprecedented spread of human misery" as one of three major causes of despair, but in fact concerns herself predominantly with responses to the nuclear threat that has captured the attention of so many white, economically secure Americans who seem scarcely to have noticed the horrifying global role of their own government in promoting death and suffering.

Is this age "worse than earlier ages"? Maybe your answer depends on where you stand. In an essay entitled " 'Fractious, Kicking, Messy, Free': Feminist Writers Confront the Nuclear Abyss," Barbara Smith focuses primarily on how women of color have viewed the threat of apocalypse.[2] There is, she points out, "an element of unsurprise" among "those of us who have experienced poverty in all its forms" when contemplating "the latest cogs in the white-European death machine" (587). She quotes Toni Morrison's *Sula*: "As always the black people looked at evil stoney-eyed and let it run" (588).

As a woman, a lesbian, a long-time dissenter from the prevailing social order, I too recognize "an element of unsurprise" in my own nuclear panic. Yet it is just that—panic: visceral, uncontrolled. And I have felt ashamed of a terror so self-interested, so abstract compared to prison or hunger pangs. Why can't *I* "look at evil stoney-eyed"? How dare I get worked up *now* about the possible end of human life on earth, the irreversible poisoning of the biosphere, when the "civilization" I can't deny is mine has destroyed so much already? I have felt torn between the enormity of the danger and my sneaking suspicion that there is indeed something "white and middle-class" about my nuclear nightmares.

Of course the threat is real. All kinds of people are afraid. Yet what I mean to suggest here is that it may not be *simply* because of the brute facts that so many white Americans and Europeans respond to this issue. What appears to be an equal-opportunity killer, entirely "universal" in its promise of total death, is also peculiarly "our" nightmare for a tortuous knot of reasons: because "we" made the Bomb, and what goes around comes around; because we secretly anticipate some form of retribution for the evils done in our name by our governments; because our top-down conceptions of power help convince us of the earth-shattering importance of all business transacted in the superpower capitals; because the imagery of nuclear holocaust is dramatic enough to impress even those inured to the most violent media spectacles; because it suits our conception of our own importance to suppose we will perish spectacularly by our own hand and take the world with us—to the bitter end, the global Main Event.

It seems likely to me that every people has its own historically rooted nightmares, and I dare to hope that even those terrifying dreams born of excessive power and privilege may have their own peculiar uses. The nuclear nightmare seems to me to be useful insofar as it helps alert "Western civilization" to the profound pathologies it has fostered. It seems to me dangerous to the extent that horror serves to transfix the citizenry, render us passive—or when the gravity of the issue gets used by relatively privileged activists as an excuse for imposing their own narrowly conceived agendas.

Anne Braden, in an excellent brief essay entitled "A White Activist's Reflections: Expanding the Notion of Peace," delivers a long-overdue rebuke to the traditional "peace movement" for its view that peace work has to involve membership in self-defined "peace organizations," which are overwhelmingly white.[3] (She might just as appropriately have addressed her comments to the non-traditional feminist peace groups whose white members monotonously lament their failure to "attract" Third World women.) Braden points out that Black organizations in the United States have traditionally linked justice and peace issues, that it is the white movement's refusal to address those issues jointly that has caused political division, and that, in any event, "it is among whites that the only mass support for our nation's arms buildup exists." She insists that effective opposition to American militarism in the eighties is going to have to mean that white people finally learn to take leadership from people of color.

I wish Braden had demonstrated an awareness of the contributions other groups traditionally marginalized by the "peace movement"—such as feminists, lesbians, and gays of all races—are making to the anti-war effort. Leslie Cagan, like Braden, a long-time activist, has written an article titled "Feminism and Militarism" which helps fill this gap.[4] In addition to suggesting how feminist theory and practice can enhance disarmament work, she considers what it means for the disarmament movement to function as a coalition of groups which may disagree among themselves on certain important issues (abortion, for example). She warns feminists against a "tendency to restate traditional ideas of maternal instinct. . . . The idea that women are in some way 'closer to the earth' seems to miss the depth of the analysis that feminism has to offer and again limits the very definition of woman."

Cynthia Enloe's *Does Khaki Become You? The Militarization of Women's Lives* is a feminist analysis of women's relationships to (male) war machines, especially the contemporary American and British ones.[5] She describes the numerous services armies exact from us and thereby debunks the militarist ideology which would have us think women irrelevant to the business of waging war. In an observation that reminded me of Dorothy Dinnerstein's conjectures about the socially destructive function of traditional female roles within patriarchy, she notes that the actual work we do may be less significant than the fact that we represent "the gender 'women'," the indispensable Others who define the soldiers' masculine mission.

Enloe traces the development of militarist policy-making from ambivalent early attempts to regulate "camp followers" to modern efforts at controlling prostitutes, military wives, army nurses, female soldiers, "nimble-fingered" electronics workers. Her portrait of a far-flung, largely Third World sisterhood of toilers in the modern weapons industry is particularly chilling. These women, she points out, are often "triply militarized":

Their labor is exploited so that their governments can go on buying foreign police and military equipment. They live in societies which are made repressive by militarised governments unwilling to confront deep-seated inequities, preferring to rely instead on coercive force and the aid of friendly powers, such as the US, to whom they give military bases. They work on products which themselves either have direct military application or are part of a larger corporate profits formula in which defense contracting plays a central part. (201)

Within the U.S. military itself, racial and sexual exploitation are equally blatant. Black women were barred or relegated to demeaning duties throughout most of World War II. Yet, "while black women are approximately only 11 percent of all American women, by June 1982 they comprised 25.7 percent of all women in the armed forces combined and 42.5 percent of all enlisted women in the US army" (Enloe, 135). In 1979 "women were six times more likely than men to be discharged from the army on grounds of homosexuality" (143).

Despite the valuable information and insights Enloe's book offers, I came away from it vaguely dissatisfied, feeling as though I'd seen lots of trees and somehow missed the forest. I felt, that is, that I'd glimpsed without quite grasping the meaning of the "militarised peacetime" she alludes to, the armed-to-the-teeth world I know is there beneath the thinning veneer of civilian life.

In part, this may be the fault of her somewhat lackluster writing style and her tendency to abandon promising theoretical points without sufficiently developing them. But I suspect there's something more at work here. My surreal sense of removal from the death establishment seems to me a characteristic American affliction, at least remotely akin to the experience of those B-52 pilots who bombed North Vietnam from nine to five, never saw their targets, and returned to the South in time for "Happy Hour." (After writing that sentence I spoke with a friend who grew up in a military family, lived on SAC bases, and now says that as a child it never occurred to her that any of this was related to wars or killing.)

And what about the fact that I'm a woman? Surely the propagandists who, down through the ages, have insisted that war is strictly masculine business have been stunningly successful. This can be seen in our own attitudes, in definitions of violence against women that ignore militarism, or assumptions on the part even of feminist peace activists that war is a phenomenon in which women participate only as casualties. It is just as hard to see that women *as women* have a real relationship to war—and begin to untangle the complexities of that relationship—as it ever was to create the consciousness that housework and mothering are real work, battering and rape are real violence. Maybe it's even harder, because housework and mothering, battering and rape at least involve the "private" sphere, traditionally our own—whereas to grapple with war is to enter the "public" arena so long forbidden to us.

Yet enter it we will, increasingly—if we're allowed to live. Despite all the dazzling horrors of this century, the spoiled revolutions, gulags, fascist states, and death camps, the tiger cages and South African "homelands," Argentinian and Chilean and Salvadoran torture chambers, despite Lebanon and Cambodia, despite America—nothing suggests that people, or even plants, give up before they have to, that any "totalitarianism" short of total extinction is going to extinguish *our* (and here I mean the very big *our*, the *our* that transcends any single species) profound and sacred capacity for struggle.

Last night as I was getting ready to watch the final installment of "Vietnam: A Television History," I caught a glimpse of the world's most powerful actor holding a news conference.

"What do you want for Christmas?" someone had to ask.

"Peace," slimily smarmed the Great Communicator.

Peace is not a gift, Mr. Asesino-in-Chief. We human beings are fighting like hell for it.

As we roll on into 1984, there's just one thing I want for all of us, for all the solstice holidays combined. And I would pray for it, if I knew how.

That gift, of course, is time.

NOTES

1. Joanna Rogers Macy, *Despair and Personal Power in the Nuclear Age* (Philadelphia: New Society Publishers, 1983) 178 pp. See the list of Small Press Addresses at the back of this book for ordering information on books discussed in this and other chapters which may otherwise be unavailable.

2. Barbara Smith, " 'Fractious, Kicking, Messy, Free': Feminist Writers Confront the Nuclear Abyss," *New England Review and Breadloaf Quarterly* V 4 (1983): 581–92. This is a special edition devoted to "Writers in the Nuclear Age" and is available from *NER/BLQ*, Box 170, Hanover, NH 03755.

3. Anne Braden, "A White Activist's Reflections: Expanding the Notion of Peace," WIN XIX 13–14 (August 1983): 4–6.

4. Leslie Kagan, "Feminism and Militarism," *Beyond Survival: New Directions for the Disarmament Movement*, eds. Michael Albert and David Dellinger (Boston: South End Press, 1983) 81–118. A number of essays in this collection are of value for activists attempting to arrive at a broad, progressive understanding of "peace-with-justice."

5. Cynthia Enloe, *Does Khaki Become You? The Militarization of Women's Lives* (Boston: South End Press, 1983) 262 pp. Another book feminists and anti-militarists might want to know about is the *Guide to War Tax Resistance* which War Resisters League publishes. This is a comprehensive guide to participation in the growing movement to resist militarization by refusing to pay all or part of one's federal income taxes. Order it from the War Resisters League, 339 Lafayette St., New York, NY 10012.

On Reading Men

When the woman I affectionately call my mother-in-law had a birthday recently, I asked her out to the theater. Besides being a gift to her, the evening was an excuse for me to see a Broadway production of Shakespeare which I undoubtedly wouldn't have gone to on my own.

As we waited in the theater lobby, I ventured a remark I figured my companion, a veteran of the Old Left, would appreciate. I said that as a lesbian-feminist writer I felt I wasn't supposed to care for Shakespeare. In reply, she told me a story: a male friend of hers who'd once enjoyed a position of some responsibility in the Communist party had taken her and several other staunch progressive types out to see the movie *Ninotchka*, which, as she explained, was on the party "Index" for poking fun at the Soviet regime. Tongue in cheek, her friend maintained that he found it necessary to familiarize himself with this deplorable piece of capitalist propaganda in order to carry on his work. And so a small group of dedicated politicos enjoyed an evening of rebellious entertainment.

And here was I, 40 years and more later, balancing my notions of feminist duty against my anarchic passion for literature.

In Ellen Frankfort's dreadful new book, *Kathy Boudin and the Dance of Death* (reactionary politics aside, this has to be the worst-written chunk of prose by a feminist which a commercial press has seen fit to dignify with cloth covers since Rita Mae Brown's tennis novel), she boasts that the founders of the *Feminist Review* made an ironclad decision never to review a man's work. Perhaps times have changed, for the *Review's* current editors reacted quite calmly to my proposal for this piece. But if so, the change is slight; though I have to assume that innumerable feminists read and think about books written by men, public discourse on the subject is still about as popular as discussion of rape fantasies was a few years back.

Why do I read men?

No: that wording doesn't quite get it. Probably only the most doctrinaire of separatists would expect me to shun men's writing altogether. The more damaging question is: why do I enjoy it? Not always, certainly, for even though I start out by being extremely selective, I still run into a lot of male writing that either offends me past interest or bores me unspeakably. Yet the embarrassing fact remains that lately some of my most intensely pleasurable literary experiences have come from reading men's fiction and poetry. (Historical, political, and other extra-literary men's writing is important to me too, but since space is limited, I'll stick to creative work here.) And nobody told me it would turn out like this, when I signed on with the feminist literati.

I've been analyzing my responses and it strikes me that one advantage of reading men is the vacation it provides from ideology, from the stuffy and untruthful atmosphere a political theory gives rise to as it becomes more and more removed from the conditions of real life. Male writers couldn't care less about the latest women's movement flap over the politics of language (or—heaven help us—punctuation!). They are impervious to feminist appeals for "positive images" of this or that group. They are not, like *our* writers, trying so desperately hard to be *good*. They either operate according to their own peculiar (and, from our point of view, largely irrelevant) notions of literary correctness, or they ignore doctrinal questions. In any event, because they are outside "the community" one does not feel duty-bound to form a political/moral judgment of their work in quite the same way one does when approaching a feminist author. No need, obviously to write denunciatory letters to *oob* or *GCN* regarding William Shakespeare, no matter how sexist, racist, or classist, anti-Semitic or homophobic his plays may prove to be.

A male writer's alien status presents the added advantage that, though one's opinion of his character may be lowered by reading his work, the reverse is rarely true—the work is unlikely to be spoiled by a too-close encounter with its maker. Sad but true confession: there are popular feminist books which I have avoided reading for no better reason than that I can't stand their authors. (And even when I do like a feminist writer personally, the prospect of having to offer an opinion of her work or even write a review deprives me, in reading it, of a certain valuable sense of freedom.) A male writer I admire retains the romantic aura which adheres to Authors before one has met any. If his feet are made of clay, I don't have to know about it.

But these are, after all, negative reasons for reading men. What about the positive ones? Whose work am I drawn to, and why?

Male writers I care about are, more often than not, outsiders in some sense. Social concerns frequently surface in their books, though these are not always overtly "political." A very few are men I happen to know personally and count as part of my extended literary-political community. Far more numerous are the strangers, the strangest of all being those who succeed in entrancing me despite my distaste for, even horror at, their politics and world views.

Certain books by men raise especially bothersome questions about distinctions between "us" and "them," about the arbitrariness of the divisions which feminists (for the best of reasons) institutionalized when we created a separate sphere of publishing and reviewing. A good example is Ernie Brill's short story collection *I Looked Over Jordan*, published by South End Press in 1980. When I read this book in 1982, I was impressed by the author's skill in conveying a work experience—that of nurse's aides and orderlies—which had made a profound impression on me when I'd had a job in a VA hospital, but which I'd never seen written about, and his success—or so I judged it—at getting inside Black characters at a level which few white American writers (including, certainly, white feminist ones) have attempted. Evidently, he was that rare being, someone equally serious about politics and fiction. With the exception of Hattie, the 65-year-old Black nurse's aide who fights forced retirement in the wonderful opening story, I wasn't especially taken with his female

characters, but I could let that pass. The book had other things to offer—
like a male perspective on literal "shitwork" (i.e., the familiar hospital
routine of cleaning up excrement, an activity as foreign to most men as it
is familiar to women).

In short, here was a rather poorly distributed, under-publicized small
press book of merit, one I knew had gotten near-zero exposure in the
establishment press and was unknown to feminists. I wanted to review it,
partly as a way of alerting my community to its existence, partly as a way
of clarifying my own impressions. Had the author been a woman, I would
have done so. But Ernie Brill is a white, straight (albeit Jewish and radical)
man. In none of the periodicals to which I contribute reviews would a
piece on *I Looked Over Jordan* have been welcome.

It so happens I got to know Ernie personally. That's unusual, as I've
said. Much more frequently I've been moved by an encounter with a
writer I'll not only never meet, but with whom I should, by all conventional measures, have almost nothing in common. Yet there it is, a sud-
den sense of kinship, a sort of absolute relatedness: intimate, essential,
and entirely unaccounted for by the crudely reductionist version of identity politics that currently dominates the lesbian-feminist literary scene.

Richard Wright, in "How 'Bigger' Was Born," an essay on the writing
of *Native Son*, recorded something similar:

> There is in me a memory of reading an interesting pamphlet telling
> of the friendship of Gorky and Lenin in exile. The booklet told of
> how Lenin and Gorky were walking down a London street. Lenin
> turned to Gorky and, pointing, said: "Here is *their* Big Ben." "There
> is *their* Westminster Abbey." "There is *their* library." And at once,
> while reading that passage, my mind stopped, teased, challenged
> with the effort to remember, to associate widely disparate but mean-
> ingful experiences in my life. . . . The feeling of looking at things
> with a painful and unwarrantable nakedness was an experience, I
> learned, that transcended national and racial boundaries. It was this
> intolerable sense of feeling and understanding so much, and yet liv-
> ing on a plane of social reality where the look of a world which one
> did not make or own struck one with a blinding objectivity and
> tangibility, that made me grasp the revolutionary impulse in my life
> and lives of those about me and far away. (xvii)

"This intolerable sense of feeling and understanding so much, and yet
living on a plane of social reality where the look of a world which one did

not make or own struck one with a blinding objectivity and tangibility." Who among feminists has said this better? I first felt drawn to Wright (whom, I'm ashamed to say, I began to read only about two years ago) because I found in him a writer, already forcibly marginalized by his race and class, who went on to become a dissident-within-a-dissident- movement. (A Communist, he eventually broke with the party, in part because it threatened to strangle his work.) In reading *Native Son* I was moved, first, by a harshly eloquent portrayal of life in a poor Black community in Chicago, and second by his courage in treating that supremely tabooed topic, the sexually charged killing of a wealthy white woman by a poor Black man. (I may say that, from a feminist vantage point, I'm rather inclined to envy the general freedom of male writers to express rage, depict brutality.) Wright's intense misogyny, while it certainly disturbed me, did not cancel the powerful impact of his work.

The Russian poet Osip Mandelstam is another writer who sometimes speaks to me so directly that I count him part of my literary family. If Wright excels in conveying the individual's experience of outsiderhood that specific oppression produces, Mandelstam incomparably renders the impersonal agony of being crushed to death by the twentieth century, as victims of an old torture were crushed by weights piled on their chests. "And to struggle for air on which to live— / this is a glory beyond compare," he wrote in one of his last poems, "Lines About the Unknown Soldier," dated 1937. And, "Must the skull be unwound entirely / from temple to temple, / so that the troops cannot but pour / into its dear eye sockets?" (*Selected Poems*, 157).

Mandelstam's work is opaque, mysterious, often highly personal in its references, at times frustratingly abstract (not in the sense of being theoretical, but as visual art is abstract). I know it partially, in translation, and largely mediated by his wife Nadezhda Mandelstam's superb memoirs, which I read first. Yet few poems "take the top of my head off" like the early 1918 "Twilight of Freedom," in which the poet with brilliant ambivalence implicates his persona in various activities symbolic of large-scale, revolutionary social experimentation: the binding of swallows into "fanatic legions" that obscure the firmament; the "screeching turn of the wheel" as navigators attempt to alter the course of the "sailing" globe. The poem ends, "We will remember even in the lethean cold / that the earth has cost us ten heavens" (*Selected Poems*, 53). It is this note of stubborn, helpless human attachment to a doomed biosphere that above all makes the poem such an uncanny and touching comment-before-the-fact on everything that has transpired between 1918 and 1984.

A contemporary writer to whom I turn for related insights into the earthly predicament is Russell Hoban, whose novel *Riddley Walker* is a fable of a technologically primitive, post-nuclear-holocaust England. Employing a rich invented jargon which is both archaic and futuristic, he creates a Möbius strip of a book in which the future seems to rush head-long into the past, in which the follies of "Western civilization" bid fair to repeat themselves—at the center of it all a terrifically appealing male protagonist who seems to embody a good many of the flaws that started the trouble in the first place. I thought *Riddley Walker* said about as much on the subjects of patriarchy and male violence as any work by a woman I'd recently read, and I would very much have liked to discusss it with other feminists—but it was, after all, by a man, and nobody had read it.

In many cases, my attraction to a writer has less to do with specific topics he treats than with the fact that he conveys a view of human exis-tence I sympathize with in language that delights me. A case in point is the American Black writer John Edgar Wideman, a number of whose fine books seem to have been issued as paperback originals, presumably for want of a more prestigious hardcover publisher. In all three of the ones I've read (*Damballah*, *Hiding Place*, and *Sent for You Yesterday*, the last being my favorite), he writes about members of a single extended family in a Black neighborhood in Pittsburgh. The language and sensibility here remind me of John Langston Gwaltney's *Drylongso: A Self-Portrait of Black America*, a nonfiction work in which a medley of voices reveals what Gwaltney calls "core black culture." Time in Wideman's books becomes a fluid, supremely human dimension; he has developed a deceptively simple method of presenting his characters wrapped in their personal and communal history, so that past, present, and future merge in a haunting simultaneity that governs everyday life.

Another wonderful writer is the late Chaim Grade, much of whose work is available in translations from the Yiddish (I've read *The Agunah* and *Rabbis and Wives*). Grade's work centers on the Jewish community of pre-Holocaust Vilna, Lithuania. He writes frequently about the politi-cal and psychological dimensions of religious disputes—conflicts that have their counterparts in any close, contentious community, even the women's movement. He excels in depicting strong, trapped women: the agunah (grass widow) who bends to intense social pressure and takes a second husband she does not care for, only to suffer because she is found to have remarried contrary to religious law; the ambitious, intelligent wife whose hectic efforts to advance the position of her husband, a modest rabbi totally uninterested in social success or power, result in misery for all. In Grade's portraits of obscure rabbis, of thwarted housewives and seamstresses, and of the struggling, vital Jewish community which is his larger subject, there is some transient satire and criticism, and a great deal of enduring love.

Now that I think about it, there are really not too many writers whose work I enjoy while detesting their politics. But it does happen now and then, as in the case of the grotesquely misogynist, racist, and anti-Semitic Balzac, whose fascinating *Cousin Bette* I read this past summer. In part, the book intrigued me because of the inner tension between what the author seemed to wish to portray and what he in fact showed. (This sort of ambiguity is endemic to literature, a fact feminists have tended to ignore.) Yes, *Cousin Bette* is a book which denigrates women and upholds patriarchy—on one level. It's also a book which presents patriarchy as corrupt, stuffy, idiotic, and ridiculous. The engine which drives the plot is the thrilling, stupendous badness of the villainess-heroine, a multiply kept mistress who enjoys a highly successful career of manipulating rich men (up until the contrived ending, in which vice is duly punished). Now, when's the last time feminist literature allowed us such a delicious revenge fantasy?

The truth is that it's all much too complicated, psychologically and politically, this business of reading men, to dispatch in one brief column. I haven't even yet touched on what I call "literary heterosexuality," by way of analogy with the other kind. For books and sex were always connected for me. In my youth, being heterosexual meant, among other things, identifying with men and being perpetually frustrated, in my sexual dealings with them, to discover that I was another category of creature, and expected to act the part. It was much the same with books: I schooled myself (fortunately I escaped most formal literary training) to identify with male characters and authors, and suffered corresponding disillusionment. Now, when I go back to "read men"—as when I meet them socially—I note that the old patterns are still there, that neither the identity "lesbian" nor my time in the women's movement has quite obliterated that 16-year-old girl in love with a latter-day teenage beatnik who plied her with paperbacks by Kerouac and Mailer. And yet it seems to me that my relative independence as a lesbian-feminist has made it possible for me to make constructive use of men's writing in a way I couldn't have done at an earlier, more dependent stage. (Or put it more cynically: I can care for men, from a safe and literary distance.)

For whatever mix of reasons, I'm going to keep reading the boys. And adopt this article of literary faith: that the most authentic and necessary literature is never directed simply to the members of one group; the deepest sympathies between a writer and a reader can never be prescribed or legislated, just as dissent can never be institutionalized—though political movements never quit trying.

To write seriously is to broadcast to the universe. To read seriously is to monitor the broadcasts in search of something that *connects*, without too many preconceptions as to what corner of the galaxy all meaningful signals will emanate from. The women writers whose work I most care for are almost invariably dissidents of one sort or another; the feminists among them more and more tend to be dissenters, even heretics within the movement itself. My favorite male authors are often far removed from me in time or place, background or circumstance. To be a lesbian, feminist, political writer, and on top of that to decline even the bleak respectability of ideological corsets is—as experience, observation, and historical analogy all persuade me—a lonely, exacting calling. Companionship is welcome from any quarter.

"A Revolution of Poets": The Impact of Nicaragua*

In 1956, the young Nicaraguan poet Rigoberto López Pérez assassinated Anastasio Somoza García, Nicaragua's first ruling Somoza; Lopez Pérez

---

*"Often, it is said that the Nicaraguan revolution is a revolution of poets." From a statement on culture by poet and Secretary General of the Sandinista Cultural Workers' Association Rosario Murillo, reprinted in *Impulse* XI 1 (Summer 1984): 7.

himself was immediately killed. Twenty-four years later, 20-year-old poet and revolutionary Leonel Rugama died fighting the *Somocista* National Guard when an entire battalion surrounded him and several comrades in a house in Managua. That these two are commonly honored by their people not only as heroes but as poets says something significant about the place of literature and its makers in contemporary Nicaragua.

The country today is at the heart of a vital Central American literary movement which is taking shape in the context of revolutionary struggles. This movement clearly differs in important respects from any and all North American counterparts (for one thing, as the above examples suggest, the conditions of its development have been far harsher). And yet it also feels strangely familiar to me. In the writings of Nicaraguans and other politically committed Central Americans, and their statements about their work, I re-encounter in changed form some of the questions about the intersection of politics and art that I first came up against in a U.S. feminist context. I recognize an energy, a faith, a revolutionary creativity that remind me of the literary/political energy generated by feminism at its best—the phenomenon that once led me to title an essay on feminist poetry "A Movement of Poets"—and I draw closer as though to a heat source that might warm my own work.

This past July I visited Nicaragua for two weeks on a trip organized by the New York–based solidarity group Ventana, at the invitation of the Nicaraguan ASTC (Asociación Sandinista de Trabajadores de Cultura, Sandinista Cultural Workers' Association). Despite the trip's focus, my most immediate, powerful impressions were hardly concerned with "culture" in the formal sense. I was stunned by the intense, pervasive, pre-industrial poverty that is the legacy of U.S.-fostered development: poverty that has urban families living in one-room dirt-floored shacks and cooking on backyard wood fires, that means hospitals without sheets, farmers without tractors, rural communities without safe drinking water. I was stunned too by the history of torment engraved most visibly, publicly, in the architecture: Managua half in ruins, never recovered from the 1972 earthquake, much less from the damages of the insurrection; and on every block in certain neighborhoods the names, hand-lettered on walls, of locals killed in the struggle.

I was much moved to witness the vitality of a society which has managed to survive and press forward, not by burying the memories of torture and death from the Somoza years, but by bringing the fallen into the living present through countless commemorative ceremonies, through the telling and retelling of the stories of the "heroes and martyrs," through organizations and community centers and cooperatives named for them. I was newly angered to realize the extent of the danger—even short of the threat of direct U.S. invasion—which menaces this fragile, so-costly revolution; how much hurt the Reagan-sponsored contras have already inflicted on a nation of three million defended by a minimally equipped teenage army and a citizen militia. I was enormously relieved to be someplace where I needn't be forever subconsciously tensed against the onslaught of reactionary propaganda that so thoroughly permeates every corner of public life in what guerrilla leader Augusto César Sandino used to like to call "the United States of North America." Which is not to say that Nicaragua is flawless, or that I didn't also view radical state propaganda with my usual crabby skepticism, but that it was an exhilarating and quite unprecedented experience to find myself in a country where social momentum right now belongs to the forces of life, not death.

But this column concerns books as well as life, and I want to discuss some things I learned about Central American writing, both on the trip itself and through reading done before and since. I do this with a sense of intense excitement about the work, what North Americans can gain from it, and the possibilities for a respectful interchange through which we might begin to repair some of the damage inflicted during our long history of cultural—as well as politico-economic—imperialism. I do it also with a sense of my own limitations as a speaker of minimal Spanish, and an anglo, someone contributing to the problematic pattern whereby it has usually been non-Latino, white North Americans who have "interpreted" Nicaragua and its neighbors to a U.S. audience.

Nicaragua's literary tradition is strongest in poetry. The late nineteenth/early twentieth century poet Rubén Darío, whose work was influenced by European sources yet expressed pronounced anti-imperialist sentiments, is now looked upon as the forerunner of modern Nicaraguan poetry. North Americans have also exerted an important influence, with poet-priest-revolutionary Ernesto Cardenal's translations of Whitman, Dickinson, and others playing a significant role. Cardenal, currently Nicaragua's Minister of Culture, is himself one of the finest living Latin American poets. For anyone who hasn't read his work, and wants to do so in English, I strongly recommend *Zero Hour*.[1] The long poem "Oracle over Managua" is, with its fury, its irony, its ruthless cataloguing of the brutal details of slum life during the Somoza years, its tenderness for "the dusty soap-opera / neighborhoods / with walls on which a kid is scratching / asshole cunt prick" (62), is quite simply one of the most brilliant, devastating political poems I've ever read—despite tiresome references to Che Guevara's "new man."

While Nicaragua possesses a sophisticated indigenous literature, it is also a country which in 1979 at the time of the revolutionary triumph was estimated to have a 50 percent illiteracy rate (since said to have been reduced to 13 percent by a literacy campaign of heroic proportions). Under these conditions, the meaning of reading—as of writing—is bound to be different for the average person than in a society like ours where basic literacy, though by no means universal, is and long has been the norm. A story I heard which poignantly symbolized the obscene power the United States has exercised in Central America was related by a North American college student who'd spent a number of weeks traveling around Nicaragua. He told of a conversation with a young *campesino* who had inquired in all seriousness whether North Americans are *born* knowing how to read.

I got a strong sense that many "ordinary" Nicaraguans are now actively involved in making literature—and, as in the early stages of the U.S. women's movement, it is frequently poetry. When our group took an overnight trip to the north of the country to visit areas which have been damaged in contra attacks, we stayed in an agricultural training center. Several women got into a conversation with a Nicaraguan studying there who later wrote them a poem which expressed his own support for the revolution and his gratitude for our solidarity; he ended with a bittersweet, regretful line in which he referred to himself as "this crazy bohemian who wanted to be a poet." In the university town of León, I visited one of a number of Popular Cultural Centers out of which poetry workshops, theater groups, art classes, etc., are organized for interested citizens. Of course it is hard to tell how many actually participate in such programs or benefit from the frequently mentioned provision whereby artists are encouraged to pursue their calling while on active military duty. Still, I got the message that Nicaraguans care about writing, visual art, and music, and are making these things a social priority despite tough times and a war on.

One of the most interesting conversations I had about poetry and the role of poets was with a 26-year-old woman named Angela who occupies a highly responsible position doing cultural organizing for the Central Sandinista de Trabajadores (Sandinista Workers' Federation). From a large working-class family, she joined the revolutionary struggle as a young teenager, doing student organizing through singing groups and other cultural activities. When I mentioned (rather defensively, as I'm used to doing at home) that I was a poet, she very seriously and matter-of-factly inquired what I planned to write about Nicaragua. Somewhat taken aback, I tried to explain in my very limited Spanish that for me writing poetry is not quite such a cut-and-dried process. She responded optimistically that surely I must have seen some things at the July 19 celebration of the revolutionary triumph which I could write about. Later, in a group discussion, when I told her through an interpreter that I frequently do clerical work in order to buy time for writing, she seemed genuinely astonished. In Nicaragua, she explained, I would be able to work as a poet developing literature among the people.

Two things impressed me in this. One was Angela's apparent conviction that making revolutionary culture is a relatively uncomplicated process: if you support a revolution, you should be able to "write poems about it." In the United States this is a viewpoint I tend to associate with sectarians and other dogmatic folk, but Angela was not in the least dogmatic. Because of her evident sincerity and faith—because I liked her so much—I found myself re-examining my assumption that poetry written with a definite purpose in mind is liable to be little more than a rhetorical exercise. I had to stop and try to imagine what it would be like to be a *non*-alienated artist.

The second thing that struck me was the notion of a universal state subsidy for artists (which is, according to Rosario Murillo's statement in *Impulse*, more a goal than an achieved reality at this point).[2] The prospect alarmed as much as it intrigued me, for I found it impossible to believe that there wouldn't be a conflict between my employer's definition of socially desirable poetry and my own obligation to certain inconvenient themes. (Most obviously, it was very hard to imagine being an openly *lesbian*, state-subsidized poet in Nicaragua or anywhere else!)

Another worthwhile encounter was with the poet Vidaluz Meneses, who has published two collections of her work; individual poems appear in translation in the Summer 1984 *Bomb*, in the anthology *Volcán*, and, together with a fascinating interview by Margaret Randall, in *Ikon*.[3] She works on libraries in the Ministry of Culture, and I visited her in that ambitious if modestly housed organization. (The day I was there they were lugging the typewriters—manual, of course—from desk to desk since evidently there weren't enough to go around.) Meneses spoke of the need to make Nicaraguan poetry available as widely as possible on account of the urgency of the political situation, at the same time expressing regret that frequently the work is not as good as she feels it will be, given more time for development.

I was particularly pleased to have the opportunity to meet Claribel Alegría, since I already knew and admired her work, which is a unique poetic synthesis of personal experience and unsparing confrontation with the political evils that beset her homeland. Alegría was born in Estelí, Nicaragua, but was raised in El Salvador and considers herself Salvadoran; after many years in the United States, Europe, and other parts of Latin America, she now lives in Managua. She is a well-recognized poet with at least seven collections to her credit as well as *Suma y sigue*, a volume of selected poetry published in Spain in 1981. Yet her work is just now beginning to get a bit of attention in the United States, where a bilingual edition of nine poems, *Flowers from the Volcano*, appeared in 1982.[4] Alegría says she plans a U.S. reading tour for spring 1985. As those who heard her fine reading in New York last spring can attest, it will be well worth the effort to go and hear her.

Alegría's small but comfortable home is clearly a sort of informal literary center for the Americans. My visit there gave me a sense of the importance of Nicaragua as an oasis where Latin American radicals—artists and otherwise—can meet, talk, exchange ideas, breathe freely for a time, before returning to their respective struggles. Her U.S. guests were introduced to an Argentinian writer as well as to a number of Salvadorans who were either living in exile in Managua or were based elsewhere and had come to town for the July 19th celebration. One of the latter was Manlio Argueta, author of the beautiful, harrowing novel *Un día de vida* (published in the United States as *One Day of Life*).[5] Told largely from the point of view of a middle-aged peasant woman, the story concerns a Salvadoran family's attempts to cope with a reign of terror visited upon them because of several members' radical activism. I was particularly impressed that Argueta had managed to infuse this heartbreaking tale with a rare sense of affirmation—and that he'd pulled off the woman's perspective with such sympathy and conviction. (All those who think political fiction has to be written out of "one's own oppresson," narrowly defined, take note!) Argueta says he has finished another novel which will be available shortly in the United States.

When I got back to New York I discovered several publications I wished I'd read before my trip. One was *Volcán*, a bilingual anthology of poems from El Salvador, Guatemala, Honduras, and Nicaragua. The editors—one of whom states in the introduction that "this is not an anthology at all, but a contact bomb"—have stuck to a fairly conventional notion of revolutionary poetry. Despite the inclusion of, for instance, Nicaraguans Giaconda Belli, Rosario Murillo, and Daisy Zamora, women are poorly represented (maybe, I speculate, because our work too infrequently treats of guns and guerrilla warfare). There's little background information to help the North American reader place the poets in literary / political context, and the selections are too brief to give an adequate idea of any one contributor's work. In fact, the anthology reminds me of one of those nightmarish marathon readings by 47 poets in which the good, the bad, and the mediocre jostle one another in a numbing succession of two-and-one-half minute segments. Still, the inclusion of poetry from a number of Central American countries makes an important statement about the region's unity; given the general unavailability of this poetry in English, *Volcán* is a useful resource.

Far more successful overall is the Canadian magazine *Impulse*'s Summer 1984 issue, subtitled "Culture of Nicaragua." Again, women are sadly underrepresented, with all nine fiction selections authored by men. Still, with its attractive, visually arresting format and its variety of genres (fiction, poetry, drama, interviews, and articles, with the first two categories printed in both English and Spanish), the issue offers a tantalizing glimpse of Nicaraguan cultural ferment.

I learned a good deal from the various discussions of the interplay between culture and the revolutionary struggle both before and after the triumph. Omar Cabezas's entertaining account of the ways in which theatrical training helped revolutionaries who had to "act in front of the enemy," and his description of his discovery that swear-words could be an effective organizing tool, inspired me with a renewed awareness that political work, *successful* political work, can be a highly creative affair. I was much distressed by Alan Bolt's play "The World, the Devil, and the Flesh," in which the misguided counter-revolutionary protagonist is a gay man whose furtive, twisted sexuality impels him to wreck innocent lives. Nevertheless, it was intriguing to find the gay theme so openly addressed (Bolt claims his theater company was criticized at a festival in Havana for *advocating* homosexuality!), and I wished I'd been aware of the piece when I was in Nicaragua so that I could have used it to ask some questions about how gay people are perceived and treated.

Some fascinating contradictions surface in *Impulse*. Repeatedly, Nicaraguan officials speak of the goal of mass participation in the arts, and at the same time make it clear that they seek "professional" excellence in full-time, salaried artists. I don't think these goals have to be mutually exclusive, but my experience in the women's movement suggests a certain inevitable tension between them, and I wonder how this will be resolved in Nicaragua. I also wonder about the long-term implications for poetry of the fact that so many poets and writers occupy official positions. This is quite a different matter from their simply supporting the revolution as private citizens and cultural workers, and might make frank expression more difficult.

I wonder, too, about the relationship between the frequently articulated desire for art to be unfettered by dogmatic prescriptions regarding either style or content, and the view Rosario Murillo expresses in her statement, "We emphasize that we are a weapon for the people in the capacity as artists. Our slogan is that art is a Sandinista trench, that art is a weapon for the people in defense of the revolutionary process" (*Impulse*, 8). The problem with this, it seems to me, is that the tools of war are those of expedience; they are necessarily as efficient as possible, whereas art is almost never either expedient or efficient, any more than a dream can be praised for efficiency. This intractable quality is suggested by Alan Bolt:

> We think that, even when theatre is a means to changing society, it is always a celebration of uselessness. I don't know if you understand the idea. Art is useless. Art is for nothing. We, human beings, fight for this, for beauty, not only for what is useful. We need a chair, but not just a chair, we need a beautiful chair. We fight not only for the chair but for its beauty. (*Impulse*, 57)

All my own experience of political movements suggests to me that eventually these two formulations—"Art is a Sandinista trench," "Art is a celebration of uselessness"—are likely to clash. If this happens, the conflict will be painful, particularly for the younger, less-established, more highly impressionable writers who will be called upon to resolve it in their own work.

For the moment, I find it extraordinary that the two statments can be made almost simultaneously, and by two artists each of whom is fully involved in the revolution. Together, they seem to me an appropriate symbol of the Nicaragua I saw: an open, fluid society very much caught up in a revolutionary *process*. Undoubtedly much more will be revealed about Nicaraguans' thoughts on these matters by Margaret Randall's forthcoming collection, *Risking a Somersault in the Air: Conversations with Nicaraguan Writers.*[6]

Nicaragua reminds me in a very immediate, powerful way of something the women's movement taught me in the first place: that there is no such thing as a creative development in a social vacuum, that certain explorations, certain achievements, come only in the context of collective forward motion. It reminds me as well how sorely I've missed that momentum in North American progressive circles of late. Which brings me back, unfortunately, to military topics. What U.S. citizens can do to help make sure the Nicaraguans are able to savor their hard-bought time of cultural flowering is to get our goddamned government off Central America's back. Then both life and art will develop in new directions, free at last of the need to hunker down in trenches.

NOTES

1. Ernesto Cardenal, *Zero Hour and Other Documentary Poems.* Selected and edited by Donald Walsh, introd. by Robert Pring-Mill (New York: New Directions, 1980). Also available from New Directions are *Apocalypse and other poems* and the prose work *In Cuba.*

2. *Impulse* XI 1 (Summer 1984). Available from *Impulse*, Box 901, Station Q, Toronto, Canada M4T 2PI.

3. Alejandro Murgía and Barbara Paschke, eds., *Volcán* (1983). Available from City Lights Books, 261 Columbus Ave., San Francisco, CA 94133. *Ikon* Second Series #3. P.O. Box 1355, Stuyvesant Station, New York, NY 10009.

4. Claribel Alegría, *Flowers from the Volcano,* translated and with an introduction by Carolyn Forché (Pittsburgh: U of Pittsburgh Press, 1982). Also available is *Suma y sigue,* selected poems with an introduction by Mario Benedetti (Madrid, Spain: Visor, 1981). Check Spanish-language bookstores or order from Schoenhof's Foreign Books, Box 182, 76A Mt. Auburn St., Cambridge, MA 02138.

5. Manlio Argueta, *One Day of Life*. Available in paperback in the Vintage Library of World Literature Series.

6. Margaret Randall, *Risking a Somersault in the Air: Conversations with Nicaraguan Writers* (San Francisco: Solidarity Publications, 1984). Includes interviews with Giaconda Belli, Tomás Borge, Vidaluz Meneses, Sergio Ramírez, and others. Order from Solidarity Publications, P.O. Box 40874, San Francisco, CA 94140.

The Political Morality of Fiction

I

Renaissance man felt he had the power to transform himself because he had the power of language. Words were units of energy. Through words man could assume forms and aspire to shapes and states otherwise beyond his reach. Words had this immense potency, this virtue, because they were derived from and were images of the Word, the Word of God which made us and which was God. . . .

Because words, like men, were fallen, however, they contained, as we do, shapes of evil within them. Fallen words, like men, are unstable elements; thus they are, as we are, such dangers to us. As we must always check that impulse to deformation in ourselves, so we must constantly be aware of the beast in language—Spenser calls it the Blatant Beast, whose rabid bite is vicious slander—and we must know that when we unleash a word and let it soar, we run the risk of loosing an evil force as well, one that we cannot control. . . .
—*A. Bartlett Giamatti*

The virtuous rage of Mrs. Stowe [in Uncle Tom's Cabin] is motivated by nothing so temporal as a concern for the relationship of men to one another . . . but merely by a panic of being hurled into the flames, of being caught in traffic with the devil.
—*James Baldwin*

If I were writing an essay with this title for a mainstream audience—a most unlikely premise, but let's pretend—my first task would of course be to demonstrate that politics and fiction indeed have a legitimate rela-

tionship to one another, that a commitment to something I call "political
morality" in art not only reflects a well-developed sense of reality, but is
quite compatible with creative excellence. For the U.S. literary establishment is untiringly hostile to overtly political writing, and even a few
of its members who eagerly applaud the political courage of selected foreign authors tend either to ignore or to patronize North American political artists, those embarrassing, supremely unchic prophets-in-their-own-
country.

Things are, of course, far different within several of the literary subcul-
tures served by alternative presses: Third World, leftist, feminist. In writing on this topic in the *Feminist Review*, I assume I share with most readers
a belief that all writing is political on a number of levels; that discussion
of the politics of both language and characterization is essential to the
development of feminist fiction; that writers from a range of oppressed
groups whose experience has largely been excluded from published writing in the past are making an immense contribution to our literature; that
an explicit (and explicitly radical) treatment of political themes is appropriate in novels and short stories.

So much for first principles, which will not get us far. This is not going
to be yet another piece about how to write in such a way that nobody
(except, of course, Patriarchy) is threatened or offended. Eventually, in
Part II, I am going to explore possible constructive implications of my
title, but first I have some things to say about the moral*ism* which, in my
view, at times fatally restricts what feminist fiction writers are willing to
trust to paper—not to mention what feminist presses and periodicals are
prepared to publish. In too much feminist fiction and critical response I
see at work a desire to prove obvious points and teach righteous lessons,
a craving to *do* good and *be* good that I believe is likely to result in a fatal
misunderstanding about what fiction is "for," what nurtures it and what
kills it.

In particular, some lesbian-feminists seem to have adopted the physi-
cians' motto "First, do no harm" as their guide to literature. In so doing,
they have helped create an atmosphere in which the effort to write well
and honestly rather resembles setting out to cook a gourmet meal, but
only after fire, knives, and every other aid or implement which might be
injurious to a two-year-old child has been removed from the kitchen.
Perhaps a few anecdotes will help clarify what I mean:

Item: A feminist publishes a short story which describes, from the victim's point of view, an act of torture carried out by an anonymous group of men. Each of the men is described by a stock phrase on the order of "the bald one," "the short one," "the leader," etc. One man is known as "the fat one." The editors of the periodical in which the story appears receive an article-length letter from a reader objecting to the story as fat-oppressive.

Item: A Black lesbian-feminist has written a series of stories whose delightful and fascinating heroine is a Black lesbian vampire. One day another Black lesbian-feminist takes the author aside and inquires how she can be writing this sort of thing; don't we have enough negative images of Black lesbians already?

Item: A Jewish lesbian-feminist expresses dismay at the efforts of other lesbians, Jewish and non-Jewish, to return to print *The Changelings*, a novel published in the 1950s by Jewish lesbian and radical Ruth Seid (pen name Jo Sinclair) which deals with a friendship between two young girls, one Jewish and one Black. Saying that she considers the book to be full of self-hatred, this woman (who in fact is in a position to exert some influence on feminist publishers' decision-making) implies that she would prefer to see it remain safely unavailable; in other words, she would deny to a new generation of readers the chance to form their own opinions of a work which *some* contemporary feminists have found extremely valuable. (In reflecting on this episode, I grew particularly indignant at the thought that, given the well-known tendency of radical and women's fiction to go quickly out of print, a few years hence some twenty-first-century feminist will probably use similar reasoning in suppressing my own and my friends' work.)

Item: A WASP lesbian-feminist signs a contact with a feminist press for a novel she has partially completed. Suddenly the publishers inform her that they have a political objection to her depiction of several characters whose ethnic identity she does not share. They say they had not made the criticism before signing the contract because they had not read the chapters she submitted to them, or at least not carefully. They proceed to circulate to selected, prominent lesbian-feminist writers a denunciatory memorandum in which they quote out of context and without permission portions of the unfinished manuscript and supply their own highly damaging interpretation of the motives behind the writing. An uproar ensues; news travels far and wide; years later, when the author submits her completed manuscript to other feminist editors, she receives confirmation that they too have heard extremely negative things about her work far in advance of laying eyes on it.

Item: Women returning from a lesbian writing conference report on their attendance at a workshop on the politics of language in which, in addition to more conventional suggestions, participants were advised to avoid "dehumanizing" collective forms (worksheet example: "The company has decided to lay off 200 workers") and "egocentrism—assuming one's reality is shared by everybody" (worksheet example: "The weather was really terrible over the weekend"). Participants expressed considerable doubt as to whether it's ever okay to write fiction about someone whose oppression the author doesn't share.

The Politics of Purity: Taming the Blatant Beast

Some of the attitudes about writing revealed in these examples have a good deal in common with attitudes toward similar issues familiar from non-feminist political contexts. In particular, the pressure on writers from certain racial and ethnic groups to be very careful about how they represent their people to the outside world is hardly specific to the women's movement; it's an important problem I want to come back to later. But there's something else involved here as well, I think: a background of radical feminist ideology which must be made explicit if its implications for fiction are to be understood.[1] My treatment of it here is necessarily schematic, since a full discussion would require its own lengthy article.

Basic to this ideology is the translation of the radical feminist conviction that women's oppression is the root of all social suffering into a worldview which equates patriarchy with evil and so-called female values with good. The result is a dualistic cosmogony which in its most basic preoccupations replicates a Christian moral/theological framework (and probably elements of a Jewish one as well). Variations on it may be studied in the work of, among many others, Mary Daly, Andrea Dworkin, and Susan Griffin.

Rather than admit the essential ambiguity of human experience, rather than view even those "female" traits we most value as having evolved in a patriarchal context—which strongly suggests there's no state of innocence to go back to—feminists of this persuasion tend to focus on correcting woman's fallen nature, tainted by patriarchal values but potentially salvageable. Obsessed with purification, they seek to eradicate manifestations of patriarchal influence which they find incessantly cropping up in themselves and other women.[2] They elevate victimology to a precise science; their accounts of the female condition emphasize suffering and powerlessness as though these were evidence of moral worth. Frequently they abandon—at least on paper—the messiness, contradiction, and moral complexity of struggles for power in the material world in favor of a symbolic effort I call "the quest for innocent power." Fiction is, as we shall see, one arena for this search.

Such radical feminism has been an influential—and extremely well-publicized—theoretical tendency among white feminists throughout much of the last decade. During the same period, Third World feminists have largely emphasized identity politics, which the Combahee River Collective defined in the mid-1970s in terms of their belief that "the most profound and potentially most radical politics come directly out of our own identity, as opposed to working to end someone else's oppression" (Combahee, 275). They have emphasized, too, the importance of practical, political means of fighting oppression on all levels. Some white feminists have learned from this example, have increasingly rejected earlier white feminist generalizations about female experience, and have begun in many cases to re-examine their own, multi-leveled identities.

Both for Third World and for white feminists, the identity politics approach has contributed to important new directions for political action, indispensable theory, valuable personal insights, and exciting fiction and poetry. On the other hand, particularly among some white feminists, it has upon occasion produced only a partial grafting of the new understandings onto the same old explanations of good and evil, the same old quasi-theological politics of purity that radical feminism promoted; consequences include an objectifying reverence for the oppressed and a narcissistic approach to one's own identity which are far from constituting a solid basis for either political work or writing. In surveying current lesbian-feminist fiction, I find that sometimes both positive and negative influences of an identity politics approach are observable in one and the same work.

Similarly, both identity politics and radical feminism have informed recent feminist discussions of the politics of language. I agree with and use in my own work a number of precepts which have emerged over the years since feminists first challenged the generic "he": for instance, elimination of a variety of expressions which equate "black" with "bad"; avoidance of terms like "handicapped" which have pejorative connotations; qualification of the authorial "we" when it is not truly inclusive. It seems to me, however, that the basic principles involved in this approach to politically responsible writing can be learned in an hour or two by anyone with a grasp of the relevant political issues—and that there are far deeper questions about how and what to write for feminists to address. It alarms me to see the inquiry carried to levels of refinement I can only describe as exhibiting political prudery.

I have been advised not to use the expression "myopic" in a negative metaphoric sense, have encountered criticisms of "Indian summer" as racist and "heavy-handed" as fat-oppressive and "paddy wagon" as offensive to the Irish.[3] I have read how the editorial collective of *The Lesbian Insider/Insighter/Inciter* changed the publication's title after being advised that the positive use of the word "insight" is insensitive to the visually impaired. I have watched the terms "physically challenged" and "differently abled," which seem to me euphemistic (is there something shameful in the fact that disabled people are in fact limited or lacking in a given capability?) gain currency.

The point here is not simply the merit of one or another specific usage; probably no two women will draw the line between appropriate criticism and tortured correctness in quite the same place. What concerns me more is the message behind the emerging method; the clear implication that because our writing, like our lives, has been tainted by patriarchy, the road to politically meaningful literature lies by way of cleaning up our act, purifying our utterances. Do we really believe, with the "Renaissance man" of my epigraph, that "when we unleash a word and let it soar, we run the risk of loosing an evil force"?

How can a writer express what is most vital in her experience while anxiously watching her tongue lest she let slip the wrong word? How does she tap the deep sources of feeling which nourish art while conforming to some abstract formulation concerning a desirable direction for political writing? These disturbing questions intensify for me with a reading of an essay published in *Common Lives/Lesbian Lives*, "White Lies and Common Language: Notes for Lesbian Writers and Readers" by Catherine Risingflame Moirai with Merril Mushroom.

The authors begin with the observation that "the equation 'light is good, dark is evil,' is so basic to the old patriarchal culture that for most of us it goes totally unquestioned" (47). Though they mean here the light the sun sheds, and the darkness of an electrical power outage, in fact a good percentage of the examples of racist language which they cite in support of their argument that we need to be very careful about light / dark symbolism involve familiar color (black/white) imagery. I don't dispute their contention that white Westerners have frequently embraced a rigid, racist dualism according to which white=light=good and black=darkness=evil, and I agree with them that in talking about light and darkness we should "think about what really happens, what we really experience" (56). The trouble is that when I do just that, some of their arguments won't wash. I find them much too eager to reform—on far too casually argued grounds—expressions of ancient, biologically based responses to the sun's rising and setting, the patterns of the seasons; for I think that some rich and valuable cultural meanings have been attached to those responses, as well as the destructive ones we'd be better off without.

Moirai and Mushroom are like prosecutors in such haste to secure a conviction that they are ready to consider their suspect—in this case, light/dark imagery which has *sometimes* been associated with a constellation of blatantly racist symbolism—guilty until proven innocent. Thus, they find fault with some beautiful, evocative lines from Jewish and Christian religious texts (which of course far predate the modern racist ideologies primarily at issue here): the description of Moses' face shining "horns of light," the expression "valley of the shadow." They do not discuss the existence of non-Western cultures in which sun worship or other expressions of reverence for light have been important. Nor do they consider that the light of morning and the darkness of night may have taken on their conventional associations with skin color at least in part because of a propaganda victory on the part of white supremacists, who have effectively promoted a rather far-fetched identification of their own pallid skin tones with one of the ancient and fundamental powers of the universe.

Certainly excellent writing can result from a reversal of the expectation that darkness will have negative connotations. Black writers in particular have often used this approach effectively; Langston Hughes's "Dream Variations" ("Night coming tenderly / Black like me" [427]) is one example. On the other hand, Black and other Third World writers have rarely been so squeamish in avoiding allusions to the negative properties of darkness as Moirai and Mushroom advocate. Hughes has another poem, "As I Grew Older," in which he implores "dark hands" to "Help me to shatter this darkness, / To smash this night, / To break this shadow / Into a thousand lights of sun, / Into a thousand whirling dreams / Of sun!" (426).

The expression "dark as the grave," assailed by Moirai and Mushroom as pertaining to "the old white male Christian scripts" (56), may be a cliché, but it still speaks powerfully to aspects of my own perception of death which I am not about to deny—notwithstanding the fact that, particularly in the nuclear age, I can easily image death as light, white, and bright, and will do so when appropriate. By the time I reach the closing observation that "comments that dark is 'scary because you can't see in the dark' reveal again how temporarily able-bodied people can fail to understand the experience of the disabled" (56), I begin to foresee a point at which almost nothing will be allowed to be said or written because of fear of what it *might* be taken to imply, a point at which experience and intention count for nothing and form is everything.

I have discussed Moirai and Mushroom's article at some length because I think it fairly clearly shows how the emphasis on purification tends to lead to the renunciation of more and more vocabulary, images, metaphors—and, as I'll discuss later, more subject matter as well. This renunciation represents, it seems to me, a fearful narrowing of the imagination in place of the brave expansion which many feminist writers have talked about as a goal. Sadly, the sacrifice of literature is unlikely to have the desired political benefit since, contrary to the more extreme claims of some radical feminists, words and images do not rule the world. Radical activity is not a matter of perfecting on paper some blueprint for faultless thought and practice, but rather of plunging head-on into the ambiguities and contradictions attendant upon what Baldwin terms a "temporal concern" with the relationship of human beings to one another—another name for which is love.

Is and Ought

Stung by the disapproving public reception accorded his treatment of the theme of illegitimacy in *Tess of the D'Urbervilles*, Thomas Hardy wrote an angry "Preface to the Fifth and Later Editions" in which he remarked:

> Let me repeat that a novel is an impression, not an argument; and
> there the matter must rest; as one is reminded by a passage which
> occurs in the letters of Schiller to Goethe on judges of this class:
> "They are those who seek only their own ideas in a representation,
> and prize that which should be as higher than what is. The cause of
> the dispute, therefore, lies in the very first principles, and it would
> be utterly impossible to come to an understanding with them."
> (n. p.)

Though the controversy which prompted this statement may seem remote to us, Hardy identified a problem which has historically been of
great interest to political writers and is central to feminist fiction today:
should our work reflect the world as it is or the world as it ought to be?[4]

Undoubtedly Hardy's position on this issue needs some qualification,
since theoretically an author could defend any reactionary or sexist or
racist or gratuitously violent piece of writing on the grounds that it shows
some part of "what is." But I don't think it was any such abandonment of
concern with ethics in literature that Hardy intended (in fact, his novel is
on one level an impassioned indictment of sexist, classist nineteenth-
century British social standards), and it's not what I intend, either. I want
instead to suggest that a groundedness in social and emotional realities is
indispensable in order for a work of fiction to be ultimately believable, in
order for it to nourish readers in some lasting way.

Good writing, I believe, begins with a passionate and imaginative love
for the world *as it is*—however fervently we might desire to change it. But
since the aim of politics is generally understood to be improving upon
this world's considerable imperfections, the possibility of a shortcut
immediately suggests itself: why not use novels and stories—so much
more manageable, after all, than real life—to create a fictional world-as-
we-would-have-it? Particularly if you believe that words have tremendous power over the material world, to create "positive images" of one
or another oppressed group—women in general, lesbians, Black women,
old women, Jewish women, working-class women, for example—would
appear to constitute empowerment of its members, while any less attractive portrait seems to reinforce their oppressed status.

Certainly we need literature in which oppressed people emerge as re-
spectfully portrayed human beings rather than all-too-familiar, negative
stereotypes. The problem is that sometimes the search for the "positive"
translates into psychological, moral, and/or political oversimplification.

Two popular works by white lesbian-feminists, Sally Miller Gearhart's *The Wanderground* and Maureen Brady's *Folly*, suggest some of the pitfalls awaiting fiction writers who seek to improve on a flawed world.

The Wanderground is a collection of explicitly utopian short stories set in a fantasy world in which women live apart from men in a state of harmony with nature and possess extraordinary telepathic powers, while *Folly* is an ostensibly realistic novel about working-class women, white and Black, living, struggling, and organizing in a contemporary Southern town. The first book has been criticized for evading consideration of racial and cultural differences among women which would necessarily remain an issue in any post-patriarchal society;[5] the second has been praised for its depiction of white and Black women trying to work together despite problems posed by the white women's racism.[6] Despite their many dissimilarities, however, each book can be read as embodying one version of the feminist theme I identified earlier as "the quest for innocent power." Therein lies a clue to a certain cloying moralistic tone which crops up from time to time in both. Plainly put, the women in these books are often too good to be true.

Elsewhere in her writing, Gearhart has maintained that there are positive female values and social capacities which, whether innate or socially produced, are inherently different from—better than—men's. *The Wanderground*'s "Hill Women" illustrate this conviction. They have found—in fact, they embody—"innocent power." They have succeeded in creating a society that is just about 100 percent noncoercive, noncompetitive, nonviolent, nurturing. They have survived, and continue to hold at bay, a patriarchy which is cruel, violent, and unremittingly hostile to them without being in any way corrupted themselves; without, apparently, even having to make the painful choice to resort to any of the enemy's morally problematic methods—as real-life revolutionaries have so far always had to do to some degree. It's not the Hill Women's ability to transcend the usual physical laws by means of their magical powers that I find so incredible, but rather the fact that they have also escaped the moral and political laws alluded to in Cherríe Moraga's suggestive remark that "oppression does not make for hearts as big as all outdoors" (*Loving*, "A Long Line," 135).

In fact, the Hill Women with their "spanners" and "mindstretches" are *literally* "as big as all outdoors." As critic Catherine Madsen has pointed out, they're identified with an essentially sentimentalized nature,

nature which is reliably benevolent and supportive as they themselves are benevolent and supportive. (There's no evidence here of the undomesticated force which "brought forth green beans *and* botulinus bacteria [and] obviously doesn't care whether she kills us or not."[7]) These are women to whom violence is so utterly foreign that one, for example, can be completely devastated by such evidence of patriarchal perfidy as the news that a slain deer has been discovered—a reaction which struck me as more a symptom of moral naiveté than an indicator of advanced development.[8] Although Gearhart's fantasy has many appealing elements, when considered in light of the ethical and political questions raised by actual attempts to survive in and change this world, it shows up as pure escape fare.

Folly opens promisingly with a compact, humorous, touching sketch of Folly's relationships with her children and with Martha, her closeted lesbian friend in the neighboring house trailer, but it soon veers away from the quiet strength of the initial realism. Brady is frequently excellent at capturing the nuances of her characters' interactions. Yet her genuine and appealing affection for Folly and Martha and their friends is spoiled for me by my sense that she's using them to prove a point, that her shaping of their experience throughout the book is dictated less by what she *knows* of their lives (which after all enabled her to create them in the first place) than by her determination that they do a good job of representing their respective identities.[9]

Every female character we get to know at all well is terrific, with the possible exception of Lenore's mean alcoholic mom who scabs in the strike, and even she's going to AA meetings and being much nicer to her daughter long before the last page. The Black women are strong and wise to a degree that makes them seem more symbols than characters. (This is only one of several novels by white feminists I've read recently in which the Black characters' main function appears to be to educate the whites about racism.) The major white characters are prompt to recognize their own white solipsism and earnest about correcting it. Homophobia is quickly overcome: by the end of the book the women who were lesbians at the beginning have read *Sappho Was a Right-On Woman* and become more open, more accepting of their sexuality, while Folly herself has come out, and her daughter Mary Lou may also be leaning in that direction. Not only does Folly's first attempt at labor organizing go off about as smoothly as could be expected, but when the gains achieved with the help of a white male union organizer prove insufficient, she and Martha are instantly ready to sacrifice their first chance at a bit of security, a longed-for house of their own. Instead, they plan to pursue a cooperative work project, which would be a highly precarious undertaking in real life, though in Brady's fictional town of Victory it appears virtually guaranteed to succeed.

Brady has tackled some extremely risky themes, and in one sense I find it understandable that her impulse seems to have been to draw their sting, to disarm them rather than chance having them blow up in her face. Yet that choice ultimately diminishes both *Folly's* artistry and its political depth. I think of the far tougher, bleaker view of a community of white working-class British women presented by Pat Barker in her fiercely imagined *Union Street*, and realize Barker *makes* me believe her account of her characters' lives. In Brady's case, too often, I only feel I *ought* to.

II

The Surrender of Ultimate Ends

In Part I of this essay, I distinguished between two sorts of readers: those who ask fiction to reflect what ought to be and those who want it to represent what is. Good writing, I suggested, begins with a passionate and imaginative love for the flawed world we live in—however fervently we might wish to amend the flaws. I offered examples of feminist fictional worlds which I said seemed to me too good to be true. In asking for characters and situations I could believe in, I was and am advocating not "realism," literal mirroring of physical, social, and psychological fact, but rather a certain indispensable correlation between the feel of lived life and the patterns of literature.

Perhaps I should have added that I not only *could* not believe in those idealized fictional worlds; I did not *want* to believe in them. For "ought" fiction always strikes me as implying a desire on the author's part to strip the world of much of its denseness, opacity, and chaos—characteristics I too sometimes chafe at yet recognize as inseparable from life's mystery and richness. Although I count myself a materialist, and respect enormously the practical talent for some measure of control in the social arena, I am at the same time increasingly impressed by the importance of the unexpected in human affairs, as throughout the biosphere. So I want fiction that, while reflecting the simplest, most profoundly political laws of social life (oppression and injustice breed resistance, for example), at the same time leaves room for ambiguity and surprise, takes into account the way people have of being so often both worse and better than they ought to be.

Fiction which is this supple, this anti-deterministic, seems to answer the twistings and turnings of the universe not by imitation but by sympathetic magic. In it, feeling precedes analysis; imagination, not theory, is at the core of the work. And in order for feeling and imagination to be so central, I think that political writers frequently have to come to what I will call here a "surrender of ultimate ends." That is, much like parents with non-literary offspring, they have to give up their cherished ideas of what their fiction is going to accomplish in the world. They must accept that they cannot know what it will teach readers, or what action, if any, it will inspire. They may, indeed, have to give up the idea that writing fiction itself is a form of action, if by action is meant behavior calculated to bring about a specific result. For how can a writer know how her imaginings will affect other people when, as frequently happens, she herself is still in the midst of uncovering their meanings?

In the realm of fiction and other art forms, a surrender of ultimate ends is not at all the same as indifference to those ends—the latter being the classic stance of the "apolitical" artist, often caricatured as "art for art's sake." Nor do all really good political artists consciously renounce specific political goals for their art; some are lucky enough to find that their deepest imaginings happen to coincide with a political movement's propaganda requirements, while others have an amazing knack for convincing themselves and others that what they need to create is the perfect illustration of theory or party line. Still, dependence on the idea that one's art is going to coincide with a political program is probably at least as dangerous to the imagination as dependence on the idea that one's art is going to sell.

The existence of a certain number of prescriptive manifestoes notwithstanding, the feminist, or lesbian-feminist, "program" for fiction is less a set of clearly articulated requirements than a cluster of dim yet powerful assumptions, the existence of which may be inferred from reviewers' offhand remarks, from authors' introductions, from feminist publishers' lists and feminist editors' rejection letters, from a study of what feminist novelists change or delete between first and last drafts. (As one who has

often been intrigued by what gets crossed out in both my own manuscripts and others', I fully expect that one day, far too late to do us any
good, our movement's well-meaning political self-censorship will fur-
nish fascinating grist for doctoral dissertations.)

One such assumption that troubles me greatly is revealed in the frequent, casual practice of evaluating fiction in terms of the perceived presence or absence of "positive" or "negative" characters, "positive" or
"negative" portrayals of experience. Such terms may upon occasion constitute a convenient, harmless shorthand—provided what is meant by
them has been previously spelled out, and especially when the material
under discussion is close to stereotype or caricature in the first place. But
to use them as ready-made labels to be applied without further thought to
authentic fiction with all its nuances seems to me as insultingly inadequate as it would be to go through one's private phonebook and classify
each acquaintance listed there as either "naughty" or "nice."

In "The Power of the Old Woman," a 1983 review essay published in
the *Feminist Review*, Barbara Macdonald points out one major problem
with the positive/negative approach to fiction. Writing of Valerie Tay-
lor's *Prism*, which portrays an older woman's triumph over the various
social, sexual, and financial difficulties which beset her upon retirement,
Macdonald comments:

> When you have carried a negative popular image around in your
> head all your life, as most of us have, who can resist turning it
> around in a positive way to prove the answer is Yes not No? All of
> the answers Valerie Taylor gives us are true in a sense, but, in
> another sense, her answers are not true. Yet she feels forced to give
> them. . . . perhaps it's inevitable that when we react to a stereo-
> type, that reaction ricochets and we end up smack in the middle of
> another. (2)

"Perhaps it's inevitable," yet Macdonald's remarks (and her subsequent
praise of *As We Are Now*, May Sarton's far less sanguine treatment of old
age) raise the question of whether a "positive stereotype" really provides
much more satisfactory matter for fiction than does a negative one. My
own answer to that is an unequivocal no. And it seems to me that the
most dangerous aspect of positive/negative labeling as a critical approach
is its implication that stereotyping of one sort or another is the natural
and appropriate basis of all fiction.

The complexity of Macdonald's analysis—particularly her recognition that fiction often conveys several different, even contradictory levels of meaning—is light years removed from the familiar, dreary appeals for feminist writing to enspirit and uplift its audience.[10] Also writing in the *Feminist Review,* Vivian Walker-Crawford takes the second approach in her treatment of Cheryl Clarke's *Narratives,* a poetry collection which frequently presents situation and character very much in the manner of fiction. In several cases, Walker-Crawford seems especially disconcerted by the multilayered texture of Clarke's characterizations:

> Although I respected Grace's ability to adapt I bemoaned Clarke's rendering her to a position of heroine when she was truly a victim. . . .
>
> But although Althea and Flaxie were out of the closet and very definitely in love their story weaves a cloth of contradictions.
> Flaxie loved Althea but got pregnant in 1955. Why? I assume it came about through dealings with a man, but then why was Flaxie dealing with a man? The motives behind Flaxie's and Althea's behavior are not made fully clear. (4–5)

Walker-Crawford concludes with a hope that Clarke's next book will provide her and other Black lesbian-feminists with "exciting visions of empowerment" (18). It is not, she makes clear, that she disputes the authenticity of much of Clarke's material, but rather that she finds this material too painful and ambiguous; she fails to see anything particularly nourishing or "empowering" in Clarke's vision of a gritty, difficult, contradictory world of Black womanhood which blossoms into joy at unpredictable moments: in the dazzling cartwheels of 14-year-old Grace, who has borne her stepfather's child, or in Althea and Flaxie's courageous, pre-feminist loving. Walker-Crawford is a partisan of "ought" literature.

Sometimes the "ricochet" from negative to positive stereotyping seems more automatic the harsher the preceding oppression has been. And there is a corollary fear, not mentioned here by either Macdonald or Walker-Crawford, but historically never far from the thoughts of writers conscious of belonging to a threatened group: "negative images"— including those which, while not themselves stereotypes, somehow touch on the same material that stereotypes are made of—can and will be used by their group's enemies. In his essay "How Bigger Was Born," Richard Wright describes all the different kinds of readers he feared would get the wrong message from his portrait of Bigger Thomas in *Native Son:* racist whites, bourgeois Blacks, his own radical colleagues. At least one of I. B. Singer's author-personas alludes wryly to acquaintances who complain that his writings provide ammunition for anti-Semites. As Wright explains, and Singer demonstrates in practice, the overwhelming need to tell the story, to get the felt truth into fiction, was finally stronger than these internal or external cautionary voices.

A related problem emerges when a writer sets out to portray a character from an oppressed identity not her own. To begin with, the politically conscious writer will naturally and appropriately be concerned with the possible uses of her work; the issue isn't necessarily simplified by the fact that this concern is likely to be both less emotionally freighted and less historically well informed than it would be if she shared the identity in question. In addition, and far more gratuitously, the feminist writer in this position is liable to be burdened on the one hand by modern feminism's one-sided emphasis on writing from direct personal experience,[11] and on the other by the unfortunate habit of reverencing oppression which *some* feminists have developed as their version of identity politics. The end result of all these pressures may once again be that the writer feels intolerably constrained in the exercise of her imagination.

I certainly do not think fiction writers of whatever identity should be indifferent to the politically dangerous uses that might be made of their work (though I do frequently feel that the advocates of extreme circumspection considerably exaggerate the power of fictional images). And in fact I believe that concern with public perceptions can do more for writers than help them avert catastrophe: it can sometimes improve their fiction by keeping the writing honest, insuring that it springs from authentic feeling, that they truly mean what they say and are prepared to stand behind whatever is controversial in their work. I think risks must be calculated, but not avoided. The ability to distinguish unerringly between being responsible and being chickenshit would be a fine talent indeed, but in its absence I far prefer occasional lapses to perennial cowardice. I find that radical clichés and positive stereotypes are not nearly so far removed from the conventions of reactionary literature as appears at first sight, for both provide neatly pre-classified images and ideas which rescue the insecure author from the unpleasantness of possible misunderstanding, while saving the reader the trouble of feeling and thinking for herself.

Some feminist writers whose fiction is far above the level of cliché nevertheless inadvertently diminish the impact of their work by adopting didactic narrative strategies which interfere with the reader's autonomous responses.[12] Thus in the novel *Abeng*, author Michelle Cliff frequently punctuates her vivid, morally compelling story of young Clare Savage's coming of age in Jamaica with intrusive comments which supply a ready-made political analysis of her material. Passages like the following correct Clare's unsophisticated perceptions:

> Clare's mind got caught in a tangle with her mother and the mistresses and *she didn't realize* that the creole and white teachers at St. Catherine's were different from Kitty in ways other than lady ways. At the bottom—as it usually was—was race and shade. *It was easy to lose sight* of color and all that went with it within the imitation-English quadrangle of brick buildings. (99, italics added)

Elsewhere, Cliff abandons her narrative altogether in favor of undigested masses of historical information:

> Slavery was not an aberration—it was an extreme. Consider the tea plantations of Ceylon and China. The coffee plantations of Sumatra and Colombia. The tobacco plantations of Pakistan and the Philippines. The mills of Lowell. Manchester. Leeds. Marseilles. The mines of Wales. Alsace-Lorraine. The railroads of the Union-Pacific. Cape-to-Cairo. All worked by captive labor.
>
> To some this may be elementery—but it is important to take it all in, the disconnections and the connections, in order to understand the limits of the abolition of slavery. The enslavement of Black people—African peoples—with its processions of naked and chained human beings, whipping of human beings, rape of human beings, lynching of human beings, buying and selling of human beings—made other forms of employment in the upkeep of western civilization seem pale. . . . (28)

The problem with such passages as these is not that the information and analysis they offer are in any way "elementary" or unimportant, but rather that fiction works far better when the focus is on the specifics of experience; the meaning that emerges on its own from the material is far richer and deeper—because it is *felt* meaning—than any meaning an omniscient narrator can announce in a few summary sentences. I wish Cliff had trusted more her own ability to convey "the limits of the abolition of slavery"—and of Clare's understandings—in terms of her characters' own poignant experience, as she does in this fine brief passage in which Clare's friend Zoe's mother explains why she feels the light-skinned Clare is not to be trusted:

> "Clare is de granddaughter of Miss Mattie. Dem is rich people. Dem have property. Dem know say who dem is. She can't be wunna true friend, sweetie. Fe she life is in Kingston. She no mus' have friends in Kingston. In fe she school. Wunna is she playmate. No fool wunnaself."
>
> "No, Mama, we be friends."
>
> "Den why she no let wunna borrow she bathsuit? Sweetie, mus' not get too close to buckra people dem." (102)

Another recent feminist novel which illustrates some of the pitfalls of interrupting narrative flow with didactic commentary is Ruth Geller's *Triangles*. Here a frank, lively, sympathetic portrait of a Jewish extended family is spoiled in places by the author's efforts to educate the (presumably ignorant) reader about the facts of Jewish life and culture. So, for example, she prefaces her descriptions of the Rosenthal family gatherings with dry summaries of the history and significance of the particular Jewish holiday they're celebrating. Why not let the account of Sylvia Rosenthal's struggles preparing the latkes speak for itself, and leave the reader to look up Chanukah in the glossary?

Of course fiction does educate. I've learned a lot about history, a lot about oppression, and a lot about the varieties of cultural experience from novels. But I've generally preferred to feel that the lessons were by-products, not the narrative's explicit, grim, or preachy purpose. I'm encouraged by the work of lesbian-feminist authors like Paula Gunn Allen (*The Woman Who Owned the Shadows*), Dodici Azpadu (*Saturday Night in the Prime of Life*), Andrea Loewenstein (*This Place*), and Judith McDaniel (*Winter Passage*), who have chosen narrative strategies which give readers a good deal of latitude for independent judgment, and allow them to take in information gently, more, as it were, by osmosis than force-feeding.

Pleasure and Danger: The Fictive Imagination

Why should a "surrender of ultimate ends" so frequently seem problematic for feminist fiction writers and readers? Why should works of the imagination be required to do double duty as analysis, theory, teaching aid, or organizing tool? As I've indicated, I think part of the answer has to do with the healthy desire, common to politically oriented people, to change what's wrong with the world, an urge which prompts us to harness all potential energy sources. But in addition I think we at times tend to react as though there were something alarming or dangerous or illegitimate in the act of raw imagining itself—a less obvious explanation I'll investigate in a moment.

First, however, it's time I clarified the extent to which these issues are anything but abstract ones for me. I have experienced on the most personal level—had inscribed in my very flesh, I want to say, like that Kafka character—some of imagination's perils. I was trashed by feminists for a work of fiction—and no, I'm not talking about nasty reviews or any other sort of *criticism*, whether public or private, kind or unkind, responsible or irresponsible; but about attack, denunciation, humiliation, shame; about having my motives impugned, my work quoted out of context, my fundamental political integrity vociferously questioned; and all this by lesbian-feminists who had professed to support my writing. What's worse, their campaign was effective thanks largely to the support, tacit and otherwise, of a wider circle of women who would never have initiated it themselves, but who accepted it once it was underway because at least for a time it seemed to coincide with their own consciousness-raising efforts, their mood of renewed ideological scrutiny. As a result, I found my sense of my writing's basic worth—not to mention my publication options—eroded to the point where a psychic separation from what I had hitherto regarded as my political community began to seem essential to my survival as a writer.

As I write this sketchy description of an episode now some years behind me, I can hear in my words the echoing pain and rage, and know that the breakage is only partially mended. Yet I've often thought that under slightly altered circumstances I myself might have stood by and watched some other feminist writer pilloried. For an atmosphere of political moralism is not the creation of any one person or clique, but rather the collective product of a great many individual hankerings after virtue. And I know my own desire for righteousness ("Jan's a *good* girl," I'm supposed to have protested at the age of three or four in reply to some maternal accusation), just as I know that the public preachings would lose much of the power they still have over me if it weren't that they echoed certain messages from within.

Let this bitter anecdote, then, stand in evidence of my claim that a climate in which literature is under incessant, suspicious political scrutiny harbors the most serious and hurtful potential consequences for fiction writers. And may I remember that "Jan's a *good* girl" is not and never has been the voice of a writer of worthwhile stories and novels, but merely the voice of a hack propagandist motivated by "a panic of being hurled into the flames," as James Baldwin complained of Harriet Beecher Stowe.

The endeavor to be good works against the operations of the imagination in at least two ways. On an obvious level, it confirms that deep down we think we are bad. The imagination is dangerous, therefore, because it springs from our erring nature undisciplined by conscious control. As I observed in Part I of this essay, such a reaction is sometimes evident in the politics of language debate, when feminists behave as though words were capable of unleashing an evil force. The most exhaustive feminist discussion of the dangers of the imagination has certainly been in the context of the sexuality controversy, in the course of which some women have suggested that we should be training ourselves not to have politically retrograde fantasies.

Though it has rarely been discussed so openly or heatedly, the issue of imagination in fiction is, I think, closely related. For fiction, like desire, cannot really be made "safe." Though we may not choose to publish every word or perform every sexual act that pops into our heads, neither can we, so to speak, run out in front of our imaginations and arrange their contents to conform with our mere *ideas*. If we cease to give feeling plenty of leeway, we will be dealing with hackwork and correct sex, not fiction and desire.

The second way in which an effort to be good may thwart the imagination is by reinforcing that fundamental distrust of the imaginative act itself which I alluded to earlier. The basic idea here is an old one in western culture: that virtue and pleasure are incompatible. There may in fact be some psychological link between fictive imagination and sexual fantasy, and therefore a taste of the forbidden in the former as in the latter. I know that a puritanical part of me suspects there's something not quite right about the intense pleasure I derive from conjuring up scenes and situations which, though their taproot is sunk in the stuff of my real life, exist not of necessity as real life seems to do, but because I have chosen them. And I infer from observing the hostility with which imagination's fruits are sometimes treated that others share my suspicions.

Other common cultural and social factors may play a role as well. A society which has for centuries been geared to remorseless, unreasoning production is naturally opposed to those activities which, like imagination, exist for their own sake without resulting in something useful. In religious terms, since God loathes competitors (or at least the Jewish and Christian gods clearly do), no wonder the act of creation that occurs in fiction writing feels more than a little risky. And oh yes, we are women; if anybody were authorized to arrogate to himself the powers of the Creator, it certainly wouldn't be us. (The restriction is reinforced by all forms of oppression; I think of Gloria Anzaldúa's "The voice recurs in me: *Who am I, a poor Chicanita from the sticks, to think I could write?"* ["Speaking in Tongues," 166].) All reasons why it may seem most attractive to keep imagination in the background and fill its place with dutiful formula material.

What Is Political Morality in Fiction?

Over many months as I contemplated writing this essay, I was hampered by a not-quite-conscious feeling that if I were going to criticize what I felt to be destructive notions of political morality in fiction, I ought to be able to offer some alternative, if no doubt more liberal, creed. I should be able to say, for instance, "It's racist to use black to mean bad, but there's nothing wrong with having a sunrise symbolize hope," or, "Here are three techniques to offset the ill effects of including an unsympathetic character from an oppressed group."

Of course, once I consciously formulated this idea, I realized immediately that any set of abstract rules would be incompatible with my basic conception of fiction as supple, multi-faceted, unpredictable, and rooted not in analysis but in feeling. Instead, I want to offer a few thoughts which take as their starting point the assumption that there is some intrinsic connection between political morality and a habit of questioning, a tolerance for doubt, a willingness to proceeed in the absence of fixed coordinates.[13]

Frequently, political people speak of writing as a form of action. I would like to propose an alternative metaphor. I think that the best fiction may be understood as a form of praise: a gratuitous outpouring that accomplishes no objective, moves no mountain, sends no reader rushing to the barricades, yet somehow binds those who are touched by it more firmly to the beloved universe. This is obviously a religious idea, possibly akin to Shug Avery's observation in Alice Walker's *The Color Purple* that "more than anything else, God love admiration" (178). I happen to believe it belongs to the part of religion that even the staunchest materialists and most committed politicos can't very well get on without. Political fiction that deeply moves me does so not by providing new facts or arguments, but by strengthening my conviction that what happens on this earth *counts*, gorgeously, terribly; and that even certain failures embody values infinitely more enduring than the successes certified by our shiny official culture.

When I wrote that good fiction begins with "a passionate and imaginative love for the world *as it is*," I referred as well to what I take to be the underpinnings of the only authentic political morality of which I can conceive: the feeling that links us irrevocably to others, that proves to us beyond the power of any analysis that we are not *essentially* isolate particles drifting in the ether; and that other, at times apparently countervailing, instinct not to be satisfied with less than the truth of things, no matter how inexpedient. Love and honesty—how worn, overused, the words. Yet the impulses they stand for are indispensable in situations in which sophisticated theoretical calculations are useless, or worse than useless—as witness the rigidity, cruelty, and abuse of power that plague the most well-intentioned political movements.

Of course actual human love is a lot more specific than I've made it sound here, and spottier, often marbled with ignorance or malice. ("God love everything you love—and a mess of stuff you don't," Shug Avery tartly observes [Walker 178].) And honesty may be ugly or unkind, and is seldom unadulterated either. That is why doubt and ambiguity are endemic to politics—and writing. Nevertheless, in thinking about the ethics of political fiction, I am far more apt to base my evaluations on the presence or absence of some spark of real caring, real interest, real enthusiasm, real anger, than on any outward forms.

One example is my reaction to the depiction of Telecea in Andrea Loewenstein's novel *This Place*. One of four characters from whose points of view the author presents the action, Telecea is an inmate of a women's prison; she is mad; she is Black; her sections are in the first person, in Black English. As a white woman who has never been jailed herself, Loewenstein breaks several obvious rules when she writes in the voice of a Black woman whom she portrays as violent and homophobic, acutely damaged rather than ennobled by a harsh childhood and subsequent oppression; nor does she balance Telecea by including any equally important "positive" Black character, or authorial comment which would make it explicit that she doesn't intend this portrait to represent all Black women.

If my reading of *This Place* suggested to me that Loewenstein was exhibiting Telecea as a freak, or had written as she does in order to impress white readers with her virtuosity, or really *did* think Telecea was representative, I would be extremely put off by this characterization. Instead, the writing persuades me that she cares for her character, who emerges as a figure of memorable power and authentic, though damaged, creativity, caught at the very margin of survival. I judge it a mark of respect that she has dared to portray this woman with such intensity of imagination—and that, so far as my limited ear can discern, she writes Black English rather well.

All this is by no means to claim that *This Place* is the ultimate in fictional treatment of Black women in prison; there's no doubt that Loewenstein explores white women's experience far more comprehensively. But I think she has written honestly, with love, in creating Telecea, and therefore I find her risks justified: without those qualities, I would fail to be impressed by a far more conventionally "positive" depiction.

Of course it's possible, even likely, that other readers will dispute my evaluation, not necessarily out of correct-line-ism, but perhaps because their reading of the novel reveals something that strikes them as false or exploitative. Though we each may marshal evidence in our favor, we may not be able to arrive at any agreement, for we're grappling here with fiction's opacity and density, its many layers, and the perplexing way its parts sometimes contradict each other, much after the fashion of life itself. Hence, troublesome doubt. We are no longer dealing with slogans, which may not mean much but at least mean it very plainly.

I wish that we feminists (and I really do mean *we*, for I speak of my own reactions as much as of what I've observed to be typical political behavior) would learn to be more relaxed with these complex demands of fiction. I wish we could more often approach it in a spirit of exploration, not in that gut-clenched mood I associated with the Letters columns in feminist newspapers, with their pressure to make an instantaneous judgment, decide who's right on, who's fucked up, and which side to support.

To this end, I propose that some of the categorical responses to novels and short stories which have been flung about lately be tested out through careful reading and detailed discussion of books that weren't born and raised in the hothouse of the feminist press movement. Writers shouldn't write about oppression they haven't directly experienced? Very well, let's keep that in mind while we go read, say, *Life in the Iron Mills* and *The Confessions of Nat Turner* and *One Day of Life* and *Famous All Over Town*[14]; afterwards we'll discuss which parts of each novel struck which of us as problematic or admirable, and see if the generalization still holds. We need positive characters to empower women? Okay, let's investigate how *Sula* and *Tell Me a Riddle* and *The Dollmaker* and *The Salt Eaters* and *The Golden Notebook* and *Meridian* and *Enormous Changes at the Last Minute* fill that particular bill—and if some of them don't, do we take them off the shelf of beloved political classics? If we leave them there anyway, why? What is it in them that feeds us?

One day a while back as I was rehashing resentful old thoughts about how art ought not to be required to imitate practical politics, to be as simple as a slogan, or accomplish what action does, I suddenly had a new thought for a change: maybe practical politics ought to imitate art. Not, I meant, that activists could or should ever abandon attempts to get things done in this starving, bleeding world; the surrender of ultimate ends is not for them. But perhaps they might, even in the midst of emergency, learn from art to accept more ambiguity and doubt. Maybe the certainties frequently sought in political work—of identity, of community, of moral righteousness and ideological infallibility and the perfect justice of this or that cause—are just as misplaced in the world of action as in the world of imagination. Maybe demonstration-goers don't deserve the slogans, either.

A final thought, by way of consolation: I believe that to submit ourselves to moral uncertainty becomes far easier if we are able to believe that, in Barbara Deming's phrase, "we are all part of one another." Whoever we are, whatever our struggles, the solutions we arrive at will be partial, flawed, subject to correction from angles of experience and understanding we may not even realize exist—and yet they do exist. This knowledge is the beginning of a political humility which seems to me inescapable, given history. "I don't know what can save us / I don't know how to save / the porous world that breathes and can be killed.'"[15] Yet our love for this world continues, as action and as praise.

NOTES

1. In reference to the development of feminist views of the relationship between politics and fiction, it seems relevant that Kate Millett's *Sexual Politics*, surely one of the most influential books of the early Second Wave, couched its arguments about women's subordination largely in terms of representations of women in male literature. It might be instructive to trace the connections between Millett's critique of misogynist writing and subsequent feminist views of what our fiction should be; clearly, from the very first many women have perceived stories and novels to be vehicles for either our liberation or subjugation.

2. It has often struck me that a fascinating study could be done on the incidence of imagery involving cleanliness in feminist writing. I had supposed that this popular enthusiasm for purification was a relatively recent phenomenon, probably coincident with the heyday of radical feminist theory in the late 1970s, and so was amused to encounter the following passage in an *off our backs* editorial which accompanied the publication of "C.L.I.T. Statement #2" in July 1974: "These papers are a tool for analysing, understanding, and exorcising the patriarchy in our souls, our heads, and our lives. Only when we have purified ourselves can be begin to create a positive woman-defined politics and culture" (IV 8: 10).

3. For the latter, see the letter from M. Gray Cahill in the November 1984 *Sojourner*, pp. 3–4. Cahill advances the argument, new to me, that at least in certain circumstances we should avoid using words with non-offensive meanings if they have an unrelated but derogatory meaning as well; she gives the example of the use of the word "chink" (meaning "crack") when Chinese women are present.

4. After writing this paragraph, I picked up the November 17, 1984, issue of *Gay Community News* to discover an interview with Jane Rule, "Finding Truths in Fiction" by Larry Goldsmith, in which she's quoted as stating the problem in similar terms: "It does seem to be that literature is about what *is* . . . and a lot of people in the movement would like literature to be about what ought to be or what we'd like it to be" (8).

5. See Catherine Madsen's review in *Conditions: Seven* (1981): 134–39.

6. See, for instance, Cindy Patton's review "Crackers and Queers," *Gay Community News Book Review* (June 1983): 1, 5.

7. Madsen, 138 (note 5).

8. See Monique Wittig's *Les Guérillères* (Avon edition, trans. David Le Vay,

1971) for an interesting contrast. Wittig has no compunctions about associating the women who populate her fantasy with violent imagery, playfully deployed.

9. For a discussion by Brady of some of the challenges and difficulties she encountered, see her article "An Exploration of Class and Race Dynamics in the Writing of Folly" in *13th Moon*, VII 1-2 (1983): 145-51.

10. Macdonald refreshingly combines an analysis of ageism in *Sister Gin* with the remark that she enjoyed the story so much she almost forgets its political shortcomings. I wish feminist critics would more frequently consider works of fiction as something other than monolithic units—as Marx did when he expressed an appreciation for Balzac because, despite thoroughly reactionary opinions, that novelist had so accurately depicted the workings of the capitalist social order.

11. See my essay "A Movement of Poets: Thoughts on Poetry and Feminism" in this volume for a discussion of this emphasis in the feminist poetic tradition.

12. Didacticism in feminist writing is nothing new, though the lessons have changed a good deal over the years. See Mary Biggs's discussion of the "embarrassingly didactic" content of the early *Aphra* ("unimaginable," she claims, "in any publication today"), in her article "From Harriet Monroe to *AQ*: Selected Women's Literary Journals, 1912-1972," *13th Moon* VIII 1-2 (1984): 205. Some feminists who were concerned with a "negative image" in my fiction once proposed to me that I should add an introduction to clarify just how the situations and characters I described should be interpreted.

13. I am influenced here by Hannah Arendt's discussion in *The Life of the Mind* of the possible connections between morality and doubt.

14. *Life in the Iron Mills* is Rebecca Harding Davis's classic account of harsh industrial life in the nineteenth century; Davis herself enjoyed considerable economic privilege. *The Confessions of Nat Turner* is white southerner William Styron's fictional version of the life of the Black man who led a famous slave rebellion; it occasioned outraged protests from many Blacks when it appeared. (James Baldwin, for one, did not object, however; he only said the novel taught him a lot more about the mind of William Styron than anything else.) *One Day of Life* is eminent Salvadoran writer Manlio Argueta's novel of peasant life in his country; he narrates it largely from the point of view of an impoverished grandmother. *Famous All Over Town* is a recent novel by one "Danny Santiago" who turns out to be an anglo writing under a pseudonym; before this became publicly known he received favorable reviews for what was presumed to be his insider's account of life in a Chicano community.

15. From my unpublished poem "Trajectory and Prayer."

III

REVIEWS

When Elly Bulkin, Irena Klepfisz, Rima Shore, and I founded *Conditions* magazine in the mid-seventies, we resolved that a carefully edited review section focused on small press materials would be a part of each issue. We felt strongly that adequate critical attention was vital to the development of all women's and lesbians' writing; but because we were aware of the special difficulties in getting such attention for books lacking the distribution and promotion advantages offered by more established presses, we decided to limit our reviewing to alternative press publications—which we saw as the backbone of an emerging woman-identified literature. We took seriously the task of devising truly feminist approaches to the reviewer's craft, and often worked with authors to improve style and content through a number of successive versions.

Conditions reviewers were asked to address seriously both literary and political dimensions of books by women; among the latter, racial and class issues were emphasized, along with "women's" issues, narrowly defined. Writers were expected to be honestly critical but not gratuitously negative—to avoid, for example, the magisterial tone and destructive ranking practices of much establishment criticism. In my own reviewing I attempt to follow similar principles, and retain from my stint at *Conditions* as well a strong interest in small press books which my own history of small press publication has helped reinforce.

It wasn't always easy to locate reviewers, and each of the *Conditions* editors frequently found herself pressed into the role. The first of the items reprinted here, a review essay on Meridel LeSueur, appeared in *Conditions: Three*. Shortly after its publication in 1978, John Crawford, LeSueur's editor at West End Press, told me it was virtually the only serious critical attention her work had received in recent decades. Given my strong feelings of personal attachment to a writer so closely identified with the radical traditions of the state of Minnesota (which as my parents' childhood home has always been for me a sort of mythical Old Country), I was particularly glad to have helped remedy such undeserved neglect.

My review of This Bridge Called My Back: Writings By Radical Women of Color was one of two which appeared in a single issue of Conditions. Because of the special importance of this anthology to a range of readers, we editors asked Paula Gunn Allen to write from a Third World feminist perspective, while I had the task of presenting a white woman's point of view. Though I found this a somewhat awkward situation in which to offer criticism as well as praise, my deep respect for the book as a whole made risk and effort worthwhile.

Of the reviews included here, those of Doris Lessing's Shikasta and Andrea Dworkin's Right-Wing Women are the only ones dealing with books which received establishment media attention. In each case I wanted to raise questions about the work which I felt had not been adequately explored elsewhere. I find it especially interesting to look back now at my treatment of Right-Wing Women, which, though not so well known as writing by Dworkin focused explicitly on women's sexual victimization, significantly foreshadowed the author's subsequent involvement in a well-known antipornography crusade which brought radical feminists into discomfiting proximity to reactionary politicians. Working with radical feminist attorney Catherine MacKinnon, Dworkin developed legislation intended to encourage the prosecution of purveyors of pornographic material deemed to violate women's civil rights; their model version, passed by the Minneapolis city council, was thereafter adapted for use in other localities by right-wing legislators who sometimes employed blatantly antifeminist language.*

This history points up some very practical dangers of a theory which, as I note in my review, construes women as universal victims and proposes to fight back with a "sex-class" solidarity that ignores traditional distinctions between Left and Right. Evidently the ironic consequence

---

*See Lisa Duggan, Nan Hunter, and Carole S. Vance, "False Promises: Feminist Antipornography Legislation in the U.S." in Varda Burstyn, ed., Women Against Censorship (Vancouver and Toronto: Douglas & McIntyre, 1985): 130–51.

may be that we're placed even more squarely at the mercy of reactionary forces which—far more than Dworkin's pet villain the "male left"— exercise real power over our lives.

My review of *Woman's Worth: Sexual Economics and the World of Women* extends the critique of radical feminist theory begun with the piece on Dworkin, this time with reference to a more substantive and balanced work.

The final three reviews reflect both my growing interest in Latin America and a continued commitment to small press books. I'm very pleased with the representation in this section of titles from Black Scholar Press, Granite Press, Kitchen Table: Women of Color Press, North Point Press, Spinsters/Aunt Lute, Thunder's Mouth, and West End Press, institutions I view as being among the most important of *all* U.S. publishers for their championing of poetry and Third World and women's writing.

Women on the Breadlines, Harvest, Song for My Time, Rites of Ancient Ripening by Meridel LeSueur

"What Happens in a Strike," the first essay in *Harvest*, is an account of the Minneapolis truckers' strike of 1934. LeSueur, who herself participated, describes the weariness, excitement, and impressive organization which prevailed at strike headquarters; the strike-breaking attempts which culminated in a police massacre of unarmed pickets (48 received buckshot wounds; one died); and the increased determination with which the truckers and their families responded.

In 1934 my father was a ten-year-old living in Minneapolis. He had never mentioned boyhood memories of labor agitation, so after I read *Harvest* I asked him what he knew about the truckers' strike of 1934. He did recall, he said, that it had been a "bad strike," marked by violence; and in fact it turned out that my grandfather, who drove a milk truck at the time, was required to join the Teamsters' Union in the aftermath of the strike.

It was strange to realize that I would have had no way of finding out about this important piece of labor history which directly affected my own family if I had not happened to read about it—and in a book which was not available before 1977, given that most of LeSueur's work has been out of print since the "blacklists" of the 1950s. The experience heightened my awareness of the political reasons behind the suppression of this and so many other revealing chapters in American history. And it made me doubly grateful that, throughout the thirties, forties, and fifties, Meridel LeSueur was busy recording the experience of white Midwestern working people, an experience which has been excluded not only from conventional written histories, but from the oral histories of many upwardly mobile families who were eager to forget their struggles once they had escaped into the middle class.

Born at the turn of the century, LeSueur herself comes of a middle-class, if somewhat unconventional, background. Her stepfather, a lawyer, was the first socialist mayor of Minot, North Dakota. She was raised in the Midwest and has spent most of her life there; she now lives in St. Paul. During the 1930s she became a Communist; she also achieved a national reputation as a writer, particularly as a writer of short fiction. But she never attempted to confine her impressive energies to a single literary form. She has written novels, a biography, a history of the upper Midwest, poems (Hampl, 62).

LeSueur's early literary success ended with the McCarthy era. Her publishing options became limited almost entirely to Communist periodicals, but she continued to write. A West End Press publicity sheet accompanying *Song for My Time* quotes her remark on this period: "I raised two children by myself, and had to have jobs. . . . every night I stuck my head under the water and wrote for two hours, because I thought the working class needed new expressions of American experience!"

It is only during the past several years that LeSueur has once again begun to receive recognition from a limited but enthusiastic circle of leftists and feminists. As her recent publication history shows, this renaissance has been made possible by "small" presses dedicated to publishing work of literary and political merit without regard to its commercial possibilities. The Communist press International Publishers last year reissued the story collection *Salute to Spring*, first published in 1940. The Feminist Press is planning a collection of fiction and essays. Of the books reviewed here, three—*Women on the Breadlines* (journalism from the 1930s), *Harvest* (journalism and fiction, 1929–1946), and *Song for My Time* (journalism and fiction, 1947–1958)—were published in 1977 by the small, leftist West End Press, which plans to reissue several more of LeSueur's early works in the near future. And *Rites of Ancient Ripening* (recent poems) was put out by Vanilla Press, a Midwest-based collective of poets, artists, and printers.

Women on the Breadlines (Journalism from the 1930s)

One of LeSueur's most exciting contributions to a reconstruction of our forgotten—or rather repressed—history is *Women on the Breadlines*, which will be of special interest to feminists. The pamphlet contains four non-fiction pieces, including three remarkable first-person narratives which are essentially oral histories of women trapped in the Depression; "I did not write these stories. I recorded them," LeSueur states in her introduction. Here I was particularly fascinated by the documentation of sterilization abuse and the use of mental institutions as prisons, issues I had naively supposed were "discovered" by contemporary Third World and women's liberation movements. "Sequel to Love," for example, begins:

> I am in the place where they keep the feeble-minded at Faribault. This place is full of girls moanin' and moanin' all night. . . .
>
> They won't let me out of here if I don't get sterilized. I been cryin' for about three weeks. I'd rather stay here in this hole with the cracked ones than have that done to me that's a sin and a crime. . . .
> (n. p.)

In "Women on the Breadlines," the longer title essay (also reprinted in *Harvest*), LeSueur records in direct, spare language her impressions of destitute working-class women encountered in the city employment bureau. The piece is politically effective because it reflects LeSueur's passionate interest in the living world and in individuals; she never sacrifices people and events to the necessity of proving a point. The lives she observes are hard ones, and she conveys their hard realities with a remarkable combination of carefully observed detail and vivid imagery:

> A scrub woman whose hips are bent forward from stooping with hands gnarled like watersoaked branches clicks her tongue in disgust.
>
> Her legs are thin but the runs in her old stockings are neatly mended clear down her flat shank.
>
> She is thin as a worn dime with her tumor sticking out of her side.
> (n. p.)

Yet LeSueur's own optimism—evident throughout her work, but particularly striking in the context of the Depression—makes her sensitive to the pleasure many of these women still take in their lives. Here is Bernice, a young Polish woman who has been "working in people's kitchens for fifteen years or more":

> When you speak to her, her face lifts and brightens as if you had spoken through a great darkness, and she talks magically of little things as if the weather were magic, or tells some crazy tale of her

> adventures on the city streets, embellishing them in bright colors
> until they hang heavy and thick like embroidery. She loves the city
> anyhow. It's exciting to her, like a bazaar. . . . (n. p.)

LeSueur's acute examination of the psychology of destitution is always
a sympathetic one. Her speculation on women's peculiar response to
economic catastrophe has special resonance for a feminist audience:

> If you've ever been without money, or food, something happens
> when you get a bit of money, a kind of madness. You don't care. You
> can't remember that you had no money before, that the money will
> be gone. . . . A lust takes hold of you. You see food in the win-
> dows. . . . You know it is suicide but you can't help it. You must
> have food, dainty, splendid food and a bright hat so once again you
> feel blithe, rid of that ratty gnawing shame.
>
> It's one of the great mysteries of the city where women go when
> they are out of work and hungry. There are not many women in the
> bread line. There are no flop houses for women as there are for
> men. . . .
> . . . A woman will shut herself up in a room until it is taken from
> her, and eat a cracker a day and be as quiet as a mouse so there are no
> social statistics concerning her. (n. p.)

Throughout the essay, LeSueur's intense but respectful curiosity
about other people's situations contributes to her impressive ability to
write about lives very different from her own. Although the attempt of an
educated, relatively privileged woman to place her writing in the service of working people is necessarily fraught with contradictions, it
seems to me that here she succeeds remarkably well.

Harvest (Journalism and Fiction, 1929–1946)

In addition to "What Happens in a Strike" and "Women on the
Breadlines," the two essays already mentioned, *Harvest* contains six fiction pieces written over a period of more than fifteen years. Though all
are set in the Midwest, they treat an interesting range of life experiences
and social circumstances, often expressing LeSueur's love of the prairie
and its people, and her sense of the deep but fragile connection between
the two.

"Harvest" is a portrait of life on a traditional Midwestern farm about
to be transformed by mechanization. "Fudge" is a middle-American horror story; the horror lies in a young girl's discovery that her stultifying

small town is incapable of producing even one authentic sexual scandal. In "Autumnal Village" a young mother realizes the barrenness of her existence as the property of a wealthy husband, while in "To Hell with You, Mr. Blue" a very different sort of woman undertakes her own insurrection against male tyranny.

The remaining two stories, "God Made Little Apples" and "We'll Make Your Bed," are told from the point of view of men, one a farmer and one an unemployed lumberjack. Here, despite my dismay at Le-Sueur's rather sympathetic depiction of some obnoxious male supremacist behavior, I often found myself both convinced and moved, particularly by the portrayal of the aging farmer who must come to terms with the limitations of his existence. Here is LeSueur's description of his encounter with an old sweetheart, unseen in decades:

> When he stood by the door looking into the cool, dark summer kitchen, flavorsome, smelling of piccalilli, and—did he imagine it?— the lavender perfume Effie used to use, he grinned sheepishly to feel his heart hammering as he waited for an answer to his knock. But he wasn't prepared for the woman who strode from the darkness, peering at him through the sunlight as if from the grave. She was wearing an old hat and the face of Effie as he remembered her hung like a dream in the layers of old flesh. (63)

These stories are engaging, rich in striking descriptive passages, and—with the exception of the heavyhanded but very early "Harvest"—expertly written; but they lack the tragic depth of some of LeSueur's nonfiction. Their strengths derive from her imaginative use of language, her ear for spoken English, and her ability to empathize with many varieties of experience.

Perhaps it sounds presumptuous to say that as I read and enjoyed this book I found myself wishing for some stories based more closely on LeSueur's personal life. I imagine I catch glimpses of her here—in the mother of girl children in "Autumnal Village," in the small-town adolescent of "Fudge," perhaps. But for the most part she is elusive. I think of such left-feminist writers as Doris Lessing and Tillie Olsen, and wonder whether, had LeSueur chosen to write more directly from her own experience, she might have achieved a deeper synthesis of her politics, her observations, and her inner reality. Certainly this would have meant examining her middle-class background—about which, as a Communist identified with the working class, she was understandably ambivalent.

And it might have involved an evaluation of her experience as a woman which could have led her to a more conscious and consistent feminism, a stance perhaps in conflict with her evident desire to present images of working-class solidarity.*

A word on sexual politics is necessary here. LeSueur is now being billed as an early feminist, and she was that; but she was and is also, to my mind, a curiously inconsistent one. Clearly she has always been strong in her own female identity and deeply interested in the situations of other women. Yet time and again her fiction comes across as an endorsement of—almost as an advertisement for—traditional sexual arrangements.

It is not her heterosexuality I question here; rather, it is her tendency to represent the virility of man and the fertility of woman as the natural correlates of the earth's glorious abundance. The duality of the sexes is seen as symptom and symbol of the life force.

So pervasive is this sexual imagery that it prevents any recognition of heterosexuality as a social institution, a power relationship. "Harvest," with a sexual scenario embarrassingly reminiscent of D. H. Lawrence, is the most blatant offender:

> But he came close to her and she was bewitched still of his body so she let herself be led straight to the giant and saw all its shining steel close to her . . . (35)

In the more subtle "Autumnal Village" the ruling-class husband is presented as sexually distasteful, his kiss a "thin peck," while the wife is haunted by the "strong male brogue" of the farmer who gave her a ride. The farmer's "maleness" thus becomes identified with the vitality and authenticity of working-class life, and the embryonic feminist critique clearly present in the story goes undeveloped.

I want to make it clear that I offer these criticisms because I take Le-Sueur seriously, and not in any attempt to discourage potential readers. Perhaps a passage from "To Hell with You, Mr. Blue," my favorite of the stories in this volume, will be convincing on this point. It is an amusing but essentially serious tale of a woman's rebellion against her misogynist

---

*LeSueur is a prolific writer. It is entirely possible that among work of hers which I have not seen are pieces which would belie these generalizations. However, though my remarks here are based primarily on *Harvest*, I feel they also apply to the material in *Salute to Spring* (International Publishers)—a more comprehensive collection and probably the best introduction to LeSueur's fiction.

gambler-husband and the equally misogynist Mr. Blue, another gambling man she encounters on a bus trip she takes to get an abortion she doesn't want. The dialogue, some of LeSueur's best, is exactly what you would expect to hear on a long bus trip:

". . . So you knew Dempsey."

"Did I know him! We were just like that. Oh, a king, a prince, a man among men. I was with him, I came right out of the ring with him after that pretty knockout. . . ."

He wasn't describing love. "Did you know his wife?" she said.

"Sure, of course, natural. I knew his wife."

"What's the matter? You look like you tasted something bad."

"It's bad for a great champ like that to get himself hooked up. A bird like that should never get himself married, that's what I say."

"That's what you say."

"Sure, I say it and I mean it. A bird like that shouldn't do it. It's a crime."

"Sure," she said, "a crime."

"Sure, a crime. What business is it of a fellow like that hooking up? Oh, that night I'll never forget it. Why should he get spliced after a thing like that?"

"I don't know, I'm sure," she said. She felt pretty bitter against him. "She's a nice person," she said feebly. (78–79)

Song for My Time (Journalism and Fiction, 1947–1958)

The writing collected in *Song for My Time*—one short story and six pieces of journalism—reflects the experience of a very different era from that which produced the exultant political certainties of *Harvest*. In the title story, set in the immediate postwar period, a grieving woman grasps the political significance of her brother's life and his death in World War II, and is thereby enabled to look beyond the present "dark time" to a future of renewed struggle. But the volume is subtitled "Stories from the Period of Repression," and in fact the country was entering upon the era not only of McCarthyism but also of the Korean War, and of a cancerous economic expansion which was to transform ever more rapidly the social organization and landscape of LeSueur's beloved Midwest. This was also a time of great tension within the Communist Party, culminating in a mass exodus in the wake of Khrushchev's public admission, at the Twentieth Party Congress in 1956, of the atrocities of Stalinism.

Given the context, it is unsurprising that those essays in *Song for My Time* which exhibit a clear organization and political assurance reminiscent of LeSueur's earlier nonfiction look back on the experiences of older people whose lives were dedicated to struggle. In "The Return of Lazarus," for me the most successful piece in the book, LeSueur accompanies an old socialist on his return, after many years' absence, to his boyhood farming community. He finds the town decayed, the farmhouse gone, his elderly cousins still slaving to keep ahead of the mortgage. Here LeSueur manages a remarkable portrait of a landscape and a life which remain beautiful even in their desolation. The old man lives in a furnished room in the city; he has spent a lifetime toiling for nothing, or rather for a simple understanding which has been acquired at almost infinite cost. Yet that understanding of social realities is everything to him, and despite his pain and regret he is triumphant: "I found out and stood with the people" (71).

"Of This Time, Upon This Earth," a tribute to the Black Communist leader Bill Herron, is moving also. Yet I was disturbed by its assumption, which was that of the Communist party at the time, that the solution to racism in American society could and should come through united struggle on the part of all elements of the working class, led by a primarily white Communist party. Today, passages like the following come across as both naive and patronizing:

> I realized how much Bill taught all of us about the Negro. He gently and firmly led us from chauvinism; he was a living example of the strength of the weave of "black and white together." (44)

The chaos and confusion of postwar America are reflected in the subject matter and rambling structure of three essays which record LeSueur's observations on bus and train trips through the Midwest. "Summer Idyl, 1949," for example, is the story of LeSueur's bizarre adventures during a flood. She observes "that genius of communal warmth which, sadly, in American life is invoked only by disaster, when some kind of reality and love rises like a submerged and magic ship" (*Song for My Time*, 26). The people she encounters are often cynical, the scenes decadent, but she draws what comfort she can from this "communal" experience so different from the unity of the Minnesota truckers' strike where, fifteen years earlier, she had described the "organization that comes naturally from the event, of thousands of men [*sic*] conducting themselves as one man, disciplining themselves out of innate and peculiar responsibility" (16).

Despite this depressing contrast, LeSueur does not lose faith in the American people. In "The Dark of the Time," she remarks:

> In the city you hear the words of contempt for our people. You even hear that our people have so many "things"—so many televisions, bathrooms, etc. Returning to the hinterland, I told this to a man who travels the Dakotas and he laughed bitterly. "The thing about capitalist 'things,' commodities, is that they are not permanent. They are an illusion, you never have them . . . now in one whole section of Dakota the outhouse has returned. . . . The killing of the REA has thrown a whole community back to oil lamps, hand milking, outhouses! Everybody knows you never own anything under capitalism—it passes through your hands and one month's backpayment on the installment and whisk—it is gone . . . gone with the mortgage!" (49)

The white working class, LeSueur is saying, still suffers, still has revolutionary potential. This reminder is relevant today; younger leftists, frustrated by the failure of "the workers" to revolt on cue, do sometimes exhibit the "contempt for our people" which LeSueur noticed in the 1950s. But that is not the whole story. One would expect LeSueur, as a Marxist, to be particularly attuned to the contradictory nature of the political reality she observes. Instead, she often seems to cling to an idealized view of the white working class. The paragraph preceding the one just quoted reads, in part:

> The people suffer under capitalism in a different way than a colonial people, for the masks are cunning and the naked wars of aggression are hidden under the words of democracy, and you are delivered into the death of wars against people you do not hate, and made guilty by Nagasakis and Hiroshimas you did not plan. (49)

There is a truth in this, but it is a half-truth. American imperialism materially benefits even the working class, and the Korean War dead, the coffined "builders, planters, begetters" whose "torn loins" LeSueur laments later in the piece, were also the destroyers, murderers, rapists of a war which foreshadowed Vietnam. On the whole, these essays are best read not for their political analysis but for their vivid depiction of an era, their vignettes of gambling rooms tunnelled beneath corn fields, pas-

sengers irritated at the delay when their "express" train keeps stopping to
drop off soldiers' coffins, and funeral mourners harrassed by "the perpetual two, blond, arrow collar, large, well-fed on the people's tax money
McCarthy twins familiar to us all" (43).

Rites of Ancient Ripening (Recent Poems)

In this poetry collection, copyrighted in 1975, LeSueur makes extensive use of Native American symbolism. She also adopts the persona of a
Native American woman throughout three sections of the four-part
book. At first glance, this approach would seem to be consistent with her
early tendency to identify herself with the most oppressed, often to the
exclusion of examining her own situation. In some of the poems she does
imagine Native American experience in a way I find moving despite my
conviction that the best thing white people can do for Third World people is to shut up and let them speak for themselves:

> I am an Indian woman
> Witness to my earth
> Witness for my people.
> I am the nocturnal door,
> The hidden cave of your sorrow,
> Like you hidden deep in furrow
> > and dung
> > of the charnel mound,
> I heard the craven passing of the
> > white soldiers
> And saw them shoot at Wounded Knee
> > upon the sleeping village,
> And ran with the guns at my back
> Until we froze in our blood on the snow.
> > ("Dead in Bloody Snow," 6)

But in many of these poems LeSueur seems concerned not so much
to understand and communicate the experience of Native Americans as
to create for heself a pleasing fantasy of a life in tune with natural
rhythms. This effort is as destructive to her poetry as it is to her political
vision, for the resultant work seems to have little to do with either the
world of the Native Americans or that of Meridel LeSueur. Because the
writing is ungrounded in the close observation that forms the backbone
of LeSueur's best work, poems which repeatedly invoke natural objects

(corn, stone, sun, water, seed) succeed in conveying only a vague nostalgia:

> Rising in pollen
> > we await each other.
> Earth roused will bring us home
> > in seed and pollen.
> Dance the ceremonial together
> > in the entire solar light.
> Sun shining on all friends.
> O meet me in the unbombed villages
> > of the earth.   ("Raise the Fruit," 39)

Many of the poems emphasize male-female "polarities." These are, according to LeSueur, intrinsic to the Native American world-view; but here the choice of symbolism seems, more than anything, a reflection of LeSueur's own sexual-political outlook:

> I lie prone   father husband,
> Open me kernel, green unfurl me
> Reach green to my hungry heart, husband.
> Potent grain and crop await your breast
> Reach green to my hungry breast
> > into my dust of fire and thorn
> And face me to your knife of love.   ("Green Unfurl Me," 12)

In "Corridos of Love," a poem in the book's fourth and final section, LeSueur abandons her persona and seems prepared to address herself directly to the question implicit in the rest of the book: what does it mean for her, a relatively privileged white woman, to say she identifies with the struggles of Third World peoples?

> Tell me—the brown woman below the border asked me—
> Can you reverse the verdict of darkness?   (47)

But rather than replying directly to the "brown woman's" question— where were you and your people when American imperialism was destroying me and mine—LeSueur answers with a list of wrongs done to white Americans. She piles incident on incident as though sheer volume of words (and exclamation marks) could obliterate the power and significance of that question:

> We have wakened screaming at the same savage face of
> > the predator, above us!

My village has disappeared in ruin and deadly wind!
I have tasted the calcium radiation of the dust,
and hear the announcement—keep your children in, today's snow is
radioactive!   (49)

"Doan Ket" ("Solidarity" in Vietnamese; the poem was sent to the
North Vietnamese Women's Union) concludes with a fantasy of solidarity which is unconvincing because it simply ignores the real forces which
keep women apart:

I saw the women of the earth coming toward each other
                    with praise and heat
                        without reservations of space.
All shining and alight in solidarity.
Transforming the wound into bread and children.
In a new abundance, a global summer.   (54)

In fact, in writing the book LeSueur seems to have directed all her energies towards obliterating reality, rather than coming to terms with it.
Quite simply, I wish she had not published these poems.

I am, of course, sorry to be concluding this review on such a note; yet
by now it should be clear that one negative judgment can do little to
dampen my enthusiasm for a writer I find so interesting, so likeable, so
intrinsically relevant to my own life and work. Perhaps a quote from
"The Dark of the Time" is appropriate here:

[The artist] must return really to the people, partisan and alive, with
warmth, abundance, excess, confidence, without reservations, or
cold and merely reasonable bread, or craftiness, writing one thing,
believing another, the superior person, even superior in theoretic
knowledge, an ideological giant, but bereft of heart and humility.
(*Song for My Time*, 58)

"Partisan and alive, with warmth, abundance, excess, confidence. . . . "
With delightful accuracy LeSueur's prescription characterizes her own
achievement. I will read her past work eagerly as it is reissued, and hope
to find her exploring new directions in the work she is said to be pursuing
now, with unabated dedication, as she approaches age eighty.

Canopus in Argos: Archives
Re: Colonized Planet 5 Shikasta
Personal, Psychological, Historical
Documents Relating to Visit by
Johor (George Sherban) Emissary
(Grade 9) 87th of the Period of
the Last Days
by Doris Lessing

Women and poets see the truth
  arrive
Then it is acted out,
The lives are lost, and all the
  newsboys shout.

Muriel Rukeyser wrote these lines in a poem, "Letter to the Front," published in 1944. I thought of them often while reading Doris Lessing's *Shikasta*, the first volume in a promised trilogy of "space fiction," for the novel—like most of Lessing's recent work—is shot through with a sense of the ease and futility of prophecy in the modern world. However, in the wake of the inexorable "truth" which she announces—the destruction of human society as we know it—there will be no newsboys left to shout. It is her insistence upon looking unflinchingly at our apocalyptic predicament which gives this ambitious, seriously flawed book its considerable power. I read it compulsively, with the frightened urgency with which I too often, these days, read newspapers.

As the full title indicates, the novel is presented in the form of a compilation of documents relating to the planet Shikasta—our Earth, as it turns out—colonized by the beneficent Canopean Empire. Many of these documents are reports by "Johor," a Canopean emissary who undertakes missions to Shikasta during various period of its—our—tragic history. To him falls the sad duty of warning Shikasta of the disruption of the

Link which ties the planet into the Canopean system (it is at this time, somewhere in our "prehistory," that the evil influence of the planet Shammat first becomes apparent); he returns to Shikasta during the "Final Days" (roughly our own era), incarnating as a Shikastan, George Sherban. Some of his reports concern these visits and related trips to the Dantean "Zone Six" where "souls" await reincarnation; some are summaries of Shikastan history from a Canopean point of view; some are case histories of individuals representative of (Western) Shikastan society during the "Final Days." Also included are excerpts from the diary of Rachel Sherban, George's sister, and various letters from one Shikastan to another, for example, "Chen Liu to his friend Ku Yuang." Amidst all this, fragments of material we recognize from Lessing's previous books—an African farm, the creatively "insane" Lynda Coldridge from *The Four-Gated City*—float by like bits of wreckage in a flood.

The narrative lurches from Johor's cosmic detachment to Rachel's helpless involvement, from pseudo-mythic tales of Giants to the super-real atmosphere of world crisis, from horror to humor and back again, producing an impact every bit as wrenching and contradictory as Johor tells us Shikasta's history has always been. There is something very impressive, very compelling in this complexity of form and perspective. Unfortunately, however, the achievement is undercut by the book's simplistic moral framework; Lessing's fable of conflict between Canopus's unadulterated Good and Shammat's unmitigated Evil lacks even the dubious explanatory power of the Old Testament—with which, as she states in her introduction, it originated.

As I read the first third of the book, I became increasingly disturbed by Johor's magisterial detachment, a detachment which seems, in a sense, Lessing's also. Not exactly renowned for my own optimism, I nevertheless found myself wanting to argue with repeated characterizations of Shikasta as utterly debased, corrupt, miserable. (It strikes me, by the way, as no accident that this almost punitively detached narrator is male, while the narrator of the antecedent *The Memoirs of a Survivor*, which treats many of *Shikasta*'s themes on a more domestic and compassionate level, was female.) I wanted to shake Doris Lessing; shout at her that detachment may be fine for cosmic emissaries, but won't do for human beings; snatch away the persona which seems to serve her as insulation from the excruciating pain of our situation. And then I came to what was for me the heart of the book, the middle portions which deal, still from a relatively distanced but somehow less judgmental viewpoint, with the sociology and psychology of our contemporary world—and I realized how little Lessing had spared herself, would spare her readers.

Here, in the form of ironic case histories, are recorded the life stories of a series of individuals helplessly enmeshed in a dysfunctional social order beyond the control of any person or group. Here is a stark description of the worldwide "generation gap," the spectacle of the young "in their hordes, their gangs, their groups, their cults, their political parties, their sects, shouting slogans, infinitely divided, antagonistic to each other, always in the right, jostling for command." Unable to learn from the experience of the old, they are condemned, finally, to the same impotence. Most important, here is Johor's / Lessing's bitterly accurate summary of the psychological consequences of the destruction we face:

> Forced back and back upon herself, himself, bereft of comfort, security, knowing perhaps only hunger and cold; denuded of belief in "country," "religion," "progress"—stripped of certainties, there is no Shikastan who will not let his eyes rest on a patch of earth, perhaps no more than a patch of littered and soured soil between buildings in a slum, and think: Yes, but that will come to life, there is enough power there to tear down this dreadfulness and heal all our ugliness—a couple of seasons, and it would all be alive again . . . and in war, a soldier watching a tank rear up over a ridge to bear down on him, will see as he dies grass, tree, a bird swerving past, and know immortality.
>
> It is here, precisely here, that I place my emphasis.
>
> Now it is only for a few of the creatures of Shikasta, those with steadier sight, or nerves, but every day there are more—soon there will be multitudes . . . where once the deepest, most constant, steadiest support was, there is nothing: it is the nursery of life itself that is poisoned, the seeds of life, the springs that feed the well. (198)

Johor concludes:

> Nothing they handle or see has substance, and so they repose in their imaginations on chaos, making strength from the possibilities of a creative destruction. They are weaned from everything but the knowledge that the universe is a roaring engine of creativity, and they are only temporary manifestations of it. . . . Shikastans are, in their awful and ignoble end, while they scuffle and scrabble and scurry among their crumbling and squalid artefacts, reaching out

with their minds to heights of courage and . . . I am putting the
word *faith* here. After thought. With caution. With an exact and
hopeful respect. (203)

Though I welcomed this conclusion insofar as it relieved the almost
unbearable tension of the preceding pages (perhaps I should mention
that I read *Shikasta* during January of this year, a month punctuated by
numerous cheery news briefs proclaiming the imminence of World War
III), it is a difficult one for me to accept, tinged as it is with a quasi-
religious escapsim, an attempt to transcend what cannot be changed. The
question arose for me here, as it did again and again throughout the book:
are things *utterly* hopeless? Is all action directed at changing the world's
self-destructive course *necessarily* futile?

Lessing, clearly, would answer in the affirmative. To this former Leftist, this woman whose fiction is as thoroughly informed by a political
sense of the forces which shape our lives as any fiction I know, all political ideas have proven equally useless, all political institutions and mechanisms equally corrupt, repressive, deadly. In this context, individuals
acquire a strange innocence, for the disaster is no one's fault. Humanity's
fatal flaw, in *Shikasta* always attributed to mystical and arbitrary forces, is
not subject to correction. Individual moral action is the only action
which makes sense, and salvation is not to be looked for except through a
miracle.

The last third of the book is devoted to an account of Shikasta's tortured "Final Days" and the "miracle" in which they eventually do culmi-
nate. The focus is on "George Sherban," the incarnation of Johor who,
Christlike, assumes human form in order to mitigate human suffering.
(Lessing issues a feeble disclaimer to the effect that, though Canopean
society is of course androgynous, Canopean emissaries to Shikasta are
generally required to assume male form because of native prejudices.)
Perhaps I'm overly hostile to male saviors, but I found George rather
obnoxious—a prig and a prick by turns. His sister Rachel, through whose
diary entries we observe both his and her own development, is by contrast a sympathetically human character, conscious among other things
of her predicament as a woman. However, Lessing seems to find this
predicament more or less irrelevant to Shikasta's sad condition.

I suppose this is as logical a place as any to lament the fact that Doris
Lessing is not a feminist. I find it hard to accept that the author of *The
Golden Notebook*, the creator of such strong, vivid female characters as

Martha Quest and the unnamed narrator of *The Memoirs of a Survivor*, the woman whose rigorous examination of the situation of certain types of women in Western society has meant so much to feminists, is simply not "one of us." But in truth she is not. For despite her fascination with the problems her female characters face precisely because they are female, these problems somehow always end up seeming incidental to the "human condition" with which she concerns herself. Woman's oppression is not causative, but merely symptomatic, of the basic malaise. I suppose she counts feminism among the host of "ideologies" which receive her impartial scorn: another cruelly misleading scheme for setting the world right.[1]

Much as Lessing declines to credit women with a basic difference in experience which could offer hope of improvement in the human situation, so she declines to credit Third World peoples with the possibility of innovative political behavior. A considerable portion of *Shikasta*'s conclusion is devoted to a proof (established by means of a mock trial over which George Sherban presides) that the white race, despite its indisputable record of pillage and murder in every corner of the planet, has only done what the Asian, the African, the Native American would do given the opportunity. I was bemused and often disturbed by this, and by her "prediction" of a Europe overrun by stereotypic Chinese bureaucrats, which seemed to me typical of oppressors' paranoid fantasies of their victims' potential violence. Not that colonized peoples do not often want and seek retribution; not that victims don't also oppress each other; but it strikes me as symbolically all wrong to shift the burden of genocide and world destruction away from the West, where, thanks to the combined efforts of the United States, the Western European nations, and the Soviet Union, it overwhelmingly belongs.

Certainly there is much that is compelling in Lessing's political nihilism. We know, for instance, that American "feminists" who acquire power in corporations or government are capable of behaving with a ruthlessness equivalent to that of their male counterparts. We know that Indira Gandhi is no less tyrannical and reactionary because she is a Third World woman. We know that both China's recent invasion of Vietnam and Vietnam's recent invasion of Cambodia had disturbing overtones of imperialism. Yet are we to conclude from these depressing observations that women are basically the same as men, Vietnamese generals basically the same as American generals, etc.? Are we to acquiesce in Lessing's reference to the U.S.S.R. and China as "the two great Dictatorships," as though there could be no differences worth mentioning between them?

The half-hidden problem with Lessing's attempt to paint a convincing global portrait is that, despite her "objective," extra-terrestrial narrator, her perspective is necessarily a white, European—and also, unfortunately, in some ways male-identified—one. While she alludes to the breakdown of world society, what in fact she depicts is the breakdown of European society. Her rejection of the possibility of human solutions to human problems springs, at least in part, from her placement at the dead center of a moribund social order. Though I am very concerned—in fact, terrified—that the world may not survive the consequences of that social order's decline and fall, I cannot agree that there are no human alternatives worth pursuing.

Shikasta's fantasy framework offers depressing evidence of what can happen when such alternatives are dismissed. As "science fiction" (or, in Lessing's preferred usage, "space fiction"), it is ludicrously simplistic, doing nothing to stretch our understanding of spatial, temporal, or evolutionary realities. For example, Lessing assumes that life on other planets would evolve in a manner parallel to human life on earth; her intelligent extraterrestrials are not only sexually bifurcated, but so closely resemble humans that interbreeding is possible. Nor does it help our suspension of disbelief that Johor's explanatory remarks often seem more clearly directed at earth-bound readers than at his supposed Canopean audience.

But far more disturbing are the moral, ethical, and political implications of Lessing's resolutely antirational system. Catharine Stimpson, reviewing the book in the February, 1980, *Ms.*, quite rightly notes the irony of the fact that Lessing, for so long an outspoken critic of colonialism, should here be asking us to believe in a benevolent Canopean Empire.[2] Furthermore, the Canopean preoccupation with genetic engineering and George Sherban's paean to traditional marriage as it was supposedly practiced in a now-forgotten time when human life spanned many hundreds of years have almost fascist overtones. That Lessing's ideal society appears monolithically heterosexual almost goes without saying. I was left entirely unenchanted by her vision of a post-holocaust world whose organic unity is reflected in the geometric shapes of its towns ("As we build, wonderful patterns appear as if our hands were being taught in a way we know nothing about"). The dream of simple unity is at best delusional; at worst, it can indeed lead to authoritarian social systems. I was left wondering uneasily whether Lessing's flight into a fantasy which negates that real human conflict and confusion which we must accept if we are to accept, fight for, human life at all is the price she has had to pay for her scrutiny of the horrors we face.

If *Shikasta* is useful neither as a historical explanation of our predicament, nor as an indication of how to escape that predicament, why read it? For three reasons, I think. First, because for many of us who have been reading and caring about women's literature and woman's fate for some time now, Doris Lessing ranks as an important, dear, and influential old friend and whatever such a friend may do, even if it's joining the Moonies or becoming a born-again Christian, we will want to make an effort to understand—not least because her behavior may contain some clues to our own situation. Second, because in *Shikasta* Lessing makes a very serious attempt to come to grips with the terror and the vast, unassuageable grief which is ours, living as we do in a world that teeters on the brink of destruction. ("I think of myself as one of the dead; I really don't believe, anymore, that I have a future," a friend of mine said at a recent meeting called to discuss the new militarism.) For the central question, the first and last question, is now whether human life will survive at all. Given that governments, social conventions, and our own terror conspire to divert us from the so-called unthinkable, to persuade us to ignore the twin evidence of our senses and our feelings, every expression which prods us to confront this question is valuable to us.

Finally—and this is more difficult for me to articulate—it seems to me that, despite the dismal effect produced by the mystical machinery whose creaking fills this book, Lessing is right to probe the possibilities of whatever may lie beyond appearances. She is right in her assertion, if not in the conclusion she draws from it, that we have reached a dead end with materialism and rationalism. This, for me, does not mean that we must discard the lessons of materialism and rationalism, but that we must go beyond them. For one of our major problems is now a problem of consciousness, one Lessing once explored in a short, ironic, highly effective story called "Report on the Threatened City" which asks the question: what does it mean that human beings, precisely foreseeing the catastrophic results of their own behavior, do nothing to change that behavior?

Most feminists would, I suspect, agree that the as-yet-elusive answer to this riddle is somehow bound up with the structure and functioning of patriarchy. Though Lessing has not chosen to make this connection, I believe it is because she is a woman that she has at least been able to frame the question. "Women and poets see the truth arrive. . . . "

Lessing's work, however flawed, places her among that company of "women and poets" who, because they are willing to credit the evidence of their senses, because they insist on feeling, and because their stake in a destructive system is less than that of the rulers and fathers, herald and make present to us the truths with which we must grapple.

NOTES

1. I am indebted to Adrienne Rich for her thought-provoking remarks about Lessing's attitude toward lesbianism, and the connections between this and her political vision: "So [*The Golden Notebook*] seemed like a very radical, very feminist book, and I remember distinctly, at one point in that book, the woman is getting fed up with her relationships with men, none of them have come off well, and then she begins to worry and she thinks, women like me become 'manhaters or bitter or lesbian.' The implication was of course that it's only from being jaded with too many unsuccessful encounters with men that you would ever turn to women. . . . Lessing has been enormously important as a quasi-feminist writer, a writer centering on women's lives, and the failure of her novels, because in many ways she's a very brilliant political novelist, but the failure of *The Four-Gated City* and of what has come after is a real failure to envisage any kind of political bonding of women. . . . " Interview by Elly Bulkin in *Conditions: One* (1977): 60.

2. While reading *The Memoirs of a Survivor*, I came across a bit of evidence which seems to point to Lessing's ironic self-awareness on this score: " . . . if you have nothing, you are free to choose among dreams and fantasies. I fancied a rather elegant sort of feudalism—without wars, of course, or injustice." Doris Lessing, *The Memoirs of a Survivor* (New York: Alfred A. Knopf, 1974): 105.

This Bridge Called My Back: Writings by Radical Women of Color edited by Cherríe Moraga and Gloria Anzaldúa

"It's like a breath of freedom," a friend wrote to me in a letter from prison, summarizing her response to *This Bridge Called My Back: Writings by Radical Women of Color*. My friend, a young white woman, expects to be locked up for years to come; she does not speak lightly of freedom. I, a so-called free white woman, concur in her assessment. *This Bridge* makes palpable the diverse and specific strengths that women of color offer themselves and each other. It embodies an emerging Third World feminism capable of immeasurably strengthening the theory and practice of "women's liberation" as these have developed within a thus-far white-dominated movement. And it powerfully challenges racism, while at the same time providing feminists of every background with support for our attempts to come to grips with personal identity as "theory in the flesh," basis for future action.

The monumental significance for Third World women of this anthology's publication is, I think, evident from the testimony of its contents alone. A deep hunger for these writings, these communications and connections, is plain in pages which movingly convey the effects of oppression intensified by isolation and invisibility—and the relief and excitement of creating a political context in which private experience can be shared and put to use. *This Bridge* is so far unique among anthologies in its woman-identified, multi-racial, multi-cultural approach to Third World feminism. Women of color will be affirming, disputing, celebrating, and supplementing its varied, sometimes contradictory perspectives for a long time to come.

One of the things I like best about *This Bridge* is its concreteness. "Theory in the Flesh," the subtitle of one section, would have made a fitting heading for the majority of pieces, both poetry and prose. At a time when many white feminist "theorists" seem to have been seduced by the heady possibilities of fuzzy, high-flown generalization, this work is, for the most part, patient with *the evidence*, with experiences and emotions which defy convenient or reassuring classification. Through the willingness of many contributors to share glimpses of their lives, I learned— as deeply, I think as one may learn from books—a great deal about a range of cultural and material realities I will never know from the inside.

Not content with merely pronouncing "Third World," "Native American," "bi-cultural," "lesbian," "Asian-American,""middle-class," "Latina," and so on, *This Bridge* speaks with love and sometimes with pain in the voice of *this* lesbian who is half Native American, half Chicana (Anita Valerio); *this* feminist who is Chinese / Korean American (Merle Woo); *this* immigrant from Argentina who is Latina and Jewish (Judit Moschkovich); *this* Cubana for whom a "middle-class" Cuban childhood meant educational advantages combined with a standard of living most Americans would consider "deprived" (Mirtha Quintanales). Occasionally the voices directly contradict one another: there is *this* Black lesbian calling for an end to put-downs of love relationships between Black and white women (Cheryl Clarke) and *this* Black lesbian ready to give up altogether on most forms of contact with white women "until these wimmin evolve" (doris davenport, 89).

Neither do these writers content themselves with abstract denunciations of racism; they make us feel its effects—by listing at least eleven ways a little Chinese-American girl longed to be white (Nellie Wong); by pointing out the astronomically high early death rate among Indians (Barbara Cameron); by exploring the implications of the fact that college students taught by a Japanese-American woman expressed surprise and indignation upon learning that Asian-Americans are just as angry about their treatment in American society as are other Third World groups (Mitsuye Yamada). The frustration and weariness of women of color who have been tokenized by white feminists are reiterated so compellingly that, if words can educate, such behavior ought to diminish instantly and markedly in white readers of this book.

Long before *This Bridge* appeared, I knew that its editors were two Chicanas, Gloria Anzaldúa and Cherríe Moraga, and that its purpose was to include the viewpoints of a wide range of women of color. Nevertheless, one of my first reactions to an initial reading was that Black women seemed somewhat underrepresented. Later I realized that I had in fact expected Black contributors to dominate the volume—and it dawned on me how symptomatic this expectation was of the characteristic American myth that Black/white is *the* color difference, *the* race "problem." The absorption of such an attitude is particularly ironic in my own case, given that I grew up in the Pacific Northwest, where my earliest experiences of color difference and racism involved Indians and Asian Americans.

The residence of many of this volume's contributors outside the boundaries of Black/white definition; the fact that a larger number are lesbians vulnerable to the homophobic disapproval of the communities in which they were raised; the mixture of cultural influences which has been formative for many—all these factors inform the approach to Third World feminism, making it richly complex. Editor Gloria Anzaldúa explains:

> The mixture of bloods and affinities, rather than confusing or unbalancing me, has forced me to achieve a kind of equilibrium. Both cultures deny me a place in *their* universe. Between them and among others I build my own universe, *El Mundo Zurdo* [The Left-handed World]. I belong to myself and not to any one people. (209)

This Bridge is divided into six sections which, as the editors say in their introduction:

> intend to reflect what we feel to be the major areas of concern for Third World women in the U.S. in forming a broad-based political movement: 1) how visibility/invisibility as women of color forms our radicalism; 2) the ways in which Third World women derive a feminist political theory specifically from our racial/cultural background and experience; 3) the destructive and demoralizing effects of racism in the women's movement; 4) the cultural, class, and sexuality differences that divide women of color; 5) Third World women's writing as a tool for self-preservation and revolution; and 6) the ways and means of a Third World feminist future. (xxiv)

There is considerable thematic overlap among the different sections; most of the pieces reflect in one way or another a commitment to "identity politics," defined by the Combahee River Collective as the belief that "the most profound and potentially the most radical politics come directly out of our own identity, as opposed to working to end someone else's oppression" (212).

A belief in self-liberation has of course been central to the Second Wave of the American women's movement since its inception. But the

"identity politics" perspective of *This Bridge* seems, in general, more in-
sistent than much recent feminist writing on the manifold dimensions of
personal/political experience. Identity is exactly equivalent neither to
race, nor to gender, nor "sexual preference," nor mother tongue, nor
cultural setting, nor country of origin, nor educational background, nor
class, nor any other aspect of experience to which a label can be affixed; it
is a subtle blend of all these factors, and of an individual's choices about
what to do with them.

One expression of this perspective which I find extremely valuable is
"Across the Kitchen Table: A Sister-to-Sister Dialogue." Here Barbara
Smith and Beverly Smith attempt to identify the points in their lives
where various oppressions intersect—to compare, for example, the effects of poverty, of racism, of sexism—not in order to establish "hierarchies of oppression," but to develop change-oriented politics truly reflective of their experience and that of other Black and Third World
women. They explore the concrete effects of an economic marginality
which, they believe, creates a very significant experiential difference between many Black and white women. (White women, they observe, nevertheless tend to assume that a Black family in which education was
valued *must* have been "middle-class.") They discuss the particularly
painful forms homophobia assumes in the Black community, while at the
same time conveying a vivid sense of their rootedness in Black culture
and social life, and the loss they experience through functioning in a
largely white context where "there is so much about Black identity that
doesn't get called into practice. . . . Because the way you act with Black
people is because they inspire the behavior" (Beverly Smith, 119).

Much of this book's strength comes from its contributors' frequent
willingness to examine many-faceted identity even when the questions
raised are discomfiting. Cherríe Moraga begins her essay "La Güera":

> I am the very well-educated daughter of a woman who, by the
> standards in this country, would be considered largely illiterate. My
> mother was born in Santa Paula, Southern California, at a time when
> much of the central valley there was still farm land. Nearly thirty-
> five years later, in 1948, she was the only daughter of six to marry an
> anglo, my father. (27)

Where she could have chosen to speak simply out of her oppression as a
working-class Chicana, Moraga takes the risk of exploring the intersec-
tions of working-class upbringing and educational privilege, of Chicana

heritage and "white" appearance, which have been formative for her. She calls on us to "seriously address ourselves to some very frightening questions: How have I internalized my own oppression? How have I oppressed?" (30).

Exploring the implications of relationships among women of different cultural and class backgrounds, Mirtha Quintanales observes:

> I am a bit concerned when a Latina lesbian sister generalizes about/ puts down the "white woman"—especially if she herself has white skin. In the midst of this labeling, might she not dismiss the fact of her own white privileges—regardless of her identification with Black, Native American, and other Third World women of color? Might she not dismiss the fact that she may often be far better off than many white women? I cannot presume to know what it is really like to be a Black woman in America, to be racially oppressed. I cannot presume to know what it is really like to grow up American "White Trash" and destitute.
>
> But I am also a bit concerned when a Black sister generalizes about/dismisses all non-black women, or all women who are not strict "women of color" or strictly "Third World." . . . Yes, racism is a BIG MONSTER we all need to contend with. . . . But I think we need to keep in mind that in this country, in this world, racism is used *both* to create false differences among us *and* to mask very very significant ones—cultural, economic, political. . . . "
> (152–53)

It feels both dangerous and important to state that I find the questions posed here by Moraga and Quintanales, and similar ones raised by other writers, to be among the central contributions of *This Bridge*. Dangerous because there is always the chance that the least hint of ambiguity in the public posture of oppressed people will be used by others to deny the reality of that oppression—as, for instance, talk about racism among Third World peoples has sometimes been used by whites to deny our own primary responsibility. Dangerous, too, because I risk failing to convey adequately the sense of deep love for and commitment to their Third World cultures which emerges from Moraga's and Quintanales's explorations, as from most of the pieces included here. Important— vitally so—because in feminist discussions of oppression, the nuances of identity and choice have too often been denied (by the "privileged" quite as much as by the "multiply oppressed"), with the effect that oppression begins to appear, in and of itself, a moral guarantee or political credential.

This Bridge clearly reaches out to all women, seeking to push us beyond safe formulations, whether those be the cozy conventions of white solipsism, the sterilities of pat, intellectualized anti-racism, or the self-righteousness of identity worn as unexamined armor.

The courage of this stance helped me immeasurably in the confrontation with my own racism that reading the anthology entailed. For, despite the fact that I'd looked forward to its appearance, I felt intimidated when a copy arrived at my house late last May. A whole fat anthology was different, I suddenly realized, from the isolated discussion group, the darker face or two or three in the pale crowd, the island article or poem or "special issue" in the familiar if boring White Sea of feminist publishing. *This Bridge* was almost unprecedentedly nontokenistic—and, despite my experience-based conviction that tokenism is destructive for *both* Third World and white women, the fact made me uneasy.

What was I afraid of? Anger, above all. "Here's a whole anthology by radical women of color, and they're going to be mad at me." It's still hard for me to confront some of that anger. However, having survived several readings of the section on "Racism in the Women's Movement," I can now better see that anger as something to be learned from—while recognizing that it is really an astonishingly small part of what *This Bridge* has to communicate. And I have to chuckle ruefully at the sardonic accuracy of Jo Carrillo's "And When You Leave, Take Your Pictures With You" ("Our white sisters / radical friends / love to own pictures of us / sitting at a factory machine . . . " [63], but are unable to deal with real live Third World women); I can recognize that Chrystos's critique of the doctrinaire rigidity of certain white lesbian-feminists speaks to aspects of my experience as well ("I Don't Understand Those Who Have Turned Away From Me").

This Bridge is very much a writers' book, though not in the rarefied sense that statement seems to suggest. Many of the contributors are committed and experienced writers, and the inclusion of the section "Speaking in Tongues: The Third World Woman Writer" underlines the dedication of the two writer-editors to writing as a means of "self-preservation and revolution." The sense of the struggles of these writers to get the work down on paper and out into the world is very graphic and powerful: "The voice recurs in me: *Who am I, a poor Chicanita from the sticks, to think I could write?*" (Anzaldúa, 166), Yet the effort is successful: for the most part, these words *live*.

The poetry is often particularly exciting. I especially enjoy Hattie Gossett's exuberant "billie lives! billie lives," a prose poem about a mysterious Billie Holiday recording entitled "gloomy sunday subtitled hungarian suicide song. . . . one of those my man is dead so now i am gonna throw myself in the grave too funeral dirge numbers (tragic mulattress division) that they used to mash on billie when she went into the studio" (110). A resourceful Billie manages to interpret this retrograde ditty in such a way as to have "them bigdaddy blip d blips leaping outta windows in droves" (111).

Chrystos's "No Rock Scorns Me as Whore" is one of the most affecting poetic meditations I've seen on the terrors of the nuclear threat, the necessity for a "deep, deep understanding of the sacredness of life, the fragility of each breath" (245). I was struck by the positioning of this sad and powerful piece at the end of the volume, in refreshing contrast to the usual practice of ending political works on a note (often unconvincing) of revolutionary optimism.

Unsurprisingly, not all of the material included in *This Bridge* is as specific, as grounded in the "flesh" of experience, or as successful in its use of words to convey that experience as the pieces I've discussed so far. "The Pathology of Racism: A Conversation with Third World Women" by doris davenport seems to me to constitute a relapse into identifying people by convenient labels and generalities: white women are weak and dumb; Black women are strong and together. (In fact, davenport seems to be addressing Black women, but uses "Black" and "Third World" almost interchangeably.) For the sake of honesty, and the further instruction of all students of the absurd and useless convolutions of racism in our time, I must add that I probably wouldn't have had the courage to state this reaction publicly had I not discovered that a woman of color whose political judgment I respect takes a somewhat similar view of davenport's piece, thus giving me "permission" to feel critical of it. Yeeccchhh!

I find Pat Parker's "Revolution: It's Not Neat or Pretty or Quick" disappointingly rhetorical, full of shopworn "radical" phrases which fail to illuminate the realities they refer to. And while I absorbed useful information from Norma Alarcón's "Chicana's Feminist Literature: A Revision Through Malintzin/or Malintzin: Putting Flesh Back on the Object," the piece doesn't succeed for me in "fleshing out" its subject matter, but remains stiffly academic.

Perhaps in part because its editors and so many of its contributors are
writers, *This Bridge* reflects an emphasis on cultural expression, consciousness-raising, and theory which has tended to characterize much of the
recent feminist movement. With the exception of a few pieces like the
Combahee River Collective's "A Black Feminist Statement," scant attention is devoted to the ways and means of effecting public, structural,
institutional change. One volume can't—and shouldn't—do everything;
the cultural focus becomes a serious limitation only if *This Bridge* is regarded as a stopping-place, rather than as the beginning its makers clearly
intend it to be.

White readers, I believe, have a particular responsibility to this beginning: to *listen accurately*, as far as we are able, to what is being said, to the
range and complexity of what is being said. For the danger exists that
because of our own preconceptions and defenses, we will hear only pain
and anger, and will miss the many affirmations and joyous moments. Or
that, on the contrary, we will deny the pain and anger altogether. Or that
we will use this volume for the old purposes of tokenism; that certain of
the contributors will be touted as "spokeswomen," and the book itself
embalmed and canonized as the last word on Third World feminism,
thereby hampering its role as catalyst and initiator.

These are hard times for all feminists. Hard times seem to encourage
the dangerous response I have come to think of as "hunkering down in
our oppressions": focusing on the very real differences in privilege and
experience which divide us *to the exclusion* of the equally real factors
which might unite us—as though, paradoxically, suffering and fear constituted the surest sign of radicalism, the most convincing proof that we
are worthy of respect and care. I am moved and very, very grateful that so
many women of color, among the least safe and privileged of feminists,
have instead chosen here to make themselves more vulnerable; to reach
out; to risk so much.

At the end of "Across the Kitchen Table," Beverly Smith remarks:

> The way I see it, the function that Third World women play in the
> movement is that we're the people who throw the ball a certain dis-
> tance and then the white women run to that point to pick it up. I feel
> we are constantly challenging white women, usually on the issues of
> racism but not always. We are always challenging women to go
> further, to be more realistic. . . . Our analysis of race and class op-
> pression, and our commitment to really dealing with those issues,

including homophobia, is something we know we have to struggle
with to insure our survival. It is organic to our very existence. (127)

This Bridge challenges *all* women "to go further, to be more realistic."
What's better yet, time and again it demonstrates that we can.

Right-Wing Women
by Andrea Dworkin

In her new book Andrea Dworkin argues that right-wing women support
anti-feminist positions because, accurately perceiving the cruel nature of
the "sex-class system" and believing that women are powerless to oppose
it, they opt for the pittance which the Right promises as reward for con-
formity to its "rules." Dworkin's call to feminists to undertake a serious
analysis of right-wing women's motivations is thought-provoking and
timely; her version of what such women think is often plausible. Unfortunately, though, it is not very well supported. She presents no evidence
for her account beyond selected quotations from a few books by right-
wing women and an affecting description of several chilling encounters
(notable particularly for their brutal anti-Semitism) with members of
right-wing delegations at the National Women's Conference in Houston
in 1977.

Not only does Dworkin fail to tell us in any meaningful depth who
right-wing women are, she neglects to analyze how they differ from
women who hold less extreme views. She does discuss at some length the
special oppression of women—the poor, the old, women of color—who
are "expendable" from the state's perspective, and are presumably not
right-wing. But she leaves us with the highly questionable and totally
undocumented suggestion that the "common woman" is a right-wing
woman: "The antifeminism of Left, Right, and center fixes the power of
the Right over women—gives the huge majority of women over to the
Right . . . because as long as the sex-class system is intact, *huge numbers*

of women will believe that the Right offers them the best deal" (my emphasis, 233–34). This depiction of the "huge majority" of women as consciously dedicated to reaction obscures both the full scope of women's struggles and the fact that much of the Right's support comes not from enthusiastic ideologues but from the disaffected and wavering: for instance, those who voted for Reagan as a "protest."

In fact *Right-Wing Women* is less about the women of the Right than it is about Andrea Dworkin's view of the female condition, one undoubtedly familiar to readers of her previous books, which have established her as a premier rhetorician of female victimization. She sets out to rub our noses in the humiliation and perils of woman's lot, and she does succeed brilliantly in conveying the emotional tone of *some* female experience. This she unfortunately presents as universal. Her innumerable references to an abstract female subject ("women feel," "women fear," "the woman who . . . ") conveniently enable her to refine away the complexities of culture and interwoven oppressions; all we need consider of the experience involved is that it is Female (as if it were ever possible really to do this). It is time for white, American, educationally and/or class-privileged feminists, in particular, to stop projecting our experience on the rest of the world. But this is impossible unless we first examine and acknowledge the way our own biases may be affecting our perceptions and resultant theory—an effort neglected here.

Dworkin's characteristic approach to the indisputable fact of woman-hating amounts to anti-analysis; her repetitive style bludgeons long after it has ceased to enlighten. Men fuck us, she informs us. They fuck us, they knock us up. They fuck us over—and over—and over—and over—and over. In this book as elsewhere, Dworkin is rarely concerned to tell us *why*; to examine how social structures have ameliorated or intensified woman-hating; to show how women have resisted and sometimes overcome. At times she does put forth intriguing suggestions: for example, that the new reproductive technologies threaten to assimilate motherhood to the "brothel" model of exploitation; that homophobia and anti-Semitism are paired in significant ways in the New Testament. Elsewhere, her argument can be startlingly over-simple, as when she suggests that the economic exploitation of women is entrenched, not largely because men make money from it, but only because it keeps women sexually at their mercy.

Dworkin asks us to read all human history as the chronicle of sexual injustice: "In patriarchal history, one passion is necessarily fundamental and unchanging: the hatred of women. The other passions molt" (121). While she alludes to the importance of differences among women, she ultimately asks us to believe that only each female's pledge of allegiance to a theory of "sex-class" as the fundamental category of oppression will save us from the apocalypse she forecasts in her chapter on the "The Coming Gynocide." And yet she never spells out the concrete political implications of "sex-class" solidarity, never says how organizers seriously concerned with a range of oppressions can make use of an alleged bond with women consciously dedicated to homophobic, racist, anti-Semitic, or classist philosophies.

A further problem arises with her discussions of the experience of women of color (usually Black). In the few places where they are separated out from the homogenized female mass, they are generally presented as super-victims. The one substantive discussion of the impact of racism specifically on women involves Black women on welfare, which risks producing the distorted impression that welfare is the typical Black female experience.

Her only clear conclusion is that feminists must go it alone politically; we can expect nothing whatsoever from "male" movements. This position seems to me indefensible from the point of view of anyone whose experience of life teaches her there are forms of oppression irreducible to women's oppression—or from that of anyone who realizes that every movement, even feminism, needs allies. From these perspectives, certainly, Dworkin's incessant potshots at a straw-man-of-the-Left, her implication that Left, Right, and center are all the same to women, are entirely objectionable. Such categorical attacks are in the mean and dangerous tradition of Left-baiting, and are not to be confused with the critiques of actual Left sexism which feminists must always be prepared to offer.

Nor does Dworkin's go-it-alone approach stop with dismissing potential male allies. A portion of her final chapter, "Antifeminism," consists of a thinly veiled attack on feminists who do not share her view that pornography is the cornerstone of women's oppression.

Andrea Dworkin's righteous anger on behalf of victims of sexual oppression is sometimes painfully compelling. Her work contains valuable insights. But her rage is not theory. Her vision of monolithic male power and universal female victimhood is not analysis. And her isolationist rhetoric will be heeded by feminist activists at the gravest peril to our life-and-death effort to prove right-wing women—and the power they serve—wrong.

Woman's Worth: Sexual Economics and the World of Women
by Lisa Leghorn and Katherine Parker

Since the late 1960s, American feminists of the "Second Wave" have searched for answers to a few basic questions: Why are women subordinate to men? What are the characteristic forms of abuse and exploitation that flow from and in turn maintain that subordinate status? How can women use our collective strength to change, fundamentally and forever, the conditions of female existence?

What has distinguished the radical feminist approach to these questions has been an insistence on viewing women's oppression as primary in the grand and depressing scheme of inequities and atrocities which the panorama of human history reveals to us. By focusing on the oppression of women as women, American radical feminist analysis has helped put women's oppression on the political map. It has excelled in picking out from the staticky background of daily life, and documenting, a broad range of abusive practices (such as battering and sexual violence) and constraining, inequitable institutions (such as motherhood and heterosexuality) which had previously seemed natural and inevitable.

While much of radical feminism's attractiveness as a theoretical approach surely stems from this success in making sense of specific areas of female experience, it possesses another appeal: the allure of ideology, of a world-view which promises to explain *all* experience. Socialist-feminism may seem not one theory, but a dubious hybrid of two; Third World feminism likewise introduces a complexity of variables. Radical feminism, by contrast, offers an enticingly coherent account of how the world got into this mess, anyway.

Unfortunately, radical feminism has not escaped the characteristic tendency of ideologies to oversimplify, to force untidy realities into a rigid framework, to sacrifice breadth of vision for intensity of focus. And much radical feminist analysis has been marred by a lopsided idealism, a habit of concentrating on psychological and moral factors to the exclusion of attention to the material conditions of women's existence and the public, political means of changing those conditions. More and more in recent years, radical feminists have tended to portray women as victims, mere hapless consumers of an unending diet of punishments dished out by an abstract, monolithic "patriarchy." Often such theorists have aspired to a universal perspective on woman's fate, yet their subject matter and conclusions have revealed their racial, ethnic, and class-bound assumptions, their ahistorical and American biases. They have demonstrated what Indian feminist Kalpana Ram, writing of the inadequacies of radical feminist theory to describe Third World experience, has called "the tendency in the Western women's movement to project its own preoccupations and terms of analysis onto vastly different historical realities" (13).[1]

Woman's Worth: Sexual Economics and the World of Women offers a radical feminist economic analysis which avoids some of these pitfalls. Within the limitations of the available data and their own position as white Americans, authors Lisa Leghorn and Katherine Parker have attempted the formidable task of attaining a cross-cultural perspective on the economic status and role of women, a view which takes into account differences in women's experience from society to society as well as similarities, and seeks to identify factors which make for limited female power within patriarchal contexts, as well as those which contribute to victimization.

Their materialist perspective is refreshing. It avoids, for instance, the absurdities of a statement I heard a prominent radical feminist thinker make recently, to the effect that the reason why society as constituted will never grant "equal pay for equal work" is that with women earning 59 cents for every male dollar, men retain the power to use us sexually (apparently she entirely discounted the notion that the pocketbook, quite as much as the penis, might motivate male supremacist behavior). Woman's Worth asserts that women's enormous, minimally rewarded economic contributions to men's life and leisure, and children's livelihood and well being, are indeed primary motivations for "keeping women down." The more dramatic forms of physical abuse and sexual exploitation must in part be understood in terms of the way they function to keep women economically subservient.

Perhaps partly because its subject matter is less emotionally charged than that of a number of influential books which have focused on crimes against women ranging from rape to infibulation, from footbinding to incest, *Woman's Worth*, published in 1981, has been scantily reviewed in the feminist media. It contains much important information about women's economic condition in a range of societies, a good deal of this necessarily obtained from relatively obscure sources. This information and the conclusions drawn from it would be most properly evaluated by a feminist trained in the social sciences, who would be familiar with related material in the field. Unfortunately, I have no such expertise. Nevertheless, I have chosen to write this review, both because I want women to know of the book's existence and because of the ways I feel it exemplifies both the strengths and weaknesses of a radical feminist approach.

Leghorn and Parker begin by stating their intention to demystify "economics," to "begin from women's perspectives" in an effort to understand those factors in the organization of material life which form women's experience. This cannot be a simple process of generalization, however: "It is exceedingly difficult, when talking about women's experiences cross-culturally, to understand the impact that customs have on the life of a woman living in a specific culture, unless one has an understanding of how those traditions fit into the entire social and cultural context" (31). They propose to investigate the determinants of women's lives in several cultures, including examples which demonstrate the range of female power. This discussion, they state, will form the basis for a later consideration of the commonalities in female experience.

First, however, they provide an excellent chapter called "Shouldering the High Cost of Development." Here they show that the economic "development" which has come to most of the world in the wake of Western colonial exploitation and, more recently, neo-colonial and imperialist domination, has usually been a vicious, socially destructive process which has created wealth for a few at the expense of breakdown in traditional economies which had provided for many—and that women have frequently borne the brunt of this disintegration. Women's suffering, they point out, has in part resulted from gender-specific consequences of economic decline: for example, the colonial burden of taxation frequently meant that men had to leave home to earn cash for taxes; women remained behind to support themselves and their children, doing the work the men had done previously in addition to their own. At the same time, such educational opportunities and new technologies as have been made available to some men are usually denied to women, and the limited power women held in their traditional societies has been eroded by the imposition of Western institutions. The authors do not romanticize precolonial cultures; they state that in most of them women were second-class citizens. Nevertheless, the effect of their powerful indictment of Western, capitalist-generated development is to raise serious questions about their decision to compare women's power cross-societally without reference to "male-defined" economic categories—a point I'll come back to later.

Following their discussion of development, Leghorn and Parker make use of a system apparently adapted from one devised by Carolyn J. Matthiasson to describe and classify varying levels of women's power. (They use the terms "minimal power," "token power," and "negotiating power" to characterize the three levels Matthiasson identified.) This approach is valuable because it provides a framework for considering women's options in different social circumstances; acknowledging that "patriarchy" is not a monolith, it seeks to identify the factors which foster women's power and autonomy. The criteria used for evaluating the societies considered are (1) valuation of women's fertility and physical integrity; (2) women's access to control over crucial resources; and (3) women's networks. Societies discussed as examples of "minimal power" for women are Ethiopia, Peru, Algeria, and Japan; "token power" societies are the United States, Cuba, the U.S.S.R., and Sweden; and "negotiating power," the highest level, is analyzed in contemporary Chinese, Iroquois, and Ewé (African: Ghana and Togo) societies. The authors point out that within the four different varieties of "male-defined economies [nontechnological, third world, capitalist, socialist], women's experience varies from minimal power to negotiating power" (32).

I wish that they had gone on to develop this comparative analysis of women's power, and particularly to investigate in far greater detail how change has been achieved by women in the specific circumstances they describe. This might have been especially useful because of their access to primary source material (for instance, an unpublished thesis by and interview with Alemnesh Bulti on Ethiopia, and unpublished research conducted by Lisa Leghorn in the south of Togo). Instead, they proceed to a far less rewarding section in which they attempt to use their cross-cultural analysis as a basis for discussing common factors which shape women's lives in all societies.

The result, a chapter entitled "The Personal Is Economic," is a hodge-podge of generalizations about women's oppression. Providing little fresh analysis of *how* oppressive institutions and practices function economically, Leghorn and Parker frequently mingle summaries of familiar analysis by such writers as Kathleen Barry (on "sexual slavery"), Susan Brownmiller (on rape) and Adrienne Rich (on compulsory heterosexuality), with seemingly random examples of the phenomena. Their analogies here (for instance, their extended comparison of marriage to literal slavery) belie their earlier emphasis on "the entire social and cultural context." Vague statements imply that all female experience is pretty much the same:

> Women as a group are socialized to be supportive and sensitive to the needs of others; and partly as a result of this socialization, women give and look for in others a high standard of emotional giving and intensity. Men, to the contrary, learn not to verbalize or express their feelings because they are afraid of being vulnerable. (113)

Unsupported and unqualified, this assertion certainly reads like the "projection" of American experience and concerns that Kalpana Ram objected to.

Unquestioned American assumptions about Arab cultures surface in the section on "Female Seclusion and the Veil." Looking up a footnote to a dire statement that in "Arab culture" a man will kill with total impunity a female relative whose sexual "honor" has been questioned or violated, I found a reference to Kathleen Barry's *Female Sexual Slavery*; looking further, I discovered Barry's source—apparently the statement of a single Arab woman who had testified at the International Tribunal on Crimes Against Women. While such atrocities may indeed be prevalent in one or many Arab societies, one woman's testimony is not sufficient documentation for such a sweeping characterization. In their discussion of "Female Seclusion and the Veil," Leghorn and Parker portray women in purdah as "household slaves," defined as the "property" of father or husband; they refer to women married to wealthy men "in many of these cultures" as "domestic slaves" and "status symbols" and say of Moroccan women who earn money that they are victims of "the mythology that they are worth nothing and produce no value." I mistrust such passages because they help to perpetuate a sterotypic view of Arab women as super-victims, one which bolsters the racist American image of a backward—and undifferentiated—Arab world.[2] (The discussion of "Polygyny," by contrast, seemed respectful of the variety of ways women experience an institution which ethnocentric westerners have viewed with righteous horror.) The scattershot approach of this chapter as a whole may be judged by the fact that "Racism" is sandwiched between sections on "Beauty" and "Love and Emotions." Though the authors clearly identify racism as a grave problem for women, their six-page treatment here is utterly inadequate to begin to account for its impact on women, American or otherwise (in fact, most of their examples focus on Black American women). Worse, they offer as fact a highly misleading version of women's history when, quoting remarks made by Elizabeth Cady Stanton in 1860, they hold up the suffrage movement as an inspiring example of "a progressive vision of change for all women," and explain that the suffragists' commitment to Black people's civil rights "began to be watered down" only after 1890.

What they do not mention is that, following their break with abolitionists who favored a strategy of obtaining votes for Black men at the expense of women's claim to the franchise, Stanton and Susan B. Anthony accepted as an ally the blatantly racist financier George Francis Train, who assisted them in the Kansas campaign for the vote of 1867 and initially backed their feminist paper, the *Revolution*.[3] Feminist historian Ellen DuBois details Stanton's racist and elitist opposition to the Fifteenth Amendment (which gave Black men the vote) on the grounds that "it was wrong to elevate an ignorant and politically irresponsible class of men over the heads of women of wealth and culture, whose fitness for citizenship was obvious. . . . While ostensibly defending the rights of all women, Stanton spoke only on behalf of those of the white middle and upper classes."[4] The episode, surely one of the most complex and controversial in the history of American feminism, can hardly be charac-

terized adequately by *any* brief summary, much less one which describes
the suffrage movement as the champion of both racial and sexual equal-
ity. Such a description not only distorts the past, it fools us about the
nature and gravity of the obstacles contemporary feminists face in our
efforts to oppose an interlocking system of oppressions.

In keeping with this oversimplified view, Leghorn and Parker reiterate
the classic radical feminist position on white women's racism: "Racism
as an ideology and institution creates the distorted notion for white
women that they truly belong to, and thus have a stake in, male-dominated institutions that thrive on racism's inequities" (110). In fact, the
history of the suffrage movement provides one of the most convincing
illustrations of the ways in which white women do derive enormous economic and social privileges from a racist social order; it was not merely
because of "distorted notions" that Stanton and Anthony made deplorable choices, but because, as practical politicans who were both white
and class-privileged, they took advantage of concrete opportunities for
financial backing and political support. To the extent that feminist theorists continue to "reduce" racism and other oppressions to sexism—to
understand every earthly evil as a manifestation of patriarchy in which
women have sometimes colluded, but in which we are not fundamentally
implicated—I believe they are no closer to an adequate account of real
experience than doctrinaire Marxists who, viewing male supremacy as
the product of capitalism, might argue that working-class men who abuse
women subscribe to the misguided idea that they truly have a stake in
capitalist-created hierarchies that thrive on sexism.

Following their chapter on the economic dimension of personal experience, Leghorn and Parker discuss the "invisibility" of women's economic contribution under male-devised systems of computing value.
Though they are certainly not the first to raise this criticism of traditional
economics,[5] the point is an important one, and I found much of their
material on women's real economic role both valuable in itself and suggestive, in larger terms, of the monumental extent to which women are
exploited. In most societies, they say, "not only does women's work raise
the entire family's standard of living to the culturally defined minimum
when husbands are living with their families, but when husbands live
apart from their families, women's work sustaining the biologically defined minimum often indirectly makes possible a higher standard of living enjoyed only by the absent husbands" (187). They offer wide-ranging
evidence to support their claim that women make possible children's and

men's leisure, and that women often suffer most from hunger because of cultural assumptions that their requirements are less, and/or inadequate attention to their special nutritional needs.

Unfortunately, the two closing chapters, which focus on the future and possibilities for change, are, along with "The Personal Is Economic," the weakest in the book. Leghorn and Parker frequently depart from their analysis of material conditions to indulge in sweeping remarks about women's superior moral and emotional endowments. Wisely reluctant to specify exactly how feminist change should come about in other societies or what new social structures might best meet women's needs, they substitute platitudes:

> The magnitude of change that is necessary cannot come all at once, it takes generations to build. In most cultures around the world, the changes will be small, as women make discoveries and assert their dreams step by step. But if each woman retains her vision of change, and makes sure that the changes she makes bring her closer to that vision, she will help to slowly erode patriarchy's foundations. Gradually, around the world, women can begin to define and create the basis for the new order they envision. (215)

This is the traditional idealist—and individualist—approach: change people's minds, thoughts, assumptions, and you will change their behavior and thus ultimately their circumstances. A materialist approach, by contrast, assumes that it is by changing social and economic structures, and thereby altering behavior, that people's minds are changed. Feminism needs a synthesis of the two approaches, a synthesis which this book's opening chapters seem to promise but which is disappointingly absent here.

At times, Leghorn and Parker seem totally confused about what sorts of changes are actually progressive for women. At one point they caution us to evaluate whether altered circumstances:

> provide women with necessary tools for survival and change yet reinforce women's oppression more subtly by making the male system more viable. . . . (213)

A few pages later, they assert:

> when women start with almost nothing, *any* changes that give them self-respect and tools with which to fight, though perhaps temporarily reinforcing the existing power structure, pave the way for more fundamental change. . . . (my emphasis, 222–23)

Their discussion of "transitional strategies" reflects their assumption that change must come gradually. This seems contradicted by their own evidence that in some revolutionary societies, notably China and Cuba, improvement in women's lot has come with astonishing rapidity. (Of course the process has been inadequate and incomplete, with conditions remaining especially bad for lesbians, as is duly pointed out.) Despite militant language—women must "fight" for change—Leghorn and Parker maintain that to employ "patriarchal means—such as centralized, hierarchical social organization, or violence . . . is a contradiction in terms" (301). Here they imply that the universal female condition approximates that of women (particularly white women) in Western democracies, where a *relative* degree of economic security, social stability, and institutional flexibility (purchased largely at the expense of colonized peoples) makes gradualism seem feasible. Nowhere do they admit that where the conditions of life are desperate for almost everyone, political choices are liable to be desperate as well.

I mean here neither to advocate nor to romanticize "revolutionary" violence, which I suspect has been as often misperceived by its American proponents as by its American detractors. I too am the product of a Western democracy, not just of "patriarchy" in the abstract, and I have inadequate equipment with which to comprehend, for instance, the choices which must confront the Salvadoran woman, member of the Salvadoran revolutionary women's organization AMES, who recently informed me that her group does not work for feminist goals because it is only through the success of the revolution that the situation of her countrywomen can be improved. My experience convinces me that no male-dominated revolution will *by itself* liberate women, so any deferral or renunciation of feminist struggle makes me highly uneasy. Yet in the midst of my skepticism I have to credit this woman's testimony—born of *her* experience— that her own liberation cannot be separated from the specific revolutionary process now going on in her country. And the example brings me back to Leghorn and Parker's chapter on women and development, to my earlier question about what it means to acknowledge the devastating role of capitalist imperialism in the world economy while seeking to develop a framework for economic analysis that ultimately discounts "male-defined" forms of economic organization.

Certainly it says something important about the commonality of women's subordinate economic status that

> In looking at the lives of women and their families around the world, we have felt that . . . families within each category of women's power [i.e., minimal, token, negotiating] receive about the same percentage of men's resources in time or money, depending on which they have more of. The criteria we have discussed and the status of women in a culture are factors which, as a composite, have a great deal more influence on the proportion of female to male participation in meeting family and societal needs than the class structure of a society (or the class of a woman's husband or father). (209)

However, this statement in isolation may lead us to ignore the fact that the "same percentage" of the resources of, for example, an American aerospace engineer and a tenant farmer in northeastern Brazil will represent vastly different *quantities* and therefore a vastly different standard of living for wife and children—in some cases, the difference between luxury and starvation. (A similar disparity clearly exists from class to class within a given country.) Leghorn and Parker have developed no way of integrating their important observations about the global role of capitalism in subjugating women into their theoretical model of women's economic role within patriarchy. As in their discussion of racism, the interplay between and among irreducible systems of oppression is discounted in the effort to portray gender-based oppression as primary. This results in a distorted picture, not merely of how many women experience their lives, but of how they struggle for change.

For the choice—as Leghorn and Parker hint in several places, but without elaboration—is not either/or. Sara Evans has written of how Vietnamese women's separate organizing within their revolution raised consciousness among pre-feminist American women (188–89). Writing of Dalit and Adivasi women in contemporary India, Kalapana Ram states:

> It has to be emphasized that their mobilisation as women has been intricately intertwined with the mobilisation of their caste and class as a whole. The fight for minimum wages, for work in times of drought and famine, for the harvest from land illegally occupied by the landlords, and against specifically caste forms of oppression—all these struggles have as much relevance and importance to the women as the men from the same class. But based on the strength and impetus gained from general class struggles they have been able to go on and push for issues unique to them as women. (14)

Had the authors of *Woman's Worth* discussed examples such as these, and analyzed their material on Cuba and China more specifically in terms of how women improved their status within the revolutionary context, their "vision" of the future might have gained both in concreteness and in credibility.

In their concluding chapter, Leghorn and Parker elaborate a clichéd definition of "female" and "male" values which attributes nurturing, caring, sensitivity, etc., etc. to women, and aggression, competitiveness, territoriality, and individualism to men. Attempting to explain the existence of numerous patriarchal cultures (for instance, African, Asian, and Native American) in which aggression, territoriality, and so forth have not been rampant, they employ circular logic to conclude that these were "rooted in more female-based values," rather than entertaining the possibility that, under a different form of economic and social organization from those familiar to us in highly industrialized nation-states, "male values" themselves might be substantially different. Thus, despite their contention that positive "female values" are rooted in women's material lives, the net effect of their treatment is to posit those values as essential, seemingly innate female qualities.

They quote Marilyn French's paean (in *The Women's Room*) to female "selflessness" and write approvingly of women's "civilizing" influence. I always wonder which branch of the women's movement feminists who talk this way have been hanging out in, what exotic brand of women they know, so different from the humanly self-interested, frequently competitive, occasionally unscrupulous females of my acquaintance. But here, too, ideology has an answer: when women behave well, they are exercising "preferred" (read "real") female values; when they get nasty they are displaying "adaptive" values, regrettable but necessary for survival within patriarchy.

Conventional wisdom has had it for a long time now that women are the world's civilizers and savers, and so far the world has become neither appreciably more "civilized" nor closer to "salvation." I am getting increasingly tired of the wishful thinking which, masquerading as theory, seizes on the ancient stereotype of virtuous womanhood and posits it as the basis of a social change movement which is supposed to eradicate not only male supremacy but all earthly injustice. The problem goes far beyond a couple of chapters in *Woman's Worth*; most radical feminist analysis seems these days to depart from or arrive at some version of the notion that women reside in a different moral category from men, and relies on that assumed difference to produce political change. But though I am not surprised, I am disappointed: I had hoped a work of radical feminist *economics* would display more depth, more rigor—and thereby come close to describing the world I think I actually inhabit.

And yet *Women's Worth* has value. If it falters as a theoretically comprehensive account of the economic and social factors which form women's experience cross-culturally, if it fails as a guide to social change, still its initial attempt to grasp the basic facts of women's material lives in widely differing societies points feminists in the right direction. It succeeds—in language considerably more accessible than that of most economics—in helping lay bare to our scrutiny the vast underpinning of sweated female labor on which so much of human life rests.

NOTES

1. Also see Heidi Hartmann, "The Unhappy Marriage of Marxism and Feminism: Towards a More Progressive Union," in Lydia Sargent, ed., *Women and Revolution* (Boston: South End Press, 1981) for a discussion of radical feminism's ahistorical bias.

2. See Leila Ahmed, "Western Ethnocentrism and Perceptions of the Harem," *Feminist Studies* VIII 3 (Fall, 1982): 521–34, for a detailed discussion of this issue. "Just as Americans 'know,' that Arabs are backward, they know also with the same flawless certainty that Muslin women are terribly oppressed and degraded. And they know this not because they know that women everywhere in the world are oppressed, but because they believe that, specifically, Islam monstrously oppresses women" (522).

3. See Ellen DuBois, *Feminism and Suffrage: The Emergence of an Independent Women's Movement in America, 1848–1869* (Ithaca, New York: Cornell UP, 1978) and Philip S. Foner, *Women and the American Labor Movement 1* (New York: Free Press, 1979).

4. DuBois, 178. See note 3.

5. Socialist-feminists and Marxist-feminists have done a great deal of work in this area. See especially Zillah Eisenstein, ed., *Capitalist Patriarchy and the Case for Socialist Feminism* (New York: Monthly Review Press, 1979). I was puzzled that Leghorn and Parker nowhere refer to this important anthology, though they make extensive use of other material published in the same year.

Flowers from the Volcano
by Claribel Alegría,
She Had Some Horses
by Joy Harjo

On the last page of *Flowers from the Volcano*, Claribel Alegría quotes a letter from a friend, a Paraguayan novelist who writes from Argentina "while the tanks roll by to Buenos Aires":

> Do you remember what we spoke of . . .
> . . . wishing for our America
> like that in the singular, a destiny that
> would not shame us? ("My Goodbyes"; my translation,* 82)

Toward the end of *She Had Some Horses*, Joy Harjo hopefully describes an explosion of "horses, / bursting out of the crazy earth" to "sweep away the knived faces of hatred":

> . . . some will see the horses with their hearts of sleeping volcanoes
> and will be rocked awake
>   past their bodies
>   to see who they have become. ("Explosion," 69)

The first of these poets is a woman who was born in the mid-1920s in Estelí, Nicaragua, raised in El Salvador, and after many years in other countries once again resides in Nicaragua; the second, younger by a generation, is a member of the Creek tribe with roots in Oklahoma who now lives in New Mexico. Together their books suggest a continuum of historical experience, political struggle, longing for transformation: an America "in the singular" that belies cherished anglo notions of the white/ right USA as legitimate arbiter of local and hemispheric destinies.

This continuum spans vast distances and transcends language barriers, national boundaries, and historical particulars to produce a poetry of

---

*Because of the translation problems discussed at the end of this review, I have, where indicated, relied on my own reading of the Spanish text in revising Carolyn Forché's English version to conform more closely to the literal meaning of the original.

volcanoes and earthquakes; of linked imperialisms—symbolized by "the golden coffee mixed with blood" that "continues / to disappear on *yanqui* ships" (Alegría) and by the Spanish conquistador DeSoto, drowned near New Orleans, who "was one of the ones who yearned / for something his heart wasn't big enough / to handle" (Harjo); of the great spaces and rugged geographies of the western United States and of Central/South America; a poetry of separations, airport farewells, epiphanies at 30,000 feet.

It is, inevitably, a poetry of witness. Alegría and Harjo write from two very different, yet intimately linked, Third World perspectives: in Harjo's case, that of an internally colonized people at the bottom of the U.S. racial/economic hierarchy; in Alegría's, that of an educated class which is relatively privileged by Central American standards, yet has suffered enough at the hands of repressive oligarchs who represent North American imperial interests to be acutely sensitized to the plight of workers and campesinos. Thus the first section of Harjo's book is entitled "Survivors," while several of Alegría's poems are reprinted from her collection *Sobrevivo,* "I Survive." Harjo keeps alive the memory of Native peoples massacred by white soldiers in other times and mourns as well the contemporary targets of "casual" social violence: suicides, alcoholics, Native and Black men shot at on street corners. Alegría is haunted by the historical and contemporary martyrs—among the latter are personal friends— of a Latin America she describes as a "slab of pained stone."

Yet each book is far more than a cry of pain or defiance. These poets who so clearly "take sides," who do not shy away from delivering righteous judgment where indicated, are also courageous in their exploration of ambiguity, their expressions of ambivalence. The work of each not only affirms the political nature of art, but hints at the potential of poetry to expand the limited, linear notions of change and struggle which too frequently beset political movements.

It especially pleases me to discuss the two books together because the parallels between them make clear the folly of the notion, current in certain U.S. literary circles, that fine and passionate political art is necessarily imported. This cliché, unfortunately reinforced by translator Forché who refers in her preface to "the luxuries of cleverness and virtuosity enjoyed by the poets of the north," is pernicious: it helps keep radical North American writers languishing in an obscurity more damaging to our political effectiveness than outright suppression would be. ("Publish anything you like, but don't expect it to be noticed." Meanwhile, Pablo Neruda's poetry sells like hot cakes and a touring Nadine Gordimer reads to packed houses.) Much of Harjo's wonderful collection (her third) originally appeared in feminist and Third World small press magazines and anthologies; she is one of an insurgent band of poet-*combatientes* here in the United States who deserve to be honored—and *read*—alongside their counterparts elsewhere.

The poems in *She Had Some Horses* exhibit a strikingly wide range of themes and technical approaches. Predominant in "Survivors," the first section, is a loosely structured, anecdotal form that serves sometimes as a requiem for the dead; sometimes as elegy for those "buried in an ache / in which nothing makes / sense"; sometimes as tribute to and celebration of the living, "those who have learned to speak."

Many of the "survivors" are Indian women, and Harjo is expert at evoking their lives with a few loving details:

> When she was young she ate wild rice on scraped down
> plates in warm wood rooms. It was in the farther
> north and she was the baby then. They rocked her.
>
> > ("The Woman Hanging from the
> > Thirteenth Floor Window," 22)

or a deft twist of metaphor:

> Early morning over silver tracks
> a cool light, Noni Daylight's
> a dishrag wrung out over bones
> watching trains come and go. ("Kansas City," 23)

These poems often seem to meander, to circle back on themselves, perhaps replicating the pattern identified in "For Alva Benson, And For Those Who Have Learned to Speak":

> And we go on, keep giving birth and watch
> ourselves die, over and over.
> And the ground spinning beneath us
> goes on talking. (19)

They tend to be more memorable in parts—phrases, lines, or single stanzas—than in their totality. Yet they give off a fine, quiet human warmth which adds a great deal to the collection.

By contrast, most of Harjo's moon and horse poems are marked by a near-mythic intensity, their effects focused with the accuracy and economy of a burning-glass focusing sunlight. A good example is "Backwards," two-thirds of a page long, with its seemingly casual, conversational tone played off against a ferociously expert juxtaposition of images and commentary. It begins with a chilly, beautiful metaphor: the moon as skeleton, glimpsed by the poet from her car. Then come an elliptical summation of the state of things ("Something tries to turn the earth / around"); a snatch of melancholy song that might possibly be coming from the car radio; and the final, brutal image which completes the meaning of what has gone before and takes it a step further:

> The moon came up white, and torn
> at the edges. I dreamed when I was
> four that I was standing on it.
> A whiteman with a knife cut pieces
> away
>   and threw the meat
>   to the dogs. (20)

Besides the many good-to-terrific poems I've been discussing, there are, unfortunately, some which fall considerably short of the emotional precision and fine-honed lanaguage Harjo usually achieves. In particular, the love poems are often laden with private references which lack meaning for the general reader, or they sink beneath a burden of conventionally romantic, vague imagery:

> But you must have grown out of
>   a thousand years dreaming
>   just like I could never imagine you
>   You must have
>   broke open from another sky
> to here, because
>   now I see you as a part of the millions of
> other universes that I thought could never occur
>   in this breathing. ("Two Horses," 65)

In addition, I'm sometimes puzzled by the way the poems are organized, with seemingly related pieces widely scattered and a general lack of coherence within sections—especially problematic given the volume's complexity and scope.

She Had Some Horses closes with a few superb, incantatory selections— in particular, the title piece and the very last one, "I Give You Back"—

which seem to me to combine the spontaneity and human feeling of some of the earlier poems with the structural rigor and mythic intensity of others. These poems are based on repetition, yet never feel "repetitious." In "She Had Some Horses," the statement of the title recurs like a refrain throughout the poem, in between paralleled descriptions—lyrical, humorous, troubling—of "horses": "She had horses who were splintered red cliff." "She had horses who licked razor blades." "She had horses who danced in their mothers' arms." "She had horses who tried to save her, who climbed in her/bed at night and prayed as they raped her." After completing this inventory, Harjo transforms our understanding of it by appending three entirely straightforward yet almost mystical summary lines:

> She had some horses she loved.
> She had some horses she hated.
>
> These were the same horses. (64)

I'm not quite sure I know what these astonishing lines "mean," but I think they are prepared for in "White Bear," a short poem in which the whole world is envisioned balanced between the bear/moon's paws:

> . . . tipping back it could go
> either way
>   all darkness
>   is open to all light. (27)

I see in both these poems an insistence on the essential unity of things which I suspect is specifically Indian; certainly it is contrary to the European method of organizing experience by means of defensive divisions in an attempt to escape the vulnerability of the admission that "it could go/either way."

Harjo's stance is a highly spiritual one; yet, as the everyday tone of some of her lines suggests, it is in no way removed from political insight or material concerns. At the risk of being a bit too literal, I must say I can't quite shake the notion that the "she" of "She Had Some Horses" is both some version of the poet and some version of god. The poem reminds me a little of Judy Grahn's "She Who" series, yet unlike that fine work, this one doesn't appear explicitly concerned to mythologize or deify the female principle. Harjo is a poet who assumes, while seemingly never needing to prove, the centrality of women's experience.

*

According to the jacket copy, *Flowers from the Volcano* "brings to the American [*sic*] reader for the first time a substantial selection of poems by a writer who has become a courageous and major force in Latin American poetry." Given that this volume will constitute a great many *North* American readers' introduction to Claribel Alegría's work, it's particularly unfortunate that it suffers from some serious editing and translation problems, the responsibility for which must be shared by Carolyn Forché and the University of Pittsburgh Press.

Most immediately apparent of these is the fact that no attempt has been made to indicate when the nine selections were written or where they first appeared; Forché's preface is silent as to her criteria for inclusion, and she neglects to situate the pieces thematically or stylistically within the larger body of Alegría's poetry. (In fact, the poems are drawn from collections published over more than two decades, as I was finally able to learn by consulting *Suma y sigue,* a volume of Alegría's selected poetry published by Visor, Madrid in 1981 with a useful critical overview by Mario Benedetti.*) Instead, Forché writes of the Central American context of political violence and torture in such a way as to attach to Alegría the emergent stereotype of the tormented Latin writer: "In her poems, we listen to the stark cry of the human spirit, stripped by necessity of its natural lyricism." This is a much less complex account than the work deserves, for it certainly displays a great deal of "natural lyricism," and is capable besides of humor, whimsy, irony, and exquisite moments of private tenderness.

"Toward the Jurassic Age," the opening poem, finds Alegría countering tyranny with an almost light-hearted surrealism. She writes of an unnamed "they" who started out iguana-sized and have grown large enough to menace the population:

> there are herbivores
> and carnivores among them
> the carnivores know one another
> by the military caps that crown
> their crests
> but both are harmful (3)

**Suma y sigue is available by mail order from Schoenhof's Foreign Books, Box 182, 76A Mount Auburn St., Cambridge, MA 02138.

Herbivores and carnivores, both harmful: one thinks of the "moderate" Duarte and outright-fascist D'Aubuisson in El Salvador.

"Letter to Time" is equally fanciful, its sinister undertones more metaphysical than political in nature. Written on the poet's birthday, the letter requests Time to lay off, cease his inexorable visits. As in "Toward the Jurassic Age," much of the effectiveness rests on the dry, flat tone and the selection of the perfect image for a menacing figure; Time becomes an older man with an "unchanging face," whose "greeting tastes of musty rooms" and who has about him a definite suggestion of the child molester: "a friend of my father's / with one eye on me."

The long, eight-part "Sorrow" and the book's title poem are the two most explicitly political pieces, if one means by this that they confront head-on the themes of repression and resistance which loom so large in Central American experience. "Sorrow" is unified by a series of invocations of poets and other artists who have been sacrificed in the liberation struggle, notably the Salvadoran poet Roque Dalton, killed in 1975. In one section Alegría describes a pilgrimage in search of the site of the murder of Federico García Lorca. In others, she merges her own identity with that of furtive, impoverished exiles who must seek refuge in museums or public baths; or she speaks in the voice of the imprisoned, listens to the screams of the tortured, inscribes on the prison wall with a piece of charcoal the unanaswerable question, "Who raised up this prison's bars?"

Perhaps in part because I know the poet's sharing of the most extreme suffering she describes is merely imaginative, in part because her descriptions lack their usual sharpness and freshness ("a gray light filters from outside / there is no sun / there are no birds, no foliage"), I was less moved by this poem than by the more personal expression of loss in "We Were Three':

> I am alone.
> My dead stand watch
> and send signals to me,
> they assail me
> in the radio and paper.
> The wall of my dead
> rises and reaches from Aconcagua to Izalco. (55)

"Flowers from the Volcano" describes a legacy of seemingly unredeemed bloodshed stretching back to pre-Columbian times ("Who said

that my country was green?/It is more red, more grey, more violent").
The poet is clearly more distant from "the dead *guerrillero*/and the
thousand betrayed faces," the "children in rags/with flowers from the
volcano," than she is from the victims of "Sorrow" and "We Were
Three." She closes with the grimly ambiguous prediction that "the cycle
is closing," "today's Chacmol still wants blood"; it's unclear whether she
expects anything hopeful to emerge from the carnage.

My favorites are two poems which combine political insight with the
exquisite skill in communicating private experience which seems to be
one of Alegría's hallmarks. In "Santa Ana in the Dark" she sketches a
portrait of the Salvadoran city in which she grew up; she achieves both a
loving tribute and a devastating sketch of the conditions and consequences of Central American "underdevelopment." Santa Ana is run by
Don Raimundo, "accustomed to command," who has defied the God of
Genesis by decreeing darkness in the city, as a result of which children fail
to learn "their 40-watt history"; meanwhile, unmarried aunts live on in a
stupefying yet charming miasma of conservative Catholicism, vanilla
sweets, and gossip; everyone halfway promising is felled by disease or
silenced by repression; DDT kills off the birds. Nevertheless,

> It didn't matter
> when we were young.
> Everything was green.
> We grew up without knowing
> of light in other places
> and we marveled when someone
> carried a lamp. (17)

The poem closes with the abrupt admission that "at times I'm assail-
ed/by a violent desire/to go back" [my translation].

"My Goodbyes," the closing poem, makes the equally dangerous admission that at times the poet desires intensely to leave behind not only
Santa Ana, which she once more evokes, but the entire "somber, green,
difficult" continent whose vastness and particularity, physical beauty
and political torment she masterfully renders. She begins with the line,
"The afternoon jet plucks me from Ezeiza." The distance the airplane
gives to her consideration of the continent and the haste of the over-flight
provide the appropriate framework for an expression of alienation:

> My America is spilled blood,
> the theater of Cain and Abel,

a struggle with no quarter given
against starvation, rage or impotence. (79)

Yet Latin America's unity is also suggested in her snatched views of the pampas, of Santiago; her recollections of the Guatemala she swallows "without tasting," and of "the phosphorescent streets of Mérida." And the poem, itself unified by repeated words and phrases, circles back from its opening among the "faces of the Río de la Plata" to a close in which Alegría quotes from her friend Roa's wistful letter (written while tanks roll toward Buenos Aires) in which he recalls their shared desire for a better destiny for their America "in the singular."

The English version of "My Goodbyes" illustrates some of the problems presented by Forché's translations. (While my own Spanish leaves much to be desired, it has sufficed for me to be able to identify omissions and alterations in a great many cases.) The repeated words and phrases noted above, for example, are lost in the English, with "la mancha morada de las pampas" ("the purple stain of the pampas") rendered by Forché as a "violet glimpse of the pampas," while "la mancha morada de Atitlán" becomes "the cobalt [!] stain of Atitlán." The repetition of the verbs "arrancar" (to pull out, uproot) and "recorrer" (to go over, travel over) is likewise lost. The phrase "nuestra América/así en singular" ("Our America/like that in the singular") is translated simply as "our America," thus omitting the poet's crucial emphasis on America's unity. Santiago in the "crepúsculo" ("dusk") turns into Santiago in the "dust." When Alegría writes of pressing her goodbyes "between the pages of a book/I don't read" ("entre las hojas de un libro/que no leo"), Forché injects a small note of melodrama, "pressing them in a book/I will never read."

These problems are repeated in other poems. No attempt has been made to reproduce certain effects—for instance, those achieved by the omission of punctuation in "We Were Three"—which might have been transferred with relative ease to English. Important words, phrases, and even whole lines are left untranslated (in the same poem, the lines "continúan su lucha/marcan rumbos" have no English equivalent). Or translations are simply wrong, as in "Letter to Time," where "Hace años que amo a otro" ("For years I have loved another") becomes "It has been years since I've loved another," while "Y había alguien más," ("And there was someone else") is rendered, "And there was something else." Finally, in many places—here, I speculate, Forché may have felt she was translating poetic feeling in preference to literal meaning—Alegría's honest details have been sacrificed to a subtly more sentimental phrasing or imagery: in "Santa Ana in the Dark," the "ciudad" ("city") of Santa Ana becomes a "village"; "El D.D.T.," which needs no translation, becomes "poison"; "algún interior" ("some interior") becomes "shacks'"; and the stars which "brillan más / en el cielo de Santa Ana" ("shine more brightly in the sky of Santa Ana") become, according to Forché, "brighter in the darkness of Santa Ana / than anywhere else in the world."

All of this is to say that *Flowers from the Volcano* falls far short of being the ideal introduction to Alegría's work. Nevertheless, it's well worth reading. More translations will no doubt follow, as commercial and university presses, their interest sparked by blood-spattered headlines, display increasing enthusiasm for Central American literature.

However ironic this enthusiasm may seem, however symptomatic of the sickness of an empire that habitually "discovers" the cultures it is attempting to destroy, the fact is that North Americans need this literature, which is both historically rich and, thanks largely to Nicaragua, particularly lively at the present moment. Its life can give us life, its agonized awareness of death sensitize us to our own monumental task— which is not, after all, primarily literary, but a very prosaic, pedestrian matter of organizing, of stopping appropriations and troop maneuvers. Meanwhile, the continuing appearance of fine small press, counter-establishment books like Joy Harjo's gives me hope that North America will be able to repay, at least in part, the debt thus incurred; in this way, rather than representing yet another instance of cultural imperialism, the process may be one of mutual respect, creative interdependence, solidarity in the struggle.

The *Granite Pail* by Lorine Niedecker, *Leaning Forward* by Grace Paley, *Where the Island Sleeps Like a Wing* by Nancy Morejón

Comes now the female poet, neglected during her lifetime, her professional reticence heavily patronized but scantily rewarded. (Inevitable cover blurb: "James Laughlin observed that if she had chosen 'to play the games of poetry politics, she could probably have ended up as well known as the ladies who are now wearing the establishment's official "laurels," but that just wasn't her way.' ") Behold the rites of posthumous reassessment. Expect the volumes selected and collected, await the published correspondence (Niedecker, *Complete Works*; Faranda). Look for respectful reviews in all the major journals.

Lorine Faith Niedecker (1903–1970) from Fort Atkinson, Wisconsin, has unmistakably arrived, her entrance trumpeted by jacket copy that twice in four lines dubs her "poetess," that retails lists of male admirers—Zukofsky Dahlberg Rexroth Duncan Creeley—to convince us her art is worth attending to. The Women's Liberation Movement, which would probably have been greeted with scant enthusiasm by Niedecker herself had she lived to note its impact on contemporary poetry, is supremely relevant to her work, yet apparently it might just as well not have happened so far as most of the folks in charge of her literary remains are concerned.

Grounded in deep silence, the poems in *The Granite Pail* have come to me amid the "buzz and burn" of my Brooklyn life like citrus in time of scurvy. So despite the heartfelt sarcasm, I'm grateful to editor Cid Corman for his decades-long interest in Niedecker's work, as well as to North Point Press for having accorded it the rare tribute of uncrowded pages, lovely classic type, and impeccable proofreading. The book is divided into three sections roughly representing early, middle, and late phases of composition. No dates are given, so that this selected volume becomes an uncluttered introduction to a transcendently uncluttered poetry.

The first thing to be noticed about Niedecker is her unwavering focus on the core of being, on first and final facts. Sometimes she expresses this with a playful impulse:

> Time to garden
>   before I
>   die—
> to meet
>   my compost maker ("Tradition," 89)

sometimes with a sobriety that makes room for the everyday and colloquial:

> The smooth black stone
> I picked up in true source park
>   the leaf beside it
> once was stone
>
> Why should we hurry
>   home ("Lake Superior," 62)

Here the last two lines surely refer both to the vacation trip which catalyzed the poem and to the rhythms of human life and death set in a context of geologic time. Niedecker seeks the unity implied by unceasing change; she is interested in natural *process*, and if the mutability of stone arrests her imagination, then her native sign is water, flood a favorite natural image.

> Oh my floating life
> Do not save love
>   for things
>   throw *things*
> to the flood ("Paean to Place," 75)

It might be argued, of course, that such insights are genderless, and in fact it was mostly to male writers and thinkers that Niedecker looked for intellectual and spiritual companionship. Nevertheless her female experience must have had a great deal to do both with her inclination towards a kind of quietly ecstatic contemplative mode, especially in her later work, and with what that contemplation revealed to her. This striking passage from a letter to Cid Corman (of February 14, 1968) indirectly suggests some of the tension she may have felt as a woman poet in a male world:

Been carrying on a correspondence with [Clayton] Eshelman. Mostly at his behest—technique, why I don't write differently, why he doesn't. I'm no good at it—I write from notes, which seem to always stay notes, grocery lists. I throw up my arms and scream: Write—cut it and just write poems. I tell him why set fire to page after page, why not arrest in at moments into quiet, enduring love? (I *dared* to say this) Also that there is such a thing as silence—and the great, ever-present possibility that our poems may not get read. Art is cooler than he thinks. (Faranda, 153)

Much of Niedecker's poetry addresses the female condition head-on, at times with pointed sarcasm ("Ten thousand women / and I / the only one / in boots"). She provides a superb sketch of the artist as a young girl. Above all, though, she's the poet of "woman's work": not cooking, for some reason, but washing, sewing, gardening, cleaning (and no wonder—she scrubbed floors for part of her livelihood). A stunning untitled poem which is said to have been composed from her mother's actual deathbed remarks comes across as the report of an astonishing blessing/curse:

> Old Mother turns blue and from us,
>   "Don't let my head drop to the earth.
> I'm blind and deaf." Death from the heart,
>   a thimble in her purse.
>
> "It's a long day since last night
>   Give me space. I need
> floors. Wash the floors, Lorine!—
>   wash clothes! Weed!" ("Old Mother," 17)

As this suggests, the work is also explicitly "North Central" (the title of one of her books), grown out of what she terms the "folk field" of everyday speech from the mouths of the working-class Wisconsinites who were her family and neighbors. Especially in the early poems she often muses on the discomforts of her situation as an artist—a woman artist, at that—belonging to these people, who often enough talk in "rehashed radio barbs":

> But what vitality! The women hold jobs—
> clean house, cook, raise children, bowl
> and go to church

> What would they say if they knew
> I sit for two months on six lines
> of poetry? ("In the great snowfall," 21)

"No layoffs/from this/condensery," she reports, attempting to construe her own artistic task in a wry analogy to waged labor.

Generations later, a state removed (my own "North Central" people wound up in Minnesota, though the half that came, like the Niedeckers, of German-speaking immigrant stock had started out in Wisconsin), my family inculcated similar precepts—taught, for example, that the only real business of life is productive work, by which is understood mostly physical endeavor: growing vegetables, chopping down forests, building houses, bearing children. There is a paradox here, for lives consumed in such tasks are full of poetry, as Niedecker clearly suggests in her many references to her fisher-father, who "knew what lay/under leaf decay/and on pickerelweeds." Yet the ingrained focus on the material, the literal eventually becomes inimical to the imagination—a fundamental tension in North American life, and one I've rarely seen so well and so lovingly expressed.

The oblique yet incisive feminism, the fascination with "folk" speech, the concern about self as artist in a work-obsessed world—these themes are most prominent in the super-condensed early poems. Eventually Niedecker developed an extended, looser form capable of taking in an extraordinary range of experience. In "Wintergreen Ridge" this includes everything from a concern with geology, evolution, and "the grand blow-up—the bomb" to an awareness of fashions in hemlines and the fate of a storm-battered sunflower. Perfectly balanced, turning on a breath, "My Life by Water" and "Paean to Place" explore a seamlessly apprehended habitat in which

> red Mars
>
> rising
> rides the sloughs and sluices
>   of my mind
>   with the persons
> on the edge ("Paean to Place," 76)

Such lines seem to come unmediated from that "silence/which if intense/makes sound."

I feel a distinctly political disappointment in the way this book ends—through no fault of the editor, evidently, for her long poems on Thomas Jefferson, William Morris, and Charles Darwin were in fact Niedecker's last major projects. "Thomas Jefferson" is a choice bit of liberal myth-making quite in line with an earlier brief laudatory segment on "J. F. Kennedy after the Bay of Pigs." Camelot and Monticello, no thanks. I find it easier to sympathize with her affection for Darwin, whose fascination with natural processes unfolding in time is so central to her own thought; still, I prefer the "folk field" to the Great Men. But then, as her letters to Cid Corman demonstrate, Niedecker was both a political liberal and in some respects almost tragically male-identified. We must take our "poetesses" where we find them.

That I do willingly, for *The Granite Pail* yields new meaning, subtler music, each time I reread. It takes me back fifteen or twenty years to when I first developed the heady notion that poetry might teach me how to live.

*

> Who saved it?
>   Women
>   of good wild stock
>
> stood stolid
>   before machines
>   They stopped bulldozers (Niedecker, "Wintergreen Ridge," 79)

Leaning Forward is the first full-length publication by Granite Press, which vows "to expand distribution and widen exposure of essential writing by feminists and lesbians." It is also the first collection of poetry by our own Grace Paley, who's been standing stolid before machines for a good many years now, and in the process has gotten to know nearly everyone on the block. It's a loose-jointed, discursive collection, though it coils up every so often to produce highly concentrated effects. For this poet, contemplation is a function of activity, and the poems celebrate both the noisy vitality of the "five exogamous boroughs" and a rural sociability with nature.

As the title's focus on the instant suggests, passing human time is a major preoccupation here. As in Paley's short stories, private moments, family life, coincide with the terrible grinding motion of history:

> My father says
>   how will they get out

> Nixon Johnson   the whole bunch
> they don't know how. . . .

  he says
> greed   greed   time
> nothing is happening fast enough ("My Father at 85," 69)

Death, personal death, is a familiar presence, but behind even the casual transformations of the city ("Macy's is nice but Klein's was the store/ and it ended") lies the tacit understanding that our world, "the green world/the green mountain," is not as immortal as it used to be.

Leaning Forward is, as they say, an "uneven" collection (are we talking poetry or orthodonture?), comprising poems as economically shaped as "At the Battery," from which the title is derived, and as slackly realized as "Illegal Aliens," which reads like promising raw material. Sometimes Paley skirts the boundary between whimsy and mere cuteness ("the risky busy labor of Repair the World"); sometimes she crosses over ("the mist/that starts the day/with drinks for all"). And in over-obvious entries like "The Sad Children's Song" ("This world is a wreck said the children/When they came home with their children") there's nothing pressing to go back to after the first quick skim.

All of which is to say that I had to do more mental editing than would have been required if either author or publisher had exercised a more rigorous approach. I turn happily to the many clear successes, poems like "My Mother: 33 years later" which evokes "the mother/out of whose body I easily appeared," the Russian Jewish family "intact talking/ . . . all of us eating our boiled egg," the deathbed pronouncement tart and unmollified as that of Niedecker's mother. There's the ferocious, funny poem-story "On the Fourth Floor," told almost entirely as overheard dialogue, with the just-right ambiguity of the ending gesture in which the censorious older neighbor takes the stoned young woman's hand. There's the gentle echo of the Communist Manifesto in the description of late flowers, "wild/because it was early September/and they had nothing to lose," and the amazing sinuous journey of "Having Arrived by Bike at Battery Park," which starts out as a birthday greeting, gives a nod to Manhattan warm-weather ambience, and then in two startling images confronts the reader with the genocidal origins of the city and the ironic fate of the "white tormented people" who came from the east

to a kind of safety there. And, from the Thetford Poems, this rare moment of solitude:

> When the wild strawberry leaves turn
> red and show the dark place of the strawberries
> it is too late
>
> I know this has a
> meaning inside my own life
> inside dark life (56)

Though it's tantalizing to be informed in Jane Cooper's afterword that
"Paley wrote nothing but poems till she was almost thirty" without having a clue as to whether any of those included here are from that early
period, I find a certain rightness in the lack of dating or chronology, for
the book as it is conveys a sense of immediacy, imparts a contemporary
feel to historical events. The two most prominent political landmarks are
the 1905 uprising in Russia and the Vietnam War, hauntingly memorial-
ized in such poems as "Two Villages," "Connections: Vermont Vietnam
(II)," and "That Year." This focus strikes me as a healthful corrective to
our habit of political hurry, the mad dash through fashions in "progressive" history which mirrors the media's sad leapfrogging from hot spot to
hot spot. The Grace Paley who can be counted on to distinguish between
what the 82-year-old people and the 92-year-old people say to the grand-
child is a good poet to have along when you're staring down the bull-
dozers.

*

> I said   is it true?   we are sisters?
> They said, Yes, we are of one family
> (Paley, "This is about the women of that country," 79)

How difficult it is to learn any non-native language, how tricky to settle
gracefully into the rhythms of a society into which one steps as a stranger
with a foreign stride and posture—but especially when unfamiliarity is a
function not merely of distance but design, when one's own country is
the historic oppressor of the other (and oppressors notoriously afford
ignorance of all they crush). I stand in this problematic relationship to
the universe of the established Cuban poet Nancy Morejón, whose
Where the Island Sleeps Like a Wing is her first U.S. publication of a full-
length, bilingual collection. (Her *Grenada Notebook*, a chapbook, was
issued by Círculo de Cultura Cubana in 1984.) The difficulty I experience in taking this work as it should be taken, not on ground of chosen-

up sides and political loves or hate but on the more subtly shaded territory of friendship, sympathy, and detailed knowledge, reminds me—if I
needed the reminder—of what I've lost through the barrier successive
generations of Rough Riders and Cold Warriors have been at pains to
construct between my experience and hers. The Black Scholar Press has
done a fine thing in publishing these poems—it's just the sort of project
that would never see the light of print without the radical small presses.

The volume appears to represent a broad range of Morejón's work.
(Here the absence of dates is more problematic than with Niedecker or
Paley, since most readers will see no other book by her.) Judging by its
contents, I prefer her singing mode, unmixed in the private moments of
the opening section, "A Patio in Havana," and recurrent later as well.
"My heart is lodged in the city and its adventure," she announces, and in
keeping with that spirit the work is romantic even at its most concrete. A
few swift strokes capture the evanescent, beloved everyday, complete
with family, neighborhood rhythms, the political backdrop:

> Dad comes in later
> with his black arms and calloused hands
> his sweat-rinsed shirt
> that gently threatens to stain my clothes
> that's father
> bent over
> so I could live
> and be able to go beyond
> where he had been
> I stop before the big door
> and think
> of the war that might break out any minute
> but I see only a man who is building
> another going by notebook under-arm
> and nobody
> nobody could resist all this ("The Supper," 5)

Master craftswoman of her own "condensery," she renders lovely images
in tribute to the women who, as she says of her mother, "Had the hand-
kerchief and the song/to cradle my body's deepest faith"; then this
obsidian-hard moment of proverbial utterance:

> Your set mouth
> pausing like a great bird

over the plain, speaks:
Death is the best misfortune,
because it wipes out all others ("Tata on the Death of Don Pablo," 15)

(By the way, it's intriguing to note the similarity of focus on the memory of parents both male and female in three such utterly different poets as Niedecker, Paley, and Morejón.)

Poet not only of family history and "the old, old neighborhood of Cerro, / and my cathedral and my port," but also of the larger history of her people—Black, Cuban—Morejón often employs her lyric talent in poems that treat overtly political themes, as in her reflections on the event that marked the beginning of her country's armed liberation struggle:

That rural night's perfume
has drifted until today,
permanent among the grasses
of the Siboney farm, and the sheen
of rifles floating in the patio well. ("Moncada's Night," 43)

It is the sense of discovery, of wonder at a completely new historic situation fraught with both hope and danger, that I relish most in Morejón's poems about the revolution. The beautiful, brief "April," its last line the book's title, conveys in images of storm and rest, of leaves and birds and bones and dust, an indelible love for her island. "Our spirits dwell here," she quietly asserts, with absolute conviction.

Often she focuses on the death of a hero: Abel Santamaría, Camilo Cienfuegos, the "brave youth, / falling, possessed by tomorrow," or the nameless murdered "Black Man" in the poem of that title, historically conceived but clearly a revolutionary forerunner. (The equally strong female figures, including her own family members, the imagined slave in "I Love My Master" and the slave turned guerrilla fighter in "Black Woman," all seem to be not martyrs but survivors.) What I miss here is more sense of the revolution as process; granted that this is a poetry collection and not a treatise on social change in contemporary Cuba, I'd still like to know a bit more about the struggles, the days of plodding confusion that surely followed "Moncada's Night." For instance: are there really no remaining tensions in being Black and female? I'm not completely satisfied by the theory, advanced by translator Kathleen Weaver in her introductory essay, that the "felt personal reserve" of

Morejón's work is simply a "strategy" for becoming "wholly open to and vehicle of a popular vision." The few poems which do seem to express a private tension, even anger and sarcasm, I find totally opaque:

> Python, lull the dialectical shit of the mosquito
> My beloved scorpion, squander your sensibility upon my act of
>   poetry
> Unite with the proletariat and its nuclear warhead.
> ("The Dream of Reason Produces Monsters," 61)

Toward the end of the collection, Morejón sometimes abandons her precise lyricism for a didactic note I've been trying quite unsuccessfully to like for a number of years now in the work of many poets whose politics I admire. Often this happens in poems expressing solidarity with revolutionary struggles Morejón presumably doesn't know firsthand. Lines like "A triumphant guerrilla fighter has now broken that / colonial circle of horror and submission" I find too schematic to make me feel either the horror or the triumph. Since I haven't read Morejón's numerous Cuban and Mexican publications, I can't begin to judge how characteristic this tendency is. In any case she's clearly a poet of fascinating range and many superb moments. I'll hope against hope that more of her work finds a publisher here.

(Translator Kathleen Weaver's introductory "The World of Nancy Morejón" provides an evocative setting for the poems, and her English versions seem generally adequate, though they creak at the joints sometimes where the supple original bends. The book is physically attractive but carelessly produced, marred by typographical errors including lines dropped here and there from either Spanish or English versions.)

*

Here then, in a desert climate (for "poetry loses money") three collections by women poets, vital as rain. Don't wait for the women's bookstores to get them in stock; "poetry doesn't sell" there anymore, either. Order directly from the publishers, to all three of whom we're much indebted. Read them slowly, more than once. Let them settle into silence.

Letters from Nicaragua
by Rebecca Gordon

In the years since the 1979 victory of Nicaragua's popular revolution, that country's policy-makers have mounted an ambitious effort to involve U.S. progressives in the transformation and defense of their battered society. This strategically canny maneuver has resulted in an extraordinary encounter between two Americas, Anglo and Latin, and two radical traditions—an experiment in consciousness-raising certainly unprecedented on the Yankee end. Some participants, of course, are simply indulging in leftist tourism. Goddess preserve us from the gringo groupie, aglow at the memory of a handshake from Daniel, his suitcase bulging with FSLN souvenirs. At best, however, Nicaragua's lessons have been far from superficial. Here is evidence that, in the words of Chilo Herrera, human solidarity can be "lovely, simple, humble—and attainable."

Rebecca Gordon quotes Herrera in *Letters from Nicaragua*, one of the most thoughtful reports available on a U.S. activist's sojourn in *Nicaragua libre*. In 1984 Gordon spent over six months there as a staffer with Witness for Peace, a Christian organization that promotes a nonviolent North American presence in regions vulnerable to contra attack and sends staffers around the country to document the war's effects. Her duties took her to remote northwestern border towns and resettlement areas, to Miskito Indian communities, and to the Atlantic coast. A lesbian with political roots in the women's movement (and a Jew with a grounding in Christian theology), she brings a useful range of progressive traditions to her discussion of freedom and revolution.

The book's backbone is a series of letters Gordon wrote to her lover, Jan Adams, supplemented by semipublic ones addressed to a circle of friends. She later added connecting passages which provide background information and allow her to elaborate on ideas raised in the letters. She includes snippets of Adam's responses, about everything from the frustrations of a termite control job to the impact of the 1984 Jesse Jackson campaign. The structure helps Gordon make organic rather than rhetorical connections between Nicaragua and the United States; she's well aware that, as Black feminist Barbara Smith writes in the foreword, "It is much easier to romanticize the situation of people who are suffering somewhere else, because that . . . entails far less individual and collective accountability" (18).

Gordon's letters display the advantages of the form. They mingle immediacy and abstraction, relevant trivia and dramatic narrative; they're rich in humor, sensory detail, self-scrutiny, metaphysics.

> The torture of these alerts is that no one sleeps, and all the important work of planting is slowed down. (63)

> . . . watched a woman teaching an avid class how to test a cow for pregnancy, of which procedure perhaps the less said the better. I only add that it requires the use of a shoulder-length plastic glove. (78)

> You know that for me the fact of Creation lies at the center of my theology—and that the continued existence of the world from moment to moment is a mystery and a miracle. (73)

> 12:45 a.m. All quiet, except for a few dogs and a pig. . . . Zinc roofs pop as they cool, but there's no confusing that sound with gunfire. As the moon rises over the roof of our house the band of light shed on the paper shrinks. Soon there will be nothing. I love you. (155)

The letters to Jan Adams reflect an intensely romantic yet practical partnership. Portraits of lesbian couples are still so rare and valuable that I find myself regretting what I assume to be the omission of some intimate—perhaps sexual—material, even though I understand the editorial choice. Gordon did not acknowledge her lesbianism to the Nicaraguans she met, and while I understand that choice too, part of her rationale troubles me. In a cryptic page and a half, she sets forth her belief that "the existence of 'lesbianism' as a cultural *identity* requires some material prerequisites. . . . This places [it] in a genuinely mixed bag of other cultural imports—from tractor to dictatorships—to which Latin Americans understandably have mixed reactions" (42–43). While I agree it would be the height of arrogance for North American lesbians to expect Nicaraguan campesinas to share their worldview, I'm skeptical of the conclusion, strongly implied here, that heterosexuality is the only indigenous sexual identity outside the United States and Europe.

For the most part, Gordon's curiosity about Nicaraguan women's lives is respectful and illuminating. Always, she asks what the political changes have meant for them. Her anecdotes convey the dailiness of a revolution: the tension and camaraderie, the drudgery and hope, the matter-of-fact heroism—and the real sadness and despair that are part of Nicaragua, too. "I wanted Corina to be a brave revolutionary and she wasn't. She was a terrified little woman with a month-old baby and a bad cough," she writes of one contra victim (109).

Gordon had little contact with Managua officialdom; valuable as it is, her grass-roots focus scants problems inherent in the necessary task of "leading" a popular revolution. In discussing abortion, for example, she acknowledges the role of traditional attitudes but does not explore the leadership's possible interest in population growth. (She does mention the racism with which the government initially treated the Miskito, and the ironies of "top-down" organizing on the Atlantic coast.) *Letters from Nicaragua* doesn't pretend to be comprehensive, though. Gordon's achievement lies in the poetic precision of her testimony, the complexity of the political questions she raises, the model she provides of a passionately committed yet flexible feminist activism.

IV

STRUGGLE

The three pieces of writing included in this section emerge from and examine three very different yet connected arenas of struggle: the feminist peace movement in which women organized as women challenged the military establishment; lesbian communities in which the political dimensions of personal relationships stand out in sharp relief; and the mixed solidarity/anti-intervention movement to which feminists and lesbians are increasingly central. Each one of these arenas has been a home to me, inhabited tentatively as all my homes have been, with a mixture of love, relief, and skepticism.

"Women and Militarism: Some Questions for Feminists" dates from immediately after the first Women's Pentagon Action in the fall of 1980. If it now reads like rather ancient history, that's largely because it was written before the threat of nuclear war briefly blossomed as a major media topic and generated activist involvement on the part of moderates as well as radicals. That movement mushroomed faster than the cloud it was intended to prevent, peaked with the massive disarmament demonstration held in New York City on June 12, 1982, and faded from sight— but not entirely; expressions of distaste at the prospect of nuclear nothingness are now less unexpected in both mainstream and leftist settings than they were at the beginning of the decade. In light of this chronology, the Women's Pentagon Action and other feminist efforts like those of British women at Greenham Common must be viewed as important precursors to later organizing which would be far less visionary in its demands and far more widely visible. The typical erasure from official histories of social phenomena like the feminist peace movement is dangerous because it distorts popular conceptions of the roots of social change—and falsely isolates radicals.

I wish now that I'd felt comfortable writing more directly and personally about my experience in the Women's Pentagon Action. When working on the article I faced time constraints as well as nervousness about publishing detailed criticisms of an organization with which I was actively involved.

"To Live Outside the Law You Must Be Honest: A Flommy Looks at Lesbian Parenting" was delivered as the keynote address at a lesbian parenting conference held in Albany, New York, in 1986. I am grateful for organizer Paula Sawyer's invitation to me to speak there, since it nudged me to address both theoretical and personal issues which I hadn't publicly tackled before except through the somewhat indirect medium of fiction.

"In Pieces: A Feminist in the Central America Solidarity Movement" is the only essay written specifically for this collection. It has been important to me to take the time to reflect on my experience as an activist during the past several years. In looking back I'm struck by the fact that the era of activism to which "Women and Militarism" corresponds seems to have passed too quickly for some of the most significant questions about the feminist anti-militarist movement to be articulated adequately, much less resolved in practice. It is not, however, too late to review the record and ask what insights it may hold for current work—or to examine thoroughly these contemporary efforts in the light of recent history.

Women and Militarism:
Some Questions for Feminists

Militarism* is the political issue of which I was earliest and most devastat-
ingly aware. The kindergarten air raid drills of the mid-1950s imbued me
with a terror of impending holocaust which has remained, often submerged but inevitably resurfacing. I believe that this early impression of a
social order so deranged that it threatens to self-destruct at any moment
has had a profound effect on my overall political development—and
probably, in sometimes hidden and subtle ways, on that of my entire
post-Hiroshima generation. However, it's only recently that the emergence of an anti-nuclear, anti-militarist movement in which other lesbians and feminists have played a visible role has made activism in the area
feel possible for me.

In August of 1979, along with members of Lesbian Energy, an affinity
group organized through Dykes Opposed to Nuclear Technology, I participated in a Hiroshima-Nagasaki anniversary protest at the Indian Point
nuclear plant near New York City. Beginning in September 1980, I did
planning and organizing for the Women's Pentagon Action, and was arrested in the civil disobedience there on November 17. This article grows
out of these experiences and others in the women's movement. In particular, though by no means a comprehensive evaluation of the Women's
Pentagon Action, it often reflects my personal perspective on that event.
I hope that the questions I raise here (sometimes providing my own par-

---

*This term, despite inadequacies, seems the best available to indicate not just warfare
itself, but the entire spectrum of military-related projects and economic arrangements
which increasingly determine the quality and possibility of life for all of us.

tial and tentative answers) will help encourage discussion among women involved in or considering feminist, anti-militarist work.

How serious a political issue is militarism in general? The nuclear threat in particular? Should feminists be working in this area? One attitude I encountered (primarily among New York City lesbian-feminists) while working on the Women's Pentagon Action is that anti-militarist organizing is somehow less relevant or "correct" than work on what are commonly perceived to be "women's issues," or other life-and-death issues such as racism and poverty. The nuclear issue, in particular, seemed to be perceived as a "white, middle-class" concern. One white woman questioned the importance of worrying about future possible wars, given that a war is going on right now in the ghettoes of America—a point of view she said she had heard expressed by women of color. I heard frequent disparaging remarks about "anti-nukers" and "peace movement types."

I believe that militarism affects all of us intimately and daily, and will do so with increasingly deadly force as this decade continues. The effects—from cancer deaths connected to uranium mining and weapons production, to a probably renewed draft, to repression and torture visited upon citizens of Third World countries where right-wing regimes thrive on U.S. military aid—will undoubtedly fall, as they always have in the past, first and most heavily upon poor people and people of color (unless, indeed, an all-out nuclear war visits non-discriminatory devastation upon us all). So naturally I spent a lot of time puzzling over the widespread mistrust of involvement with the issue.

Evidently, for some feminisits the very possibility of such involvement has been closed off by their anger at the politics of groups (in New York, predominantly straight, male-dominated, white, economically privileged—though East Coast feminists should remember that Native Americans are leading anti-nuclear work in many Western states) which have recently been associated with anti-militarism. Perhaps some of this goes back to the sense of betrayal experienced by many women active in the anti–Vietnam War movement.

While I don't doubt that this anger is richly deserved in many cases (I've seen a fair amount of racism, sexism, class bias, and homophobia first hand), it disturbs me to find the *issue* convicted, as it were, of "guilt by association." We need not impose a hierarchy of issues; we need demonstrations at Rocky Flats *and* at Sydenham Hospital, at local welfare centers *and* the Pentagon. Nor need strong and valid criticisms of peace and anti-nuclear groups lead us to dismiss the significant work they have in fact done.

Another apparent factor in feminists' reluctance to deal with militarism is a fear that our meager resources—already spread too thin by frantic efforts to deal with issues other groups won't address—will be swallowed up by yet another movement which will ignore our needs.

I also suspect the presence of the denial mechanism which tends to click on in all of us when we are confronted with the horrifying prospect of nuclear holocaust. Rather than admit our own sense of helplessness, it's easier to make light of the threat, much as "Ban the Bomb" demonstrators were dismissed as "nervous nellies" in the 1950s.

What does the nuclear threat mean to us? How does it function in our lives and political movements to keep us passive, and how can we combat that passivity? How can we relate anti-nuclear work to other forms of anti-militarist work? Some activist women have told me, in effect, "If they press the button, they press the button. There's nothing I can do; I just try not to think about it." Doing anti-nuclear work involves finding ways to overcome this "psychic numbing," as it has been called, in both ourselves and others—a form of "organizing" for which traditional politics provides no precedent. (My hope is, however, that women, traditionally permitted to feel and express fear more freely than men, will discover ways to do this.)

Horrified at the absolute negation promised by nuclear weapons, it is easy for those of us shielded by skin and/or class privilege to forget that death by more "conventional" military means is a direct and ongoing result of our government's policies. (And nuclear murder, too, can be exercised selectively based on such factors as race—witness the nuclear "experiments" at Hiroshima and Nagasaki.) If anti-nuclear activists are to build an effective, inclusive movement, we will have to address seriously the relationships among all forms of militarism.

Maleness and Violence

Most women, certainly most feminists, assume a certain connection between war and male dominance. "Boys will be boys," we say; or, with less tolerance but equivalent contempt, "Take the toys away from the boys." But the assumption, though gratifying, leaves too much unexplained; a simple male/female, warlike/peaceful dichotomy clearly fails to account for the virtually unchallenged prevalence of war. Examining militarism in the light of existing feminist theory, we must ask over again some familiar questions: *Would women as a group, given powers similar to men's, abuse them similarly?* (Virginia Woolf thought that woman's position as "outsider" preserved her from the taint of militarism.) *Or do we oppose war because we are inherently more "nurturing" than men, perhaps as a result of our child-bearing capacity?* (Anti-nuclear activist Helen Caldicott has recently advanced this view.) How innocent is our traditional lack of direct involvement in warmaking anyway? (Dorothy Dinnerstein, in *The Mermaid and the Minotaur*, presents the haunting suggestion that traditional male/female roles function complementarily to "keep history mad.") *Just how legitimate is the concept of "male violence," given that the most awesome destructive powers are wielded almost exclusively by white, economically privileged men—often with the collusive support of women?* (Why not "white violence" or "ruling-class violence?")

Answers to these questions will shape our response to others involving the form our anti-militarist work is to take:

Will we do work in mixed groups? Women-only groups? Lesbian-feminist groups?

Is the choice to work exclusively with women based primarily on our own preference for such interactions, or rather on the belief that an autonomous women's anti-militarist group has a unique contribution to make?

Are we particularly concerned to reach other women, and if so, what specific forms of action do we want them to take?

What are the connections and/or contradictions between feminism and pacifism?

How does militarism specifically affect women? (For instance, what will be the social results if women are drafted?)

Can active, visible, feminist anti-militarist organizing advance the cause of feminism as well as that of anti-militarism?

What are the implications of being visibly lesbian in doing such work?

My work on the Women's Pentagon Action convinced me that the most crucial question facing would-be builders of a feminist anti-militarist movment is: *How inclusive—or exclusive—will this movment be?*

Unsurprisingly, so far feminist anti-militarists have been predominantly white and middle-class, many of them heterosexual. The very nature of the issue places certain limits on participation: A mother on welfare may feel, for instance, that any energy she has to spare for political work needs to be spent on welfare rights organizing. We need to find ways to support her, respecting her priorities; we also need to recognize the contributions of women who don't define themselves as feminists (for example, some of the Native American women doing anti-nuclear work). But above all, we need to examine our own privilege, whatever form it may take, to see how it affects our organizing efforts and how we can overcome that influence. Otherwise we will increasingly be "talking to ourselves." I hope we will ask, before launching future organizations and/or actions:

How can we publicize planning sessions to the widest possible range of groups and individuals before decisions are made, rather than relying on "outreach" after the fact?

What are groups unlike our own doing in related areas that we can support, rather than always expecting them to connect with us?

How can we form alliances with groups working on issues of particular importance to their constituencies, in the process supporting and educating both ourselves and them?

A closely related question is: *How do we deal with political differences amongst ourselves?* Significant differences spring from the varied experiences of lesbians and heterosexual women; white women and women of color; middle-class and working-class women; women involved in the mixed peace movement and those primarily identified with the women's movement. Other questions concern the specific form of our protests:

How can we minimize the drawbacks of mass protest and civil disobedience: abysmal quality of news coverage; difficulty of participation for those who must travel long distances, often missing work or leaving children; selective jeopardy, based on race and class, for women risking arrest; energy-draining court appearances and increasingly lengthy sentences?

What does civil disobedience accomplish?

If we do CD and go to jail, how do we relate to women we encounter who didn't choose to go there and will remain after we leave?

*What new tactics, perhaps more decentralized and accessible to less privileged
women, can we devise?*

*What steps, if any, can we take to minimize the consequences of the repression
that we (along with other activists) are sure to face increasingly as the right wing
consolidates power?*

My two brief prison experiences have served as a healthy personal
reminder of the power of the legal system and the unrealistic nature of my
previous illusions of control with respect to it. While in Alderson federal
penitentiary following the Women's Pentagon Action, I was enormously
affected by meeting other women who, because of the political threat the
government felt they represented, had received sentences of years rather
than days.

We must not be caught unprepared by a regime, desperate and often
paranoid, which takes us more seriously than we sometimes take ourselves. For if we are truly intent on survival, on the possibility of life for
all of us, we threaten it indeed.

To Live Outside the Law
You Must Be Honest:
A Flommy Looks at Lesbian Parenting*

When it comes to parenting, I consider myself a hopeless amateur, a
fact that's made me hesitate a good deal in thinking about what to say
here today, even though I'm excited and pleased to have the chance to put
together some of the scattered thoughts about lesbian parenting which
have occurred to me over the years. My primary self-chosen identity is

---

*Keynote delivered at "Mother's Courage: Lesbians Creating a Parenting Community,"
Albany, New York, April 5, 1986.

that of writer, an identity that has frequently conflicted with the demands of child-rearing. *Writer* is something I think I'm really good at, at least part of the time, whereas *parent* is something I think I do okay.

And yet: I'm a writer who, much to her own surprise, has often been drawn to use fiction as a way of exploring some of what goes on between lesbian parents and their children. I've also been, for more than ten years now, a live-in, so-called "non-biological" parent or co-parent (in our household we like to use the word "flommy" instead, since it makes me sound less like I'm made out of Teflon). I have shared daily life with my lover's daughter, have fought with her, laughed with her, traveled with her, worried about her after-school whereabouts and her migraine headaches and her TV and sugar consumption, attended karate demonstrations and open school nights and swim meets. I've watched her grow from a scrawny, barely articulate preschooler into a poised high school sophomore who towers over me—and if only she had *my* genes, I joke, her size would be more appropriate.

For me, being a parent has had more positives than negatives. It helps that I really *like* this child I'm raising—which I consider to be largely a matter of good fortune, since at bottom I'm pessimistic about exactly how much control parents have over how their kids turn out. As the years have gone by, I've come to feel much more secure in my role as this weird, socially invisible person, a flommy; much more at home in the solidity of Anna's and my ongoing, daily connection to one another—a history that no law court, no "natural" father, and no context of conventional public assumptions about the sanctity of blood ties could now erase. My lover and I and our child, all three of us, have somehow made our chosen family work. It provides us with emotional and material supports that are sometimes strikingly different from, and sometimes frankly reminiscent of, the supports to be found in other types of families.

And yet my enormous ambivalence about parenthood—about the role of "mother," no matter what name it wears—has never gone away. Every time I think I've resolved "all that" (after all, I've helped raise one child nearly to adulthood, and I'm quite clear in my mind that I don't want to have a baby or take such major responsibility for a young child again), some situation arises which shows me just how complicated my feelings still are. *Other* women, I tend to assume, are sure of what they're doing— especially those who are just now becoming parents. *I'm* the one who doesn't have it all together. (Last week, for instance, I was enormously relieved when a close friend of mine who inseminated last fall and is expecting her baby in the summer mentioned her ongoing ambivalence about what she was getting into. Though I knew her so well and had watched her difficult decision-making process, I'd somehow managed to decide that now she was pregnant she must be well on the road to being the "good" parent I think I ought to be—one who nurtures spontaneously and without second thoughts.)

The fact is that parenthood has given rise to some of the most painful emotional and practical dilemmas I've encountered in the course of my complicated efforts to figure out some tolerable way of living as a woman. There's a part of me that perceives the work of caring for children as a trap, a fatal diversion from the rest of the work I want to do in this world: the work of disciplined fantasy that is writing, the work of understanding that leads to political analysis, the work of taking care of my lover and my other adult friends, the work of getting together in activist meetings to change social conditions on this planet.

I've observed similar contradictory feelings in most of the lesbians I know who've had kids for a while now, especially biological mothers who've been parenting for 10 or 15 years already. For some, their struggle both to meet their kids' needs and to have full adult lives which include every important lesbian activity from torrid sex to political organizing has made it just too difficult even to talk about lesbian parenting at conferences like this one. (My feelings about being a mother are simply not fit to be spoken in public, a friend of mine said when she heard I was doing this talk.) And then there are the lesbians who do not live with their children, who've lost them in custody battles or backed down from custody battles or decided early on that it was better for their kids to be reared by someone else. Lesbians who gave infants up for adoption, lesbians who had kids who died, lesbians who were flommies like me and lost touch with kids they loved when they broke up with the mother. As much as any other role we ever find ourselves in, parenting points up the contradictions of being female—and being lesbian parents doesn't mean that we sidestep those contradictions. Far from it.

This morning the main thing I want to do is to think about lesbian parenting as a place where promising opportunities for women and their children intersect with ancient problems, where real freedom exists in a complicated tension with hoary stereotypes about our "place" as females.

In other words, what Adrienne Rich called the "institution" of motherhood is going to haunt lesbians' efforts at redefining our relationships to children, not only because of what society requires but sometimes because of what we expect of ourselves.

I think it's especially important to look at this intersection of opportunities and pitfalls now that larger numbers of lesbians seem to be having babies or actively seeking out parenting relationships—the phenomenon vulgarly referred to as the "lesbian baby boom." I'm not sure that the actual numbers of mothers and co-parents are radically different from what they were ten years ago, say, but the atmosphere clearly has changed. Having a baby is now an accepted activity in many lesbian-feminist circles, where back then it was something you'd done when you were straight, like shaving your legs, or performing fellatio, only motherhood had longer-term consequences. Then, lesbian custody fights were the big parenting issue; though they haven't gone away, more publicity is now given to topics like donor insemination. The lesbian mothers of ten years ago were frequently viewed by the "child-free" as martyrs to women's condition, in line with the early feminist criticism of social definitions of motherhood. And co-parents were even less well understood, scarcely perceived to exist by the women's community, let alone the straight world.

The new focus on lesbian parenting issues clearly has the potential to help create a more supportive atmosphere in which to raise children—or to be a child oneself. But at the same time, it involves the danger that we may be trying to re-invent the wheel: either by forgetting that there's already a long history of lesbian parenting which we need to look at, or by assuming that we have it within our power to create a brave new world of lesbian child-rearing which is immune to the problems and disappointments traditional mothers have faced. At times I've been concerned about what I perceive to be an intense focus on deciding whether and how to have children, with a lack of equivalent attention to the array of puzzling issues that lie in wait for lesbian parents a little further down the road. (To pick one woefully under-examined topic: what happens when co-parents break up?) I'm reminded of those civil disobedience training sessions that anticipate every conceivable thing that could happen in the half hour between sitting down in front of the nuke plant and being popped into the police van—but say not a word about what to expect when you find yourself in jail or prison for two weeks.

Besides being aware of the parenting experience of other generations of lesbians, I think that before we speak of creating a parenting community we must examine how our individual ideas about being parents, and our daily experience of living with children, differ according to our identities and backgrounds, the specific oppression we face, and the specific strengths we have that grow out of our memories of the people who raised us. To put this in the words of a Black friend of mine: "Black children are still being shot down in the streets in this country—that's something Black lesbians have to discuss when we talk about parenting."

For some of us, having kids is intimately bound up with survival issues, as it is for this friend; as it is for those Jewish women who feel a direct link between the Holocaust and their desire to raise a new generation of Jewish children; or for those Native Americans for whom the genocide of white rule makes parenting a crucial act of resistance. For a working-class lesbian who plans to have a baby by herself, economic realities and hence the entire experience are going to be worlds apart from those of the middle-class professional couple who have a baby together. For me, whose college-educated mother never worked for wages while I was at home, my assumptions about what a mother is "supposed" to do differ in crucial aspects from those of women who held jobs to help support the family. Growing up, I saw my mother as a kind of privileged servant— and it was a role I knew I wanted no part of in my own adult life.

All of these variations and many more exist among lesbians— including lesbians who don't think of themselves as feminists and would never come to a conference like this. In deliberately building a lesbian parenting community, we not only have to be prepared to explore the meaning of these differences, but to identify ways in which specific forms of oppression selectively target parents and kids. And then we have to be prepared for yet another struggle, both in our own circles and the society at large, to make the necessary changes. (Here, of course, the burden of commitment is largely on women with more relative privilege—those with less have no choice about the daily fight they wage.) Otherwise, lesbian parenting becomes yet another private enterprise, and the self-defined "lesbian parenting community" is likely to be one of shared advantage.

I want to speak briefly about some of the ways it's been for me in my time as a flommy, because I'm especially concerned that in a context where the realities of all forms of lesbian parenting have been insufficiently discussed, the experience of co-parenting has been particularly neglected. Co-parenting highlights very sharply what I call the basically "outlaw" character of all lesbian—and gay—family situations. If lesbian mothers are not supposed to exist (since everyone knows queers can't reproduce themselves), then a co-mother or non-biological parent is doubly a non-person: she lacks the blood bond to her child which our society considers so vital that it will occasionally concede that even dykes can care about the kids we birth. Audre Lorde has written of a school friend of her son's who insisted on referring to Audre's lover as "the maid"; I know I've been in countless situations where I felt Anna's and my relationship was either not seen or completely misjudged. Because of our own frequently confused feelings, our ambiguous standing with our lovers' children, co-parents sometimes have a hard time discussing our situations even amongst ourselves. A group rather oppressively titled "lovers of lesbian mothers" which was formed by the New York City-based Dykes and Tykes in the middle 1970s only succeeded in attracting three "flommies"—one of whom immediately dropped out, leaving me and another woman to be a support group of two.

When I began to write down what I wanted to say about my personal experience, I was taken aback by how many painful memories surfaced. My first three or four years as a flommy were especially hard. It was hard to fit myself into an already-established mother-child system, even though my lover welcomed the presence of another adult and genuinely tried her best to share the parenting with me on an equal basis—a willingness I believe was absolutely essential to whatever success we had later. What made things doubly difficult was the fact that often I wasn't sure whether I *wanted* to fit in.

It was hard to be with a young child who was frequently miserable, even when the reasons for her misery had little to do with me. I remember years of violent tantrums that turned our apartment into a battlefield, engulfing every room so that there was no room apart, no DMZ to retreat to. I remember the guilty anger with which I responded, sometimes hitting, more often imposing a mature, abstract punishment like taking away TV watching time that nevertheless left me feeling like an ogre. I remember the discomfort of doubting whether there'd ever be room for *anybody's* needs—mine, my lover's, our child's. I remember the awful nagging worry: maybe Anna won't be okay—and it's a terrible thing to worry that a child isn't going to be okay. I remember just wanting to withdraw, find my own separate space—but knowing that to do that would be to make myself even more of an outsider, and so choosing to stay. I remember, when I stayed, the intense anger I felt at my lover's ex-husband, our child's father, the man who was not as I was a participant in her daily life, but who was besides her mother the socially recognized parent, the one who had a legal right to her that I could never claim. (A worst-case scenario based on that circumstance became the plot of my novel, *Sinking, Stealing*.)

Ours was certainly not a well-thought-out, neatly planned arrangement. I still tease my lover about how one time very early in our relationship when I asked her about me and Anna, she replied, "Oh, I wouldn't worry about it—she'll probably just want you to read her a few bedtime stories once in a while." Yet gradually we all three developed an intense loyalty to one another. As my lover and I like to say, "We stuck together through thin and thin"—and certainly there are moments in both parents' and children's lives when "thin" seems to follow "thin" interminably. Interestingly, we still seem to work better as a series of pairs than as a threesome; when we're all together, there's too much of a chance that one person will feel left out.

With Anna I finally feel I have a secure place as someone who is a very unique relative: clearly, to us both, not her mother, even though I connect so many of my parental feelings to what I know of motherhood; certainly not a father-substitute and not a stepparent, for I'm replacing no one—I'm the only flommy she's ever had. The fact that she and her mother are Jewish and I am not underscores the chosen nature of our family; dealing with that difference has meant hard work and some painful moments, but a great deal of growth for me as well.

And now, just when I feel more comfortable than ever in the past with my family setting, and when at the same time I'm looking forward to the freedom of ceasing to be responsible for the care and feeding of a resident daughter, parenting has suddenly become a hot topic in the lesbian community. And it's not simply that a younger generation of lesbians has decided they want to do what I did and build a life with kids—so many of my peers, women from their mid-thirties on up into their early forties, are now deciding to have babies, or at any rate investing a lot of energy in contemplating that possibility. And though sometimes I feel excited by what this means for individuals among my friends, and have even begun to look forward to the possibility of being an "aunt" to one close friend's child in a way I never felt I was to my blood sister's little boy, I also have a lot of negative reactions: fear of being abandoned by specific women as they immerse themselves in the demanding, absorbing world of early childhood; fear of finding myself trapped in a community where my emancipation from the need to locate a babysitter is meaningless because everyone *else* is home with the kids.

Most interesting and most painful is a totally irrational feeling of betrayal: I thought other lesbians were with me in the decision not to give birth, in that defiance of our expected womanly role—and now here these new lesbian mothers go, showing me up, *proving* that the fact I'm a dyke is no excuse for my failure to have a baby. The nerve is such a sensitive one that in examining my reactions I'm sometimes reminded of the gay/straight split of the early 1970s—such, I fear, is the power of the entrenched social institutions that have traditionally defined us as women to come between sisters.

As I've said, I think many long-time biological mothers are even warier than I am about the positive potential of lesbian parenting. Some are angry that there was so little support from the feminist community when they themselves were raising small children—yet now they're expected to attend a baby shower every week. Some fear that interest in children is becoming a substitute for political activism, or at best that many lesbians who are new to parenting have an unrealistic notion of the extent of the contradictions between an activist way of life and the needs of infants and toddlers. Some separatists have gone so far as to pen furious manifestoes listing 15 reasons why any lesbian who dares to have a kid is a traitor to the Lesbian Nation.

Which only indicates once again what an incredibly charged topic motherhood is for rebellious women (and as lesbians, we're rebellious almost by definition). The consequent conflicts certainly won't be resolved with manifestoes, any more than were earlier controversies over everything from the length of our hair to monogamy vs. nonmonogamy to our lovemaking techniques to whether or not we ought to be doing political work with men. We don't move by rules; we move toward what we love. We don't have kids or not have them for political reasons. Having kids, being with kids, looking toward a new generation, is a part of being human, and in one sense I think the current public and publicized interest in having babies is another way the lesbian-feminist community has of stretching into a newfound sense of its rights to the full range of human and female experience.

Yet I think there are some important questions to be raised about this community trend. The flyer for this conference inquires under a workshop heading: "Does having children and building a family provide a feeling of connectedness that is missing in the women's community?" I would add to that: Are we somehow trying to compensate for the failure of the women's movement to change the world in all the ways we so desperately need it to change? Feminism, the gay movement, Third World communities, poor and working-class people, all have sustained enormous setbacks in the 1980s. Of course many of us haven't stopped fighting—no matter what the media think—but the temptation is certainly there to turn to more private, seemingly more controllable spheres of activity. Which leads me to pose the question: if there were more hands cradling rocks (to borrow the title of a poetry collection Rita Mae Brown published eons ago, before her novels started selling in airport newsstands), would there be fewer hands rocking cradles?

As lesbians, we're not necessarily immune to the oldest trap there is, the false consolation of motherhood, the notion that women can be compensated for our lack of power and standing in the adult world by the supposed influence we exert over our children's development. I think we have to be very cold-eyed and clear-headed about just how much control over kids' lives we really do have, particularly in this society. I believe that to be a parent requires the performance of that strange act of faith that's referred to in Christian scripture as "casting your bread upon the waters." You hope it will come back increased, but for all you know it might not come back at all or it might be a soggy, inedible mess. At least as lesbians we're more likely to be alive to the possibility that our children will grow up straight, reversing our sexual choices. And in that, perhaps we have an important advantage over many traditional parents. From the very beginning we know it's going to be about difference as well as sameness.

The reality is that society brings home to us its most painful contradictions not only through our internal experience of parenting, but through the experience of our children. I think of racism, class: in my case, for instance, the experience of living on a mostly Black Brooklyn block with a small white girlchild; wondering, when she was bullied by an older Black boy next door, now how do I try to protect her and help her sort this out in a way that lets her be angry at being terrorized by this kid without attaching that anger to Black people in general—how to make sure she doesn't distort the social reality entirely, misunderstanding the power of her skin color inside her real feelings of powerlessness; how to give weight to his gender-based privilege *and* his probable racial motivation.

Or how about the choices regarding schools: public schools, yes, but what did this supposedly egalitarian choice teach in the long run, given the realities of tracking in the New York City public school system? Though Anna's junior high was statistically thoroughly integrated, in fact *her* classes were heavily white middle-class; her high school amounts to a fairly exclusive prep school within the public education system. And anti-Semitism: the twinge I've sometimes felt, reading about Hitler's Europe—they'd have done this to *my* kid, and how could I have protected her? And sexism, and homophobia, and certainly economics, an issue I think lesbians interested in parenting need to discuss in far greater depth, especially in light of the many grim statistics about poverty in female-headed households: the reality is that we have to ask ourselves, not simply how will we take care of the kids and go to the meetings and demos too, but how will we take care of the kids *and* go to the meetings and demos *and* hold down a job that will support everybody in the family at the pittance most women make for most of the work we do? Is parenting a luxury affordable only by lesbians with professional incomes?

And on top of all that, what about war and peace? Will there even *be* a world for our kids to grow up in?

This litany, I know, is overwhelming. I'm certainly not saying that I think little kids should be dragged to meetings every night of the week, and of course there will be plenty of times for many lesbian parents when macro-level political concerns get tabled for long stretches. But I would like to suggest that the questions I've raised imply an opportunity as well as a burden. For one thing, they bring us smack up against some of the early-1970s women's movement agendas that are still waiting to be addressed: the need for good, affordable daycare; welfare rights issues; the high rate of teenage pregnancy that, especially in Black and Latino communities, turns the lives of so many very young women into a day-in, day-out battle for the bare minimums of survival. I believe we need to start thinking and talking about those issues we have in common with straight women, as well as those that uniquely affect us as lesbian parents.

When I told a friend that I was thinking of titling this talk "To Live Outside the Law You Must Be Honest," she wanted to know why. In closing, I want to offer an answer. First of all, as lesbian parents even more so than simply as lesbian women, I believe we are all fundamentally outlaws. That doesn't mean we all realize the full radical potential of our outsider status all the time, and it certainly doesn't mean the "law"— informal social law or the law of the court system—falls with equal weight on each one of us: other forms of privilege, other aspects of oppression are crucial. It does mean that we are doubly in defiance of the general society's prescriptions for what we should be. We're not supposed to be dykes, and if we are dykes, we're certainly not supposed to have families. Our involvement with children mixes up their categories too much. It's as confusing as the involvement of many religious Nicaraguans with that country's revolutionary process—for a reactionary, the only thing to say about that puzzling circumstance is that Sandinista priests and nuns are not real priests and nuns. By the same token, the heterosexual reactionaries would have it, lesbian mothers are not real mothers, and children of lesbian mothers are completely invisible as such, and flommies don't even exist. Like open, unashamed lesbian and gay sexuality, our chosen lesbian families call into question some terribly basic assumptions about who's important to whom, and why.

So that's the outlaw part, and considering what the laws are, I'm proud to be outside them. The honesty part is about what you do with where you find yourself. To live outside the law is to live without a script, without preformulated rules for being with other people. Living that way requires being clear about feelings, both good and bad feelings. It also requires a finely tuned awareness of the contours of the country that surrounds you.

Being an outlaw doesn't mean being a law unto yourself. It doesn't mean the luxury of being able to retreat to a safe corner, a cozy community, and forget the rest of the world. And our kids are a constant reminder of that. If escapism ever tempts us, they will be right there to bring us back home. Kids live on the block; they ride the school bus; they play in the street, in the woods, in the vacant lots with all the neighbor kids. Abstractions rarely impress them. Daily experience marks them deeply.

Along with our love for them as who they uniquely are, I believe the process of our daily struggles as women who still intend to change the world is the greatest gift we lesbian parents can give our children.

In Pieces: A Feminist in the Central America Solidarity Movement

For a while now, it seems, I've been living my life in pieces. At the same time I've been experiencing difficulty in writing on the edge of what, politically, I know. Whether in poetry, fiction, or other prose forms, I often end up producing what feels to me like a pale, partial, two-dimensional response to the densely layered reality into which I'm plunged each time I enter my neighborhood, the world. This essay, then, will be not so much an attempt at wholeness as an effort to identify the fragments in relation to one another.

An obvious reason for my sense of dislocation is the fact that, after roughly a decade in which my home was the U.S. women's movement, for the past several years what I think of as the center of gravity of my social, political, and cultural life has been shifting steadily southward. (At this rate, I joke, if I live long enough both body and mind may wind up in Patagonia.) I have fallen in love with the Americas: not, I hope, in the shallow racist-imperialist tradition of gringos who go shopping for adventure—though inevitably there are echoes of that pattern in my attraction—but deeply and for keeps, prepared to work and be changed. Like any other passion, this one both lures and frightens me with its promise of altering, unpredictably, the direction of my life.

I've often felt shy and defensive about the pull it exerts. For one thing, I cut my ideological teeth on identity politics, a theoretical framework that doesn't readily explain or justify immersion in other people's struggles. Besides, I know by heart the common criticisms of Central America solidarity work, and have to agree there's merit in all of them. Aren't there plenty of dire but less glamorous issues to keep us busy on the domestic scene? Why is it that white leftists, frequently so active on behalf of Central America's liberation, have been comparatively uninvolved in anti-apartheid organizing? Given the similarities between the Nicaraguan contras and the U.S.-supported counterinsurgency mounted by Unita, why is it that this country lacks a vigorous Angola solidarity movement? I've winced at right-on-target observations by Latinas that it's usually middle-class, Anglo feminists who have money to take off on revolutionary junkets, who form solidarity groups with romantic Spanish names— while ignoring Puerto Rican and other Latino communities right here at home. And I've asked myself what would happen to my lesbian-feminist consciousness and practice if I worked day to day in a heavily straight and male organization.

All these righteous and principled criticisms blend ambiguously with my snobbish recoil from political bad taste, now that Nicaragua is thronged with callow enthusiasts like the round-faced young woman I remember from my first trip there in 1984. How gleefully, flirtatiously she took advantage of photo opportunities to pose cuddled next to teen-aged soldiers with their AK-47s, and bragged of her ambition to study journalism in Cuba—at which a young Latina from New York quietly inquired how she planned to manage that when she spoke hardly a word of Spanish.

And yet, I've plunged ahead with an involvement which I can now see has some deep if shadowy roots in my own life, beginning with my first years in the volcanic, provincial Pacific Northwest (Oregon! I saw from the rain-split air, flying into June-green Managua the first time). On the fifties West Coast of my childhood, Europe and Washington seemed distant, legendary, and the sense of "America" as a world apart, a sovereign land mass where indigenous peoples had recently lived in freedom, was palpable beneath the overlay of the worldview we memorized with the Pledge of Allegiance, the Star-Spangled Banner. Thirty years later I'm drawing essential nourishment from friendships with Latina lesbians and Caribbean and Central American immigrants, from Latin American poetry and fiction, from feminist theory by puertorriqueñas/chicanas/cubanas, from the sounds of the Spanish language, from trips to Nicaragua, from my work in the Central America solidarity movement.

Though the color of my skin and my nation's history often make me question my right to claim the relationship, this huge chunk of New

World feels to me like long-lost kin. More and more I'm aware that my neighborhood, Brooklyn, is a product of the Caribbean and Central American (as well as African, Jewish, Middle Eastern, Italian) diasporas; only the map-maker's literal-mindedness locates it north of the 40th parallel. I conclude that my southward urge must amount in part to this: that despite my radical disillusionment, I never quite stopped being the child who loved "America," and here at last in "the Americas" North and South, a multitude of them in their glory and torment, I hope to find a nation-substitute, a home I might wholeheartdly inhabit without sacrificing truth.

Aside from attendance at some demonstrations, my first venture into Central America work was to join the Brooklyn chapter of CISPES (Committee in Solidarity with the People of El Salvador) in early 1985. I felt like a Martian walking into those meetings. I was the only out gay person (I never discovered any "in" ones, either). Though I probably knew as much about Central America as the average new member and had recently spent two weeks in Nicaragua, as a lesbian-feminist I hailed from a political tradition and a social world very different from that of others in the group. Never mind strong female leadership and a fair degree of consciousness about women's issues on the part of some of the men; this was clearly the "white male left" I'd spent so many tedious hours hearing radical feminists and separatists vilify. I wanted to experiment with this new way of working, but I knew I was in for something of a cross-cultural experience, and felt considerable anger that most of the adjustment was probably going to be on my side.

Nearly three years later the CISPES chapter has dissolved, and the focus of my political involvement has become the Brooklyn Sister City Project, which cultivates ties between that borough and San Juan del Río Coco, Nicaragua. I work with a number of lesbians and feminists, including members of a semi-autonomous Women's Committee, which has done a lot to raise my personal comfort level. I'm also more at ease with my straight associates, some of them old CISPES members; a few have become friends. Still, I'm left with an uneasy feeling of dwelling in a house divided between feminism/the "women's community" and the other realities in which I move—including not only that of the North American left, but the very different one of Central Americans I meet, to whom my lesbian-feminism is often invisible.

I know I'm not alone in this rather lonely experience. News reaches me

frequently of like-minded sisters who participate in extra-feminist progressive organizing. As women of color choosing to work in their home
communities, as white dykes involved with Witness for Peace or the
Sanctuary Movement, as members of the Rainbow Coalition or New
Jewish Agenda or Mobilization for Survival or the National Anti-Klan
Network, as AIDS educators and union organizers, they're performing
many crucial tasks—and evidently reaping more satisfactions than they
thought they could by concentrating their efforts within explicitly feminist groups. Some of them are my friends, and on occasion our discussions drift around to the fact that we're working in ways we never would
have imagined, most of us, ten years ago. For the most part, though, we
go about our business without time to figure out what it all means, how
we got from there to here, or the repercussions for our feminist agenda of
the choices we've made.

Why are so many feminist and lesbian activists choosing to work in
"male movements?"[1] I believe the trend is due partly to a lesson many of
us learned from direct experience, and which feminist theory at its best
reinforced: the fact that the complexity of oppression on this planet calls
for a broad spectrum of liberation struggles. The women's movement
strengthened us, showed us our power, gave us invaluable practical organizing experience—but at times it also left us high and dry within insular women's communities that seemed disturbingly out of touch with
events in the rest of the world. For me, at any rate, the shift in political
focus in a sense represents the fulfillment of a lifelong dream, the childhood root of my adult feminism: that I would be free to exercise my
insatiable curiosity about every aspect of this life; that, female or not,
nothing would prevent me from coming to grips with its fundamental
problems, its intricate mysteries.

Another, less positive factor which seems to me to be implicated in the
decision of feminists to work in such a range of settings is (to phrase the
matter rather provocatively) the demise of the feminist movement. There
are, of course, strong, committed feminists across the United States;
there are pockets of activism here and there; there are feminist thinkers
and feminist books, women's land and "lesbian space." Goddess knows
there are women's issues, possibly more urgent than ever. But it seems
we've passed that recent time in U.S. history when, by organizing *as
women* to confront oppression in our lives, feminists from a range of class
and racial and ethnic backgrounds were a dynamic force for change.

With very few exceptions, North American feminism in the late 1980s is not visible in the streets and does not proselytize; at the risk of sounding unduly sarcastic I want to say that it rather looks as though we planned to reproduce ourselves by solely physical means, through the lesbian baby boom. At a time like this, women's movement veterans still committed to activism have the choice of working in relatively limited ways within traditional feminist settings (while awaiting an inevitable but perhaps distant moment of resurgence, U.S. feminism's Third Wave), or going elsewhere to "bore from within."[2]

Naturally, we "borers" usually try to locate feminist support in order to minimize both our sense of personal alienation and the danger that our commitment to women's liberation will get lost in the shuffle of competing issues. Often that tends to be a private network of feminist friends, old-time activists scattered across the country with whom we can check in to air grievances and evaluate strategies. This is helpful, and sometimes the best that we can manage, but it's no substitute for an organizational base; for one thing, the private networks aren't connected to the groups we work with and hence can't exert influence within them, and for another they aren't accessible to everyone who needs them—for instance, our co-workers who could profit from exposure to feminist ideas, or newer feminists who may not have activist friends. I know that I've personally found the formation and increasing visibility of a Women's Committee within the Brooklyn Sister City Project to be vital in bringing to the Project as a whole a minimal feminist consciousness, even though the committee's energies have been limited and its impact fragmentary.

Ideally, of course, "boring from within" should mean bringing to nonfeminist groups not only an awareness of explicitly women's issues, but of the results of our long experience with identity politics, racial issues and racism, class, Jewish identity, disability, homophobia as experienced by gay men, feminist process—in short, all the useful lessons of 20 years of struggle. (Given my bias as a writer and book-lover, I admit I often feel the urge to compel on pain of having his/her mouth taped shut just about every straight person I encounter in the Central America movement to sit down and read *This Bridge Called My Back*, *Home Girls*, *Yours in Struggle*, *Loving in the War Years*, *Letters from Nicaragua*, *Zami*, *Compañeras*, *Sanctuary: A Journey*, *Borderlands/LaFrontera*, *Lesbian Fiction*, and several other key texts before attending another meeting.)[3] In practice, too often we're stretched to the point of triage by the pressures of struggling on many fronts at once. For instance, at a recent all-day meeting of the Sister City Project called to discuss the political direction of the group, Women's Committee members felt it was essential to discuss racial and class issues and coalition work; hence we didn't push to use the limited time for a discussion of a paper on the role of the Women's Committee itself.

The truth is that when we work in relative isolation from a critical mass of feminists, it's very difficult to be as "feminist" in practice as we are in theory or when among friends. It's even harder to know when it's right politically to insist on a feminist agenda at the expense of other priorities. And there's not much time or space in our crowded calendars to think it through, to hash it all out.

No wonder I end up feeling I do my work in pieces.

*

In pieces: I get this written, crank it out. Set myself to beat the bushes and round up sullen words, marshal them into sentences and then paragraphs, reliant on writerly habit and raw willpower, the thrifty resolve not to let go to waste all this experience, dammit. I'm in the midst of separating from a lover who has been for long years at the heart of my life, a life I cannot accurately partition into private and public, personal and political.

So: not my political life in fragments; not simply a matter of the unsimple web of social trends and historical forces, the ebb and flow and kiss and shock of this struggle and that; but a whole fragmented life, in which the actions and reactions of public and private, political and personal events upon one another are so complex that to chart them accurately would require a completely new science, an art the women's movement dreamed of early on but has barely begun to develop. What genius of the twenty-first century will tackle the Unified Field Theory of work and love?

As I go through the motions of coherent days, meetings, conversations, essays: a woman in pieces. And when did I decide to open up the door and let old Chaos in?

*

> You come here speaking of Latin America, but this is not important. Nothing important can come from the South. History has never been produced in the South. The axis of history starts in Moscow, goes to Bonn, crosses over to Washington, and then goes to Tokyo. What happens in the South is of no importance. You're wasting your time.
>
> —Henry Kissinger

What can I possibly say about Nicaragua that hasn't been said already, that can make any difference? That daunting question has followed me around for the three and a half years since my first visit there, creating yet another obstacle to my attempts to write on the outer edge of my political awareness. I am not of that extensive tribe of writers who appear to believe that a sojourn of several weeks in a war-torn Latin country is makings for a definitive account.

From that 1984 trip, two emblematic images. The first is of hordes of little kids who'd descend on our group of "cultural workers" every time the bus would stop, "¿Tiene un lápiz?" their inevitable question. (This request for a pencil was gracefully explained as an outgrowth of the famous literacy campaign, but we rapidly learned that it translated as, "Do you have anything for me, anything at all, rich *chele* with the camera around your neck, lucky owner of a digital watch?") The second is the look of stale matted grief, or perhaps sheer fatigue, or was it slow-motion terror, on the brown face of the blunt-bodied young woman in the shiny blue hand-me-down dress in the dust and heat of a hamlet called Pantasma that had suffered a contra attack several months before our visit. She held up her light-haired toddlers to the camera while the older woman with her voiced the ritual request, "Tell them in your country, these kids are orphans, *la guardia* killed their father." As though an orphan or two or hundreds could make the least difference in my country, where in December 1987 Congress voted additional millions for rape, hideous torture, and the manufacture of more orphans, with the excuse that the good legislators couldn't be expected to stick around Washington haggling over Reagan's contra aid request when their families expected them home for Christmas.

What, I sometimes wonder, recalling those images, can possibly be the prospect for North-South dialogue when a nation has been reduced by history—not History the impersonal, godlike force at which we can only marvel, but a crude, specific fate imposed at gunpoint, land mine-point, bayonet-point, International Monetary Fund-point, by its cynical northern neighbor—to the spare change appeal of a can rattler on the Brooklyn-bound IRT?

Of course the irresistible thing about Nicaragua is that, despite its very real vulnerability and near-desperation, it's still a place that dared to have a revolution—and has thus far been skillful, brave, and lucky enough to steer a self-appointed course. "Yanki no nos arrodillaremos por hambre jamás!!!—El Pueblo" ("Yankee we'll never kneel in hunger!!!—The People") reads a typical *pinta* (graffiti) scrawled in giant letters on the wall of a McDonald's (Téllez 131). Over and over, Nicaragua has given the lie to Kissinger's arrogant, ignorant dictum—and thereby ratified the aspirations of dispossessed people everywhere. "We have been nought, we shall be all." One day the homeless panhandlers of New York City may make history, too.

My second trip took place in the summer of 1987 under the auspices of the Brooklyn Sister City Project, a sponsorship I hoped would provide a more solid sense of purpose, a deeper connection to the people I encountered, than I'd felt in 1984. The idea behind sister city projects is to create support for Nicaragua's revolutionary process by encouraging ongoing contact between paired communities. The localities themselves decide the form of their involvement, which usually includes a variety of people-to-people exchanges, from letter writing to delegation visits. The North Americans raise material aid for their Nicaraguan counterparts, and use the sister city relationship as a basis for community educational campaigns designed to penetrate the fog of disinformation through which most U.S. citizens view Central America. The sister city concept has proved tremendously popular, with more than 70 such projects currently under way across this country and many more in Europe. It provides a positive basis for political work, a welcome alternative after years of largely disappointing campaigns against not only contra aid but a range of noxious U.S. policies in the region, such as support for military-dominated governments in Guatemala, Honduras, and El Salvador.

By June 1987, the Brooklyn Sister City Project had been organized for just a little over a year; the group I traveled with was its first annual delegation. There were twelve of us, five women and seven men. Two of the men were Black, all the other members white. Most of us were middle-class by profession if not by background. Two of us were lesbians, a fact that was not overtly an issue during the trip. (I'd made a brief coming out statement at one of the orientation sessions.) We left New

York full of anticipation, laden with our baggage limit in material aid (everything from school supplies to an autoclave), but without firm assurance we'd actually reach our destination, since our sister community, San Juan del Río Coco, lies in the heart of the northern war zone on a rough road several hours' drive from the city of Estelí, a route often made impassable by the threat of contra attacks.

As it happened, we were lucky: despite a major attack on the town of Quilalí, located a few kilometers from San Juan, which made headlines in Managua on the day of our arrival, we were able to keep almost exactly to our planned itinerary. We spent one day and night in the town of San Juan itself, then the following two nights in a settlement 18 kilometers away. This was Patio Grande, one of six *asentamientos* (resettlement communities) based around coffee production which, together with the town, form the sister "city" region.

I had joined the delegation as a representative of the Women's Committee. I took with me a scrapbook, a gift to women in San Juan, which Brooklyn women had gathered to make on the preceding International Women's Day. Each page expressed some aspect of the maker's life in Brooklyn, together with friendship for the people of Nicaragua and hopes for peace. I brought with me pens, paper, glue, and other materials (an embarrassing overabundance, it later turned out) so that the Nicaraguan women could make their own scrapbook if they wanted to. I was supposed to try to contact representatives of women's groups or individual women who might want to stay in touch with our committee, as well as to inquire about a project for which women in the San Juan area would like to see us raise material aid.

I was a little nervous about this ambitious agenda, worried that a scrapbook might seem frivolous or irrelevant in the middle of a war, and unsure how I'd manage with my limited Spanish. I was also tremendously excited at last to be meeting face to face these Nicaraguans (women especially) with whom we hoped to form a lasting connection. Up until that point all our direct contact with our sister city had been through a young North American woman named Sarah. A Brooklyn native who now lived in San Juan and worked for MIDINRA, the ministry of agrarian reform, she'd helped set up the sister city link, now served as the project's coordinator from the Nicaraguan end, and would be the delegation's guide and translator while we were in the area.

For me the heart of the trip was the time we spent in Patio Grande, which I want to focus on here for two reasons. One is that it's there I believe we glimpsed most clearly the threadbare bravery, the precarious hope that are fundamental to Nicaragua's revolution, a kind of human strength I associate with Adrienne Rich's beautiful lines, composed ten year ago in a very different context, about those who "perversely, / with no extraordinary power, / reconstitute the world" ("Natural Resources," 67). The other is that the experience suggests some important questions likely to face North American feminists—white ones especially—who choose this type of work.

Patio Grande, at the time of our visit a rough settlement of about 50 families, had been established on land that we were told had been like a "contra hotel" several years previously. Already planted in coffee, it had immediately become the largest producer of the *asentamientos* surrounding San Juan, and as such was of considerable importance to the region. In contrast to the situation in many *asentamientos* where families have relocated from areas of heavy fighting to a place of greater security, here most people had come because of the land which had productive capacity far surpassing that of their homes in the "dry zone."

They could hardly have left a physically riskier situation than the one they found in Patio Grande. Sarah described to us how the community had been established in the fall of 1986, the families going into the area accompanied by an armed convoy. She hadn't slept much that first night, she admitted. However, things went well for a few months, until on April 9, 1987, the contra attacked. They killed five civilians, including children, and burned a truck recently purchased by the farm cooperative and vital to its operations. Afterwards, many frightened families left. A major effort was now underway to persuade them to return, or to attract others in their place.

The short trip between San Juan and Patio Grande was the most dangerous part of our delegation's journey, and loud singing and many bad jokes testified to our nervousness as the open truck swung over the hilly road. Still, we knew that extra military patrols had been sent out the night before in preparation for this ride; the last thing either local or Managua officials wanted was dead or wounded internationalists. The realization that Nicaraguans had to live with trips like this on a daily or weekly basis helped put things in perspective. Too, there was extravagant scenery all around to distract us from the jitters; Patio Grande is located at a much higher elevation than San Juan, in lush green mountains, cloud-

companioned. Nobody had bothered to inform us of the politically irrelevant detail that our sister "city" is one of the most beautiful spots on
earth.

Some edited diary excerpts from the next two days:

> We were met at the truck . . . a small procession came strag-
> gling down the muddy hillside, women and children mostly, led by
> three kids with signs on sticks. A brief round of speeches. Then a
> skinny, almost toothless old woman came up to us saying they
> needed "una ropita" [a little clothing] and Sarah rather sternly told
> her that the things were being given communally. Another, much
> younger, dark, long hair and few teeth, expressed her enthusiasm . . .
> "Oh, we were so glad all day because you were coming," was the gist.
> A little disturbing—could we live up to expectations? . . . She
> asked whether it were true that U.S. women had fewer kids than
> Nicaraguan women. I thought she was going to be critical but instead
> she pointed out that "large families make so much noise."
>
> [Recorded by a snapshot, the text of one of the signs which wel-
> comed us reads: LAS MUJERES DE PATIO GRANDE LES DAMOS LA BIEMBENIDA A
> LOS INTERNACIONALISTAS DEL PUEBLO DE BROOKLYN Y ESPERAMOS COMPARTIR
> EXPERIENSIA DE MUESTRA NICARAGUA Y SU PAIS COMO LAZOS ETERNOS QUE NOS
> UNIRA ASTA EL FIN, "The women of Patio Grande extend a welcome to
> the internationalists from the town of Brooklyn and hope to share
> experience of our Nicaragua and your country as eternal bonds that
> will unite us to the end." The Spanish, in block letters and full of
> misspellings, makes me think of Dora María Téllez: "León had beau-
> tiful graffiti, graffiti of the sort that contains misspellings. Those are
> the ones I like, those with misspellings" (127, my translation). Er-
> ratic spelling is the evidence of a newly literate population fearlessly
> exercising its freedom to write.]

> They show us bullet holes in everything: in the walls of the health
> center, in the truck that was burned and still sits, a grim hulk, in the
> center of the flat open space where we made the *parque infantil*
> [playground; together with Patio Grande residents, delegation
> members spent half a day building a simple swing set]. Abel ex-
> plained how he and a companion miraculously escaped the April 9
> attack. Armed, they were surrounded and outnumbered because the
> *comedor infantil* [children's eating center] where they happened to be
> at the time was at the edge of the *asentamiento* where the attack be-
> gan. They escaped detection by knocking a hole in the false ceiling of
> the *comedor*, climbing up between that and the zinc roof, and staying

there for several hours during which they had to breathe through bullet holes in the zinc to escape asphyxiation by the smoke from the burning truck. At one point they looked out and saw *la guardia* [contras; the term is that used for Somoza's National Guard] dancing and eating jam from a storeroom and calling on people to surrender. After a while the "freedom fighters" left and they were able to go around collecting the dead and wounded. A teacher was killed firing from the window of the building that houses the health center. We were shown the bullet holes.

We painted the burned-out truck with solidarity slogans because we couldn't budge it—Nicaraguans and Norteamericanos working together at the job. There was a gender problem with the work on the playground, definitely something for the next delegation to devote some advance planning to. The women worked, of course—I did some with the machete as well as the painting—but the real physical labor the men did.

There's another, more serious sexual politics issue: the temptation for us delegation women to allow ourselves to be treated the way Sarah seems to be, as "one of the boys," more or less. Maybe that's okay for her, given the requirements of her job, but in our case it makes me uncomfortable. For instance, Sue and I are staying with Don Sebastián and his wife Marina. Both are very sweet, lovely, gentle. They have four kids, are probably in their middle to late twenties. Marina certainly doesn't seem at all weak or passive, but Sebastián does most of the talking—not at all in an aggressive or particularly "patriarchal" way, but just really sincerely wanting to explain to me his political understandings and also the material realities that are closest to his heart: for instance, his love of this incredibly rich land which could be producing so much, such a marvelous variety of food and livestock as well as the coffee, if it weren't for the war which he said had almost put an end to cultivation during the past month.

Marina is shyer, and I'm shy with her, so though we talked a little about having a meeting of women after the kids' piñata-fest (which has been indefinitely postponed thanks to a torrential downpour), mostly I've watched her prepare food and go about other tasks. (Don Sebastián just handed Sue and me about five bananas each from an enormous bunch that he's got in a sack on one side of the shelter—Marina says we'll take some down to the others when we go for the piñata.) In many ways they have a comfortable-looking domestic economy—if you like year-round camping, and if it weren't for the contra terror. The shelter is one good-sized room with three beds. Walls are tarps; roofs, zinc; floor, dirt. [Efforts to add permanent walls and other amenities had been postponed, we were told, because of the difficulty of getting construction workers to come to such a dangerous area.] There's a clay stove/oven under the roof's overhang, a wood work surface and some benches. There's a sleek cat who likes to sleep on the edge of the stove, a thin dog and some magnificent chickens which give nice little eggs. (Sebastián wanted to know if the chickens were bigger in the United States.)

In the morning Marina makes tortillas, first grinding the maize in a large meat-grinder type thing which is also in use in the barracks kitchen below. Food is beans, sometimes made like refritos; tortillas; eggs; the sweet black coffee which is ubiquitous in the *campo*; bananas. At least that's what I've seen so far. Though Marina and Sebastián have enough to share, that isn't true of many families, according to Sarah.

The Polaroid photographs were a grand and uncontrollable success. I started taking pictures of the piñata and was immediately mobbed—adults and kids alike, "¡Tome una fóto, tome una fóto de mí solita!" (As I write this Marina's oldest boy is insisting on holding my flashlight [due to a scarcity of batteries, flashlights were little used in Patio Grande] while the youngest "chigüín" watches in fascination the movements of the pen—Marina inside the shelter, Sebastián out for the night's guard duty. The murmur from neighboring households, chirring of crickets—a few minutes back a rifle shot from an "undisciplined" citizen.) It's terrible—is that the right word—sobering and moving—to see how every little thing fascinates these kids: the slide show and filmstrip made possible by the portable generator Sarah brought, Susan's song about the animals, the swings, the piñata this afternoon—from which each child received something like one balloon and one piece of candy. In the United States everybody would be bored and complaining—poor kids included—under fancier circumstances.

Funny to have a "women's meeting" here, with lots of men strolling around. We did it right after the piñata, before people could disperse. I presented the scrapbook, and a woman from one of the brigades held it up and read from it—she must be one of the women who's worked with AMNLAE [the acronym for the national women's organization, Asociación de Mujeres Nicaragüenses Luisa Amanda Espinosa] that Sarah spoke about. It was awkward, I felt

incredibly responsible and as though *I* should have been listening to
them rather than the other way around. I gave the Spanish *Our Bod-
ies, Ourselves* to Gregoria (one of the nurses) and Tom said he found
her and Fátima poring over a picture of a fornicating couple an hour
or two later when he stopped by the pharmacy; they looked embar-
rassed when they saw him. The sewing things I handed to Doña
Estelvina, along with—at the end—the materials we'd brought for
their scrapbook. There were too many things for the latter, and it
created a minor community crisis. Inez, the president of the farm
co-op, who'd been standing on the sidelines, immediately came and
collected the supplies. He said that the "junta"—governing body of
the co-op, I guess—is going to have to meet to decide how to share
them out after the scrapbook is completed. I could appreciate the
point, especially after seeing the scramble over the Polaroids.

Some of the women with young babies sat very quietly through
the meeting. Doña Estelvina had to work to make them think of
things that were needed for the childcare center [which we had
agreed would be the project the Women's Committee would try to
support; the building already existed and only equipment was
needed]. I felt she was consciously trying to educate them in more
active participation.

Inez came and talked to me in the morning. He was waiting when I
came out of the shelter, pounced on me just as Marina handed me a
glass of coffee and one of those hard white slightly sweet things they
serve with it. "Good afternoon," he said, with gentle sarcasm—this
because he'd tried to get to talk to me the previous evening, and now
the morning was wearing on. He spoke about the importance of our
coming to a place like Patio Grande as opposed to staying in the
larger cities—there he said you meet the bourgeoisie and middle
class, but out here you see the people who really understand what
the revolution is about. If we'd come before the Triumph we would
have seen obvious evidence of malnutrition in the children, for instance. Things really have improved measurably.

Doña Estelvina turns out to be one of the two Frente militants in
Patio Grande (this, as I understand it, being the highest grade of
membership in the FSLN, the Sandinista organization). There are
two brigades here right now, one of families who are considering
relocating here, another a cultural/political brigade assigned for
four months, I believe Amparo said—she's the woman who held the
scrapbook at the women's meeting. Her name means "protection."

Sarah told me she's supposed to be doing some kind of women's organizing while she's here. This morning she mentioned that she's a teacher, and that, yes, she's a bit afraid, especially at night. "One thinks of one's children"—she's the sole parent, divorced. A sister cares for her kids while she's here in Patio Grande.

Sebastián and Inez explained to me that they're planning to visit neighboring communities to raise political consciousness; some of the settlements along the river, particularly, are giving a good deal of support to the contra. They'll attempt as well to organize more economic cooperation. The incredible strategic importance—in a social not military sense, I mean—of Patio Grande and places like it has become clearer throughout our stay. The contra can be defeated militarily, but the only way to take back the land on a permanent basis is to settle families there. El Paraíso, visible from Patio Grande, had been attacked recently—no deaths but many buildings burned, folks left without so much as a change of clothing. It's a basically apolitical community with a religious orientation. The people there were unarmed but it didn't prevent an attack.

Sebastián hugged me so warmly when we left, and we kept holding hands till I was afraid it looked weird. But then Marina embraced me so lovingly, and burst into tears, and kissed me on the lips. Very very sweet. I said I'd write to them through Sarah.

As I reread my diary entries from the trip and review the memories they trigger, several impressions stand out. One is the sense that our delegation's presence, however brief, really did make a difference to people in Patio Grande. To whatever extent this was true, it certainly wasn't because of any exceptional qualities or behavior on our part. Rather, it was because people in Patio Grande were fighting for their lives and their future on such a basic level and with so few resources at their disposal that help in *any* form was welcome. They clearly felt so isolated at the time of our arrival that it was meaningful to them that we would care enough to come, to spend time with them and hear what they had to say and go home to talk about it in the country that was making war on them. I have encountered a somewhat similar attitude among women in prison who felt themselves completely forgotten by the world, a receptivity and gratitude that surpass my comprehension.

At one point I remember Sebastián saying words to the effect that, "Because you people cared enough to come here to visit us, it makes us feel we also must do something for ourselves." Acutely aware as I was in that moment of the fact that our effort was completely insignificant compared to the sacrifices made on a daily basis by every Patio Grande resident, the remark also brought home to me how miserably discouraged, sapped of strength, terrorized, the community must have felt in the wake of the April 9 contra attack. It seems to me a great gift, this generosity of spirit that could accept our sometimes clumsy gestures of solidarity without apparent bitterness—even given who we were. Yet it's an attitude that North Americans have encountered all over Nicaragua. I think it is a tremendously hopeful sign for the future of relations between North and South—though I can't help but anticipate that there will come a time for speaking much bitterness as well.

Another important lesson of the trip, and one with implications for the work of the Women's Committee, had to do with the major differences between the campesino society of San Juan–Patio Grande and the relatively urbanized world of Managua, Estelí, and Nicaragua's other cities (never mind that in the latter goats graze freely on vacant land and dawn is a chorus of roosters). Brooklyn's sister "city" is so isolated that when I tried to explain that borough's location by mentioning that it was part of New York, I wasn't sure whether my listener understood that New York was a major metropolis, let alone where in the United States it was located. I was asked, for instance, whether our delegation included any campesinos. (Now that I think of it, I'm not sure why it should have surprised me that rural Nicaraguans could be as limited and provincial in their worldview as North Americans typically are!) I recall telling Sebastián that our group had attended the opening rally of the *repliegue,* the ritual re-enactment of the "strategic retreat" from Managua to Masaya which preceded the July 19 Triumph of the Sandinista revolution in 1979. Sebastián, with a faraway look, remembered that, yes, he'd read something about it in a copy of *Barricada.* It dawned on me that this public celebration, which had been the talk of Managua, might seem almost as distant from his point of view as if it had happened in Mexico City or Miami.

Within this campesino society, women's roles are far more traditionally defined and clearly distinguished from men's than in the cities and larger towns. We could observe that gap in Patio Grande itself, as reflected in the behavior of women from different backgrounds. Amparo, the teacher who was visiting with the political and cultural brigade, wore pants. Like most of the men in the settlement, she carried a rifle for defense. The unarmed campesinas almost all wore skirts—and perhaps partly for that reason shied away from a volleyball game with the net and ball we'd brought, though the men played very enthusiastically. About half the women in Patio Grande are farm co-op members, which means they do work for which they are paid and also receive a share in the co-op's earnings. According to Sarah, many who don't join refrain in compliance with their husbands' wishes, or because they don't want to leave their children. In contrast to the more egalitarian practice in some parts of Nicaragua, female co-op members are exempted from the defense patrols which are the duty of all male members. The co-op's officers are men.

This certainly doesn't mean a total absence of women's leadership. Marina took an active role in bringing together our women's meeting. In the months since our visit, she's been put in charge of social welfare in the community, and has been instrumental in setting up a daycare project, which is now a going concern though reportedly with almost as many workers as kids, since mothers still aren't used to the idea. However, we didn't find in Patio Grande the radical challenge to patriarchal tradition which began with Nicaraguan women's historic role in the struggle against Somoza, and continues to be pressed by AMNLAE.[4] (As a matter of fact, in San Juan we were introduced to the local AMNLAE representative only as an afterthought.) It was in Managua that we were privileged to hear a fascinating talk by Amalia Dixon, a Miskito Indian woman who plays an important role in implementing the Autonomy Plan for the Atlantic Coast region. It was in Estelí that we met with a nurse-midwife in that city's Centro de Parto Natural (natural birth center) who described a woman-centered reproductive health education program. She spoke frankly about contraception and sex education, and proudly reminded us that the right of women to take time off from work to breast-feed is guaranteed in Nicaragua's constitution. Also in Estelí, we met with Georgina Cordón, an official in charge of foreign contributions to the region, who smiled when I spoke of the problems we'd had in getting to talk to women. Nicaragua, she said, had made important strides in overcoming machismo, but still had a long ways to go.

As Georgina's comment underscored, women's liberation is not simply a bee in the bonnet of die-hard North American feminists. It is an issue deeply embedded in the everyday life of revolutionary Nicaragua, where it is commonly conceptualized in terms of increasing "women's participation" in the social process. The differences and points of overlap between North American and Nicaraguan formulations of the "woman question" potentially form an important subject for dialogue, a dialogue contingent on the fact that feminist concerns emerge within and are validated by North American solidarity organizations.[5] Given the social dynamics of campesino society, in the absence of an active Women's Committee, a Brooklyn delegation might have spent almost all its time in San Juan and Patio Grande hobnobbing with the male leadership, and received a very partial picture of life there.

I felt I absorbed weeks' worth of experience in that brief time we spent in the mountains above the Coco River. Six months have now gone by, yet in the rush of my Brooklyn life there's been too little time to reflect, to let lessons sink in, or even to be clear about the questions. When I realize this, I have to ask myself about the effect of my society's habits of haste upon its social change movements. What do we forfeit in depth of understanding and solidity of practice because of our North American lack of patience, our penchant for doing fifteen things at once, our typical issue-of-the-week approach? We may not watch TV, or accept its slant on the news if we do, but our conception of events is inevitably to some degree conditioned by the pace and superficiality of the medium. And even under the best of circumstances, a dialogue between Nicaraguans and North Americans about liberating women would have to be slow in developing, probably even slower than most other aspects of the concrete relationship between communities that sister city projects seek to foster.

And there's always the war to contend with, which means that circumstances could hardly be worse. On October 4, 1987, the contra once again targeted Patio Grande. Six civilians from the settlement, two children included, were killed, and another eight were injured in the ambush of a truck which had delivered building supplies and was returning to San Juan with a full passenger load. ("We all know we could leave for San Juan any day and never come back," Inez had told me as we sat in the morning air sipping strong sweet coffee.)

As I write this in December 1987, Sarah has come to Brooklyn for a visit. She'd meant to bring with her the scrapbook that women in Patio Grande recently completed for us. However, because of the tense military situation—worse in the recent weeks since the end of the Sandinistas' unilaterally declared ceasefire than in any previous time during her three years in the area, she says—it seemed too risky for her to make the short trip up to the settlement before her departure. The scrapbook is now supposed to come with a co-worker of hers, a woman named Modesta, who will be arriving next month as part of the first San Juan delegation to visit Brooklyn. The Women's Committee looks forward to that visit as a major opportunity to educate both ourselves and others about women in our sister city.

Meanwhile, we're concerned about some issues internal to the Brooklyn project. Although at one time the Women's Committee operated in relative isolation from the larger organization, over the past half year we've made a conscientious effort to send committee representatives to general meetings, both to explain our work and so that we can better understand and participate in the group's decision-making process. Despite this, and despite some valuable support from a few individuals, the Women's Committee is often treated as though its membership and agenda were peripheral to the project. Frequently in general meetings we seem to have to speak up louder and oftener than anyone else present to avoid having our committee's existence ignored entirely.

Recently, when we held a women-only dance as a fundraiser for Patio Grande's daycare project, only one or two Brooklyn project members not affiliated with the Women's Committee bothered to attend. Was homophobia an issue here? Hard to think not. Was it an issue last year when we sponsored a reading by lesbian-feminist Rebecca Gordon from her just-published *Letters from Nicaragua*, an event open to both men and women, and only two men showed up? If so, it's hard to gauge to what extent, since lesbian and gay issues have almost never been openly discussed among the general membership. (Incidentally, by no means all of the Women's Committee members are lesbians—which of course wouldn't necessarily prevent our being viewed as a "dyke outfit.") Within the Women's Committee we've begun to consider initiating a project-wide discussion concerning the importance of our work. But it sounds like a major undertaking, and so far we've opted to concentrate our limited resources on efforts more directly related to the needs of our sister city.

Experiences like these, coupled with recent contacts with very young women who profess to feel so unconstrained that they have no need for feminism, have persuaded me that the cause of women's liberation des-

perately needs some sort of "back to basics" movement. (Whether the
time is ripe for this to have much immediate impact is another question,
one I'm afraid I answered pessimistically early on in this essay.) We need
to remind the world at large, and particularly women who've come of age
in the so-called post-feminist era, that (A) women are *still* oppressed and
in need of liberation; (B) women working together must be at the heart of
that process.

Which doesn't mean turning back the clock. In reviving some of that
"old-time religion," the surprise and outrage that come with recognizing
women's universal second-class status, we can't afford to forget how very
broad the range of female experience is, how various our oppression and
relative privilege, how important our home cultures. Nor can we afford
to short-circuit the impulse that would send us moving out, across
borders, toward other tongues or continents, other people's liberation
struggles—whose lessons for us will often but not always have to do with
freeing women.

Evidently, we have to do everything at once. Is there then, somewhere
down the road, a synthesis of what Audre Lorde with weary, tart humor
once designated "all these liberations" ("Who Said," 50)? I don't know,
but I think a step in that direction would be increased public dialogue
among feminists who are part of the "moving out" process. Ideally, I
think this should involve all of us who are in some way working outside
traditionally defined feminist groups. In terms of my own concerns, I'd
definitely like to see an initial discussion among feminists and lesbians
involved in Central America work. There are so many of us by now,
working in such a variety of settings, that we already have a great deal to
talk about. One question to start with might be what effect this choice of
work is having on relations between Third World and white feminists.
I've mentioned criticisms by Latinas of Central America work engaged in
by white women; I've noticed for myself that doing this work brings me
into much less contact with Third World feminists than some of the
work I did in the women's movement; and I think it would be important
to examine whether, in some cases, white North Americans may be connecting with Central American sisters at the expense of working with/
supporting Latinas and other feminists of color who are their next-door
neighbors.

That question is important to me especially because what I want out of
the revolution I've been describing is not a "global feminism," to use the

current phrase. That sounds to me too much like a sisterhood in orbit, a women's movement whose native habitat is the airport concourse or Sheraton conference center. Rather, I want something homegrown, slow, solid, rooted and ripened on the local level, yet flexible and daring enough to reach out to touch the world.

Until that synthesis arrives, I'll be juggling the pieces. And holding on to a glimpse here and there of what might be possible: a roughly lettered sign of welcome in the mud of Patio Grande invoking "eternal bonds that will unite us to the end"; that day, like a longed-for meeting in a dream, when we built a playground in the middle of a war.

NOTES

1. Recent books which reflect this trend include Rebecca Gordon's *Letters from Nicaragua*, Judith McDaniel's *Sanctuary: A Journey*, and Mab Segrest's *My Mama's Dead Squirrel: Lesbian Essays on Southern Culture.*

2. See Rebecca Gordon's "Five Years Later—Are We Ready for Rainbow Feminism?" *Lesbian Contradiction: A Journal of Irreverent Feminism* 21 (Winter 1988): 5. Gordon asks, "Where are all the feminists?" and considers both positive and negative reasons why so many feminists are now involved in solidarity work. She comes to a rather optimistic conclusion about the near-term prospects for a revitalization of the U.S. feminist movement as such.

3. These books—by Cherríe Moraga and Gloria Anzaldúa, eds.; Barbara Smith, ed.; Elly Bulkin, Minnie Bruce Pratt, and Barbara Smith; Cherríe Moraga; Rebecca Gordon; Audre Lorde; Juanita Ramos, ed.; Judith McDaniel; Gloria Anzaldúa; and Elly Bulkin, ed., respectively—may be hard to locate. See the "Works Cited" and "Small Press Addresses" sections at the end of this book for bibliographic and ordering information.

4. For an account of recent debate on women's issues in the context of AMNLAE's tenth anniversary celebration, see Margaret Power's "Decade-Old Women's Group Keeps Heat On," *The Guardian* (9 December 1987): 14.

5. There are, of couse, a number of all-women solidarity groups, of which New York–based MADRE is perhaps the most widely known. Most of them, however, have not to my knowledge explored in any great depth (at least publicly) the feminist implications of this type of work, beyond articulating the general idea that women as women have something in common that transcends national boundaries.

V
MENDING THE SILENCES

In the introduction to this book, I expressed my conviction that words are not enough, that the work of the writer needs to be balanced by the work of the activist. But action is only the first of language's boundaries. In the following remarks I explore the second, silence. There is a time to pause before the wide expanse of all we cannot know, accomplish, articulate; to enter the wordless place of cessation and beginning.

Mending the Silences:
New Directions for Feminist Poetry*

Good evening. I wanted to start out this evening with a slight qualification. When I was asked to do this talk about six months ago, I knew that I wanted to speak about something that I would call "Mending the Silences," and I had some ideas about what that meant but I thought I'd better add a slightly more responsible-sounding subtitle. So I came up with "New Directions for Feminist Poetry." And I will be talking about that a bit, but I don't mean to sound either comprehensively descriptive or prescriptive. Most of what I'm going to say is going to be, I think, a lot more speculative than that. For some reasons that I'll be talking about later, I'm not even sure that it's possible to have an overview of feminist poetry at this point.

My central interest tonight is going to be this question of poetry and silence, but more specifically, what are the implications of silence for the political poet? I'm somebody who's always looking for what I call a "unified field theory" of art and politics: that place somewhere a few feet down or a few yards down or a few miles down beneath our feet—if we could only dig deep enough—where the apparent contradictions between the issues that come up in a political movement and poetic questions, aesthetic questions, effortlessly dissolve.

So I guess I should say that anybody here tonight who assumes that art and politics are fundamentally contradictory will probably be a bit unnerved at my assumptions. As might anybody who thinks that there's no problem at all, no tension or contradiction. For me there's always some

*Talk delivered at the St. Mark's Poetry Project, New York City, February 25, 1987.

215

kind of contradiction and at the same time always a very intimate relationship that I'm always worrying at and worrying over, trying to pick
apart.

I'm going to start out tonight by trying to remember a little bit of the
atmosphere in the heyday of the feminist poetry movement, somewhere
back there in the 1970s. And I'm going to do that both because I think
that a lot of the poetry that feminists wrote in that period was tremendously important for its own sake, and because I see the feminist poetry
movement as a very interesting paradigm of some of the things that
happen when poetry and politics come together in the explosive way that
they sometimes do in the heat of a political movement.

Later, I'm going to be talking a little about someone whose poetry has
come to mean a lot to me over the past year: Lorine Niedecker, the Wisconsin poet who died in 1970, and whose work is just now being
reissued. Reading it has been the immediate catalyst for a lot of the thinking about poetry and silence that I'm going to be sharing. And then I'm
going to talk about mending the silences, raising some questions about
what silence is. What is the relationship of silence to poetry and specifically to political poetry? What are the politics of access to silence in the
contemporary urban world, and perhaps the contemporary world in
general? And I'll be wondering a bit whether women because of our particular experiences may sometimes have a special relationship to silence
that has implications for our poetry.

So, feminist poetry: breaking the silences.

When I was working on this talk, I had a growing sense that I could
only speak about feminist poetry in the past tense, and this really alarmed
me a lot because I am a feminist, I am a poet. A lot of women that I know
are feminists and poets. And many of the feminist poets who were active
from the late sixties to the early eighties are still writing and publishing.
And certainly the issues of the feminist movement have not gone away.
They've perhaps slightly altered, perhaps slightly intensified in some
cases, but they're certainly still there.

Nevertheless, I have a very definite sense of a scattering of women who
are feminists to many different places, many different personal and political involvements. A hundred flowers are blooming, so to speak, and
some of them have explicitly to do with what might be called women's
issues and some don't, though I think for feminist poets who lived

through that period the impact is often there in a lot of subtle ways, as well as more obvious ones.

"Breaking the silences" was of course a central metaphor of the feminist poetry movement, and continues to be so for feminist activists addressing many different issues, to the point where the phrase has become, for me at least, a rather grating cliché. Whenever I see an article with that title, or a book with that title—even books are still being titled that or subtitled that!—I reflexively cringe. And yet what that was all about, I think, was something tremendously important, and still is something tremendously important.

One thing that I did in trying to remember what all the breaking silences rhetoric was about was to go back and reread my essay "A Movement of Poets." And when I did that I found out how much I'd forgotten, myself, about what it was like to be living at a time, in a place where women's poetry was incredibly alive to the women who were involved with it, in a way that I think was only possible because of the existence of a sort of critical mass of people bouncing off each other in their work and their thinking and their activism.

Part of what was remarkable about that time was not only the way that feminist political concerns showed up overtly in the poetry, but also the way that poets showed up in the activist movement at meetings and demonstrations—and the kind of influence that they sometimes wielded there. Certainly this was not completely unprecedented; there had been the experience of the movement against the Vietnam War, and the Black Power movement, and the role of activist poets in those settings was in part a forerunner of what happened with feminism. But I think that what you had in the women's movement was a very unique fusion where large numbers of women felt that writing poetry was an important form of expression. Without the movement much of the poetry that was written during that time by women could not have been written and certainly couldn't have been published; but also without its poets the movement would have been something quite different.

I think a lot of poets at that time had a sense not only of breaking silences about personal experience but of speaking for women as a group, and for many, many silent, oppressed generations. Again, this is something that a lot of political literature does. It tries to give a voice to people who've been silent. I think at times there was almost a sense of a kind of collective pressure of silenced generations, with the poet as medium for those generations of women to express themselves.

I think for instance of Judy Grahn's "Common Woman" poems and "She Who" poems that create a sort of Unknown Soldier of a woman protagonist, and of June Jordan's stunning 1972 poem "Gettin Down to Get Over," which begins with a barrage of images of the Black woman:

> MOMMA MOMMA MOMMA
> momma momma
> *mammy*
> nanny
> granny
> woman
> mistress
> sista ("Gettin Down," 27)

and ends

> momma
> help me
> turn the face of history
> *to your face.* ("Gettin Down," 37)

And I think that many women poets coming out of a range of backgrounds and identities were trying to do some version of this: "help me turn the face of history *to your face*."

So there was a sense of speaking both from a collective and to a collective, which was incredibly liberating in the beginning and sometimes continued to be so, and also eventually became limiting when it got codified and ritualized. There was a power in the raw need to speak that shows up in the early work, when it wasn't a question of speaking out of any theoretical political idea of what you should be saying, nor speaking with an expectation that even a small audience would automatically welcome your words, but simply: you had to say this.

So the silences were not simply about being a woman—female experience in some generalized sense—but about more specific aspects of identity and oppression. June Jordan in that poem and much of the rest of her work was writing about Black female experience; Grahn frequently about the experience of white working-class lesbians. As the seventies went on, there was increasing visibility and importance of lesbian poets, both white and Third World; Third World women poets both lesbian and straight. And I think oftentimes there was a remarkable sense of the importance of diversity, at least some effort to encourage that.

And poetry really was a living force in women's lives. An experience that happened to me fairly recently, really, I see as a sort of holdover from that period and it simply astonishes me; I can hardly believe it happened. I was violently attacked when I was jogging near Prospect Park in Brooklyn, by a man who dragged me into the park and started choking me, and I was struggling and as all this was going on, I heard in my head lines from the Susan Griffin poem "Breviary," lines which go, "She fought / him off and she lived" (118). It's about a woman who's attacked by a man who stabs her repeatedly, and there's this line, "She fought / him off and she lived." And I'm not saying I was struggling in that situation *because* that poem came to me, but I thought afterwards, you know, in fact I did struggle and the man did run away. And that poem was there. And it was a fascinating example to me of how something can get embedded in your consciousness, how poetry might be there working under the surface in all kinds of situations you would never anticipate. I wonder what if I'd only had Yeats's poem that goes, "Did she put on his knowledge with his power / Before the indifferent beak could let her drop?" to fall back on (212).

And I'm somebody who inveighs against the idea that poetry is useful. But since this experience I'm willing to concede that it may in fact be useful on occasion. Maybe we simply can't *count* on it to be useful. We don't know when it will be.

So there was a raw need in a lot of this poetry, and we still see that. I think of Cherríe Moraga's recent poetic play *Giving Up the Ghost* that has the line, "I'm only telling you this to stay my hand" (3). I think a lot of feminist poetry is like that.

So if this is where feminist poets were coming from, no wonder that few of them were interested in investigating the positive qualities of silence. And in fact, silence became the movement's favorite metaphor for powerlessness, the kind of repression that results when we're forbidden even to attach words to our experience. No wonder verbal expression seemed to be synonymous with liberation—again, as it frequently has been in other political movements.

So time passed, and the original explosive force of feminist poetry began to dissipate. We saw the development of a tacit orthodoxy which I tried to analyze in "A Movement of Poets," certain assumptions about what male poetry had done, or what reactionary or patriarchal or elitist poetry had done, and that whatever that was we were going to do the opposite. And sometimes that really limited poets in what we felt able to write.

At the same time, a large sector of what had been an activist movment was narrowing its focus, turning in on itself with the development of cultural feminism and lesbian separatism. There was less of a sense of a dynamic movement that's going to go out there and change injustices in the world, and more an almost defeatist sense that it's simply too impossible out there, we can't hope to change it. And we'd better have what we can for ourselves off in this corner over here.

Concurrently, feminist poetry became more professionalized in the sense that there were a lot fewer open readings, a lot fewer crummy-looking stencilled or mimeographed periodicals and so on, which again is a kind of two-edged development. We all want books that look good and don't have typos in them, but I think there was an energy that we lost in that process.

And another thing happened that I was discussing with someone in the audience before this event started tonight. What I found myself saying was that I realized I don't have one relationship with a friend where poetry is the central thing that connects us, or even something we regularly talk about. I think that a lot of feminist poets just got so absorbed with political work or cultural activism, being publishers, a whole range of different commitments—and political movements and social networks, especially of the sort that you find among New York feminists, are tremendously noisy, busy affairs. I think that for many of us the poetry got drowned out, or it had to go underground and occupy a secret corner of our lives.

At the same time, a lot of exciting things are continuing to happen among feminists who are poets, and among women poets who in some way have been influenced by feminism. The exploration of identity that the women's movement at its best tried to encourage has had an impact on poetry, and by that I mean identity in terms of cultural, racial, ethnic, class issues, and other issues as well. An experimentation with language goes along with that, languages of origin, languages of background. You find poets using Spanish, Yiddish, Chinese. And women doing "experimental" writing in the more usual sense as well; there's a periodical called

HOW(ever) published in California that serves as a newsletter for women working along these lines.

I find there's an increasing sense of internationalism. I think of Kitchen Table: Women of Color Press's publication of a book by Mila Aguilar, *A Comrade Is as Precious as a Rice Seedling.* (Aguilar, a Filipina, was one of the first political prisoners to be released after Corazón Aquino came to power.) I think of Granite Press's *Ixok Amar.go*, an anthology of poetry by Central American women; the Art Against Apartheid issue of *Ikon* magazine; two international focus issues of *Conditions*—and the list could go on.

But at the same time, I personally—probably along with a lot of other feminist poets—at some point stopped feeling that feminist poetry could be, as it were, an all-weather home; that it was unnecessary to go out and read any of those people from the past, or poets who were not feminists, or writers coming from radically different places. I know I began to feel very claustrophobic and very bored, really, with feminist poetry—heretical as that sounds. And I don't mean to deny the real excitement that I also found with some of that work.

So I started going around looking for the letter in the bottle, the poems that would come from a totally unexpected place, the writer that I might not anticipate having much in common with, but who would turn out to give me something that I needed. Somewhere I was hoping to find poems that could do that miraculous and unnerving thing that poetry sometimes does, give me the image that would flash out at me, or the line that would hook my unconscious before my conscious mind had time to figure out what it meant in a logical or rational sense.

And a lot of different poets have done that for me, from some of the Eastern Europeans to poets like Central American Claribel Alegría, or a poet like Joy Harjo. But my most recent enthusiasm of this sort has been the poetry of Lorine Niedecker.

A little while ago I wrote in a review of Niedecker's work that her poetry takes me back 15 or 20 years to when I first developed the heady notion that poetry might teach us how to live. I was first attracted to that work while standing in a bookstore where I happened to glance at a copy of *The Granite Pail*, a volume edited by Cid Corman and published by North Point Press. Every element of the book jacket signaled to me that there might be something important going on here, both in a feminist sense and a poetic sense. Here was this small, bird-like woman in a dark coat standing in the snow, wearing 1960s pointy-rimmed glasses, and the bio note said that she had lived in rural Wisconsin all her life, and had cleaned floors in the local hospital, and then there were a series of quotes from various male admirers who were all well-known poets and publishers of the fifties and sixties, all very patronizingly calling her a "poetess" or doing some version of those little pats on the head that used to be the lot of women writers in that period. And my first reaction was, god, it must have been hard to be that woman in that scene and how did she manage? And this woman looks like she could have been my grandmother. And I want to read this book.

Her poetry is very fruitfully, very resolutely rooted in a single place, the Lake Koshkonong area in Wisconsin where she lived most of her life from her birth in 1903 till her death in 1970. Her German-American father was a fisherman there, and he left her a modest property when he died in the early 1950s. Niedecker came of a generation and of a class of Midwesterners for whom hard work and frugality were central values, people to whom the everyday workings of nature commonly seemed much more vivid and real than the cultural and political pursuits of educated people back East. I base that description on some firsthand knowledge because, though I'm a couple of generations after Niedecker, I come from people like that too.

It was not a community that expected to spawn poets, or would have known what to do with one if Niedecker had proclaimed herself locally, which she didn't. She was a college dropout, worked as a proofreader, had a series of odd jobs, never traveled much—not out of the country, except to Canada. But she practiced an exquisite economy of experience and might have paraphrased Thoreau's, "I have traveled much in Concord" by saying, "I have traveled much on Blackhawk Island."

Her literary contacts came mostly through the mail, and at least in her later life they were almost entirely *with* males; it's quite striking to read her letters to Cid Corman and discover that nearly every reference is to some male poet that she was reading or corresponding with. And yet female and even feminist concerns surface consistently in her work, alongside expressions of intense absorption in her natural environment. Her poems are full of her involvement with the philosophical implications of that environment and her continual musings on personal, collective, and natural history. "Nobody, nothing/ever gave me/greater thing/than time/unless light/and silence/which if intense/makes sound," she wrote in a late poem, "Wintergreen Ridge" (*Granite Pail*, 82).

Her work has given me back a profoundly healing sense of the meditative, contemplative possibilities of poetry, something that for all of its energy and all of its cleansing anger and all of its revelations I think I've sorely missed in the feminist poets I basically grew up on. Niedecker mentions silence occasionally in her poems, more frequently in her letters. But more important, her work welcomes silence and seems to be grounded in it. We understand the quality of light by what it reveals, and just so I think we may infer the depth of silence by what it allows us to hear.

Certainly Niedecker's feeling about silence is connected to her sense of the primacy of nature, and that's something I've been missing terribly while I've been wandering through all these political thickets. I've had a nagging sense, never verbalized, that both silence and nature are luxuries the engaged poet ought to get used to doing without, and my passionate response to Niedecker's poetry has helped me to turn around and ask myself just what my self-denial accomplished.

I don't think this is simply a question of "political correctness." I think there's also a very deeply rooted defensive reaction involved here: the reaction of somebody who grew up in the Pacific Northwest and saw the trees continually being cut down around her and the highways being built, and sort of watched it all go, and began unconsciously to attempt to divest herself of an attachment to the natural world and perhaps to certain other things that it appeared future generations of humans might have to do without.

Niedecker's work has had its effect on me despite her own unfavorable conclusions about the effect of politics and especially any kind of activism on poetry. (These are conclusions that she reached in her later life; in her youth she apparently espoused some form of socialism.) She leaves me with a feeling that any theory of political art somehow has to enlarge itself to acknowledge the relevance of work like hers; and at the same time with a renewed sense of the real contradictions between activism and contemplation.

*

Working on this talk, thinking about letting more silence into poetry and finding more silence in my life, naturally has led me to explore the question of what is silence, and of course I'm finding it a bit more complicated than it appeared at first glance. We started out with the feminist metaphor of silence as repression, either political repression or psychological repression. Adrienne Rich develops an interesting version of this in her quite well-known poem "Cartographies of Silence" from *The Dream of a Common Language* (16–20). In that poem, silence is imposed from within. She calls it "the blueprint to a life." It's a kind of avoidance or lie. Interestingly enough, she alludes to the positive potential of silence in terms of visual imagery, which she refers to as "the pure annunciations to the eye." But she seems to regard the choice of language as the medium of expression to be a choice against silence, as though the two were incapable of complementing and enhancing one another.

But the silence of avoidance is only one of many silences. Think of the overpowering silence of nature, which at one extreme shades into nothingness. This is a description from the novel *Giants in the Earth* by O. E. Rölvaag of a Norwegian woman's experience of the silence of the prairies when she arrived in this country some time in the 1870s:

> The infinitude surrounding her on every hand might not have been so oppressive, might even have brought her a measure of peace, if it had not been for the deep silence, which lay heavier here than in a church. Indeed, what was there to break it? She had passed beyond the outposts of civilization; the nearest dwelling places of men were far away. Here no warbling of birds rose on the air, no buzzing of insects sounded . . . the waving blades of grass that trembled to the faintest breath now stood erect and quiet, as if listening, in the great hush of the evening. . . . All along the way, coming out, she had noticed this strange thing: the stillness had grown deeper, the silence more depressing, the farther west they journeyed; it must have been over two weeks now since she had heard a bird sing! Had they travelled into some nameless, abandoned region? Could no living thing exist out here, in the empty, desolate, endless wastes of green and blue? How *could* existence go on, she thought, desperately? If life is to thrive and endure, it must at least have something to hide behind! . . . (37)

This kind of silence, I would suggest, is something that human beings still experience from time to time in the late 1980s, somewhere on earth. But it seems to me that in general it becomes more difficult as the decades pass for most of us even to comprehend the threat this woman experienced. In our era (and certainly in the U.S.), it's really the social noise

and the barrage of information, I believe, that for the majority have become far more overwhelming and threatening than silence—though perhaps we might fear the silence of nuclear winter as a kind of futuristic
analog to the silence of the prairie.

The novelist Eli Wiesel, whose testimony on the Holocaust has been
important to so many readers, has something else to say about the possibilities of silence in literature in this quote from a recent interview. (I find
it very interesting, by the way, that somebody whose work might be characterized as a kind of speaking out also seems to be so fascinated by the
communicative possibilities of silence.) Wiesel says:

> I am fighting words with silence, I am fighting silence with words,
> and hopefully one day I would be able to fight silence with silence,
> but then that would be the end of literature. I tell stories to escape an
> irreducible silence. Some experiences lie beyond language because
> their language is silence. Silence does not necessarily mean an ab-
> sence of communication. Imagine a great dancer motionless, for one
> hour, on stage; imagine a gifted painter staring intently, for one day,
> at the white canvas. This is the evocative descriptive silence of the
> artist. If you use silence, you are no longer silent. There is a mystical
> concept meaning talking less or using less words, surrounding words
> with silence or introducing silence in to the word. You can introduce
> silence into a word by waiting before the word comes to life so that it
> carries its own silence. (Cooper-Clark, 183–84)

And finally, Lorine Niedecker makes the following remarks in her letters to Cid Corman. In one place she writes:

> I wrote to LZ of the quiet and he wrote: "Cid at his quietest is the
> most *steadily* passionate of the young". . . . He cites your *hello* in
> Quarry Sunday and I cite "each man an empire when he enters / a
> silence." [That quote being from a poem of Corman's.] Passion in
> sound, noise . . . however, isn't it closer to art when it's still
> enough (deep enough) to become ice? (Faranda, 38)

Elsewhere she observes:

> Been carrying on a correspondence with Eshelman. Mostly at his
> behest—technique, why I don't write differently, why he doesn't.
> I'm no good at it—I write from notes, which seem to always stay
> notes, grocery lists. I throw up my arms and scream: Write—cut it
> and just write poems. I tell him why set fire to page after page, why
> not arrest it at moments into quiet, enduring love. . . . Also that

there is such a thing as silence—and the great, everpresent possibility that our poems may not get read. Art is cooler than he thinks.
(153)

I find that last, especially, suggests a certain humility: "The great, ever-
present possibility that our poems may not get read" evokes the final
silence of death which all our works return to.

I started to play a little game in word association, and it went something like this: Silence-rest / sound-work. Silence-stillness / sound-
motion. Silence-eternal / sound-temporal. Silence-death / sound-life.
Silence-depth / sound-surface. Silence-solitude / sound-society. Silence-
nature / sound-culture. Silence-useless / sound-useful. Silence-aesthet-
ics / sound-politics. Silence-the unconscious / sound-consciousness. Si-
lence-nothingness / sound-being. Silence-poetry / sound-prose.

Now obviously this could quickly get absurd, and I don't mean to
belabor it, but I'd like to consider the last item for a minute, the notion
that I have that poetry as a literary form is closest to silence. (I should say
that I'm about to make some gross generalizations, since without doing so
it's almost impossible to discuss a subject as vast as the difference between poetry and prose.)

It seems to me that the fiction writer typically creates and populates a
possible or alternative universe, almost as though she were trying to give
herself company in this world. She plays God in a sense, which is a role
that has a loneliness all its own; but that loneliness is very different from
the loneliness of the poet's naked, stripped-down consciousness that
roves through the world. Fiction's slower and more ponderous patterns
are not very much like the lightning connections of poetry, which are
capable of leaps that are like the connections that are made between syn-
apses in a brain. And I think that the fiction writer's populated, alternative universe has a better chance of competing with the noisy social world
in which it's likely to be read than poetry does. The solitude of the poet in
the poem places her much closer to silence, and gives her the opportunity
at least occasionally to "enter a silence," as Cid Corman puts it, and then
report back.

The poet is a writer who works with molten language, language that
comes directly from the core of consciousness, language which is mallea-
ble and at times seemingly dangerous in its heat. I believe that the narrative preoccupations and devices of the fiction writer usually mean a

slightly more distanced relationship to language. They even mean that some very good and compelling fiction writers can get away with taking language more or less for granted.

The poet has to achieve an immediate, compressed unit of perception and feeling and verbal expression. (Prose that aims for the same effect is usually called poetic prose.) The poet works as close as possible to the bone, the origin, the source-point of utterance, and her work constantly confronts her with the question: what is language? But to ask what language is, is also to wonder about silence. What is silence, and how does sound emerge from it, how does communication emerge?

In the beginning was not the sentence or the paragraph or the chapter. In the beginning was the word, and the word belongs first of all to poets. As a philosopher asks, "Why is there something at all, instead of nothing?" so a poet may come to ask, "Why are there sound and word and meaning and expression, when there might be only silence?"

Finally, the musical effects of poetry depend very much on the patterning of sound against the backdrop of silence.

So I think all of these things mean that in some way poets are particularly vulnerable in a noisy world, particularly dependent on the possibility of silence. Maybe available silence is to us the equivalent of a painter's available light.

Given that, what kind of atmosphere are we trying to produce poetry, read poetry, absorb poetry in? Do we have enough silence?

I don't minimize the importance of literal noise, something that in New York I'm constantly inundated with. But I'm also concerned with the metaphoric din of information and stimulus that North American culture bombards us with all the time.

Certainly this is an urban phenomenon, but I wonder whether it's not also a continent-wide phenomenon, and increasingly a global phenomenon. In terms of North America alone, it's amazing and frightening to contemplate the rapidity of change. Imagine, for instance, the pre-Columbian relationship between people and space, people and the natural environment; imagine the insignificance of people-made noise, sound, communication, against the enormous backdrop of plains and mountain forests. How drastically that balance has been skewed in just a few hundred years.

I think of Plath's phrase "the staticky noise of the new" in connection with this weight of social and technological change, and the fact that, especially in the United States, so much of the "new" consists of methods for further amplification, further dissemination of sound or information. The computer, photocopying technology, Walkman, VCR . . . we very rarely get out of range of some kind of technologically mediated verbal stimulus. And it's as though this stuff seems to have the same curse attached to it that most technology does: if it's available, it will be used sooner or later. It becomes too difficult to tune it out.

So it's gotten to the point where there's a phenomenon called "white noise" which is an attempt to fight noise with noise—in Adrienne Rich's words, "twisting the dials to drown the terror / beneath the unsaid word" ("Cartographies," 17).

I have a job that's the perfect example of this situation; I work in a tape transcription agency. And all afternoon I sit with headphones on and I listen to audio cassettes of TV interviews, conferences, medical presentations, training videos for stock brokers—a whole range of things. I type whatever I hear, and I have a sense of voices pouring through my head. And I sometimes wonder: can you erase all that chatter as simply as though it were a backup file? Or does it stay in there, and if so, what residual effect does it have over time?

After I get done with the tapes, I come home from work, I'm tired, I don't want anybody to bother me while I'm making dinner. So I turn on the all-news radio station to create some kind of space between me and the rest of the world. Fighting noise with noise.

I think there's an analogy in terms of the tremendous availability of poetry itself: good poetry and not-so-good poetry, domestic poetry and poetry in translation. Certainly I don't think anybody would want poetry to be less available. But at the same time, it's simply impossible to absorb all this in any kind of meaningful way.

And then I think the overload is further intensified for politically concerned and politically engaged people. I know I have the sense of a world flying apart at the seams, and sometimes absorbing as much information as possible about it feels like an effort to hold it all together—not that that makes any kind of logical sense, but it motivates behavior. So a lot of people simply become media junkies. They read the *New York Times* to see what the ruling class wants us to think, and they read a whole variety of alternative press sources, and have other methods of trying to keep pace with things. And there's a sense, I think, on the one hand of using our own words as stones to heap up to make a barricade against all of the threats that are coming at us; and on the other, the obligation, as it were, to respond to all the tortured voices that cry, "I am, I'm here, you can't make me disappear. This is where it hurts, pay attention to my pain."

And I think those things are all very real, on some level very legitimate impulses that can't simply be pushed away by anybody with a political conscience. The problem is that too often within political movements themselves the solution becomes a competitive attempt to raise our own noise level in order to get above *their* static.

And so politics becomes a very noisy business. The protest is noisy; the chants, the demonstrations are noisy. And the volume of information is sometimes overwhelming. Polemic and infighting generate noise of a different kind. And rhetoric I think of as the diametrical opposite of silence, total noise as it were, sound for sound's sake.

Too, I find myself wondering about the political implications of noise qua noise, quite apart from its content. What does the noise of the mainstream media block out? And I wonder about the politics of access to silence. Does silence become something that we buy by having the means and the money to, say, exit from the city for a certain length of time, or to live in a beautiful, secluded place?

It seems that, much as we've built armaments against which there can be no effective protection, so we've devised mechanisms of amplification against which our fragile societies are quite defenseless. And then the poet and the political person are left asking, "What gives me the right to remain silent?" Even occasional periods of stillness and withdrawal can feel like a luxury.

I realize I just said "we've" created these mechanisms, but I think there are real questions about the extent to which a woman can really wholeheartedly say that. So I wonder in what sense the noise that we live with can be considered manmade. And I'm not saying that I think women by nature are quiet. And I'm not saying that I think women are more virtuous than men. But it's true for us as it is for all oppressed and marginalized groups that on some level we live in a world we never made.

And so I wonder whether female experience might be considered one tool for the preservation and, if you will, the amplification of necessary silences. I feel this in Niedecker's work, that her poems express a relationship to silence that somehow is connected to her female being in the world. In the almost satirical passage I read earlier where she describes her correspondence with Clayton Eshelman, I think she implies that he indulges in a sort of phallic-aggressive noisemaking. So I wonder: was she, as a woman poet, perhaps somehow less threatened by silences, less impelled to test herself against them, or to deny what she calls "the great, everpresent possibility that our poems may not get read"?

One aspect of women's peculiar relationship to silence relates to the fact that we tend to be specifically embedded in a framework of social sound: for instance, in terms of our traditional relationship to children. I speak as someone who's spent the past 11-plus years raising a child who's now almost grown, and I know that a lot of the hardest work of that for me has had to do with being verbally available—which was often much more draining than the physical work.

I think there are a lot more questions that could be asked about cultural as well as gender-related variants in the kinds of relationships that human beings have to silence, or the kind of patterning they set up between silence and sound. I certainly don't necessarily assume that male-female differences in this regard would automatically be any greater than cross-cultural ones. Just as an obvious example, the prairie silence that seemed so sinister to the Norwegian immigrant woman obviously must have been familiar and natural to the Plains Indians.

The last thing I want to do here is to set up another hierarchy, to stand on its head the feminist dictum that silences were made to be broken, and say that silence is good and utterance is bad. Rather, I want to suggest that the life of poetry and the life of all people as well depends upon a balance between silence and language, reflection and communication; between the nothingness which is the ground of existence and being in all its aspects. And I think that silence—not the inauthentic silence of psychological repression or political repression, but the silence of nature, of night, of meditation, the silence in which the unconscious speaks in unforeseen language, Niedecker's "silence/which if intense/makes sound"—that this healing and authentic silence is in jeopardy.

When silence is no longer an option, it seems to me that words become meaningless. I don't believe we can ultimately survive in the meaningless environment that results from the destruction of a proper balance between silence and speech, any more than we can survive a radical dislocation of the balance between nature and technology. So I think the question for political poets is, how do we maintain our necessary silences? How do we arrange from time to time to "enter a silence," and yet not repudiate the world in which so much of what comes to our ears is the necessary noise of suffering?

As happens with Niedecker's work, I think poems can sometimes magically re-create an element of silence around them. But that's only if they are rooted in silence in the first place. Perhaps a whiff or a glimpse or a taste of silence, an insistence on the momentary suspension of noise that's merely noise, is one thing that poets might bring to the political environment. Across a broad spectrum of political movements, feminism included, the present moment seems to be a time for realizing how long and comprehensive and complicated the struggle for survival and freedom and justice is; not the freedom and justice that belong to any one group, or the survival of any one group, but really on a global level. With this new-found humility perhaps could come a rethinking of incessant, desperate, unreflective activity and the din that accompanies it. And then maybe we won't have to be afraid of or to scorn the fertile silences out of which new sounds, new voices, poems eternally emerge.

WORKS CITED

Alegría, Claribel. *Flowers from the Volcano*. Bilingual edition with preface and translations from the Spanish by Carolyn Forché. Pittsburgh: Univ. of Pittsburgh Press, 1982.

Anzaldúa, Gloria. *Borderlands/La Frontera*. San Francisco: Spinsters/Aunt Lute, 1987.

———. "Speaking in Tongues: A Letter to Third World Women Writers." *This Bridge Called My Back: Writings by Radical Women of Color*. Eds. Cherríe Moraga and Gloria Anzaldúa. Latham, NY: Kitchen Table: Women of Color Press, 1983.

Baldwin, James. "Everybody's Protest Novel." *Notes of a Native Son*. 1955. Boston: Beacon, 1984.

Broumas, Olga. "Artemis." *Beginning with O*. New Haven: Yale UP, 1977.

Bulkin, Elly, ed. *Lesbian Fiction: An Anthology*. New York: Gay Presses of New York, 1981.

Bulkin, Elly, and Joan Larkin, eds. *Lesbian Poetry: An Anthology*. New York: Gay Presses of New York, 1981.

Bulkin, Elly, Minnie Bruce Pratt, and Barbara Smith. *Yours in Struggle: Three Feminist Perspectives on Anti-Semitism and Racism*. Ithaca, NY: Firebrand Books, 1984.

Cliff, Michelle. *Abeng*. Freedom, CA: Crossing Press, 1984.

"The Combahee River Collective Statement." *Home Girls: A Black Feminist Anthology*. Ed. Barbara Smith. Latham, NY: Kitchen Table: Women of Color Press, 1983.

Cooper-Clark, Diana. *Interviews with Contemporary Novelists*. London: The Macmillan Press, Ltd., 1986.

Daly, Mary. Remarks transcribed in "The Transformation of Silence into Language and Action." *Sinister Wisdom* 6 (1978).

Dworkin, Andrea. *Right-Wing Women*. London: The Women's Press, 1983.

Evans, Sara. *Personal Politics: The Roots of Women's Liberation in the Civil Rights Movement and the New Left*. New York: Vintage, 1979.

Faranda, Lisa Pater, ed. *"Between Your House and Mine": The Letters of Lorine Niedecker to Cid Corman, 1960 to 1970*. Durham, NC: Duke UP, 1986.

Giamatti, A. Bartlett. *Exile and Change in Renaissance Literature.* New Haven: Yale UP, 1984.

Gilbert, Sandra M., and Susan Gubar, eds. *Shakespeare's Sisters: Feminist Essays on Women Poets.* Bloomington: Indiana UP, 1979.

Gordon, Rebecca. *Letters from Nicaragua.* San Francisco: Spinsters/Aunt Lute, 1986.

Grahn, Judy. "A Woman Is Talking to Death." *The Work of a Common Woman.* New York: St. Martin's, 1978.

————. *True to Life Adventure Stories.* Vol I. Oakland: Diana Press, 1978.

Griffin, Susan. "Breviary." *Lesbian Poetry: An Anthology.* Eds. Elly Bulkin and Joan Larkin. New York: Gay Presses of New York, 1981.

Hammonds, Evelynn. Interview. "Michelle Cliff Finds Her Own Voice." *Sojourner* (June 1981).

Hampl, Patricia. "Meridel LeSueur, Voice of the Prairie." *Ms.* (August 1975).

Hardy, Thomas. *Tess of the D'Urbervilles.* New York: New American Library/Signet.

Harjo, Joy. *She Had Some Horses.* New York: Thunder's Mouth Press, 1983.

Hughes, Langston. "As I Grew Older." *Black Voices.* Ed. Abraham Chapman. New York: Mentor/New American Library, 1968.

————. "Dream Variations." *Black Voices.*

Jordan, June. "For the Sake of a People's Poetry: Walt Whitman and the Rest of Us." *Passion.* Boston: Beacon, 1980.

————. "Gettin Down to Get Over." *Things That I Do in the Dark.* New York: Random House, 1977.

————. "Poem About My Rights." *Passion.* Boston: Beacon, 1980.

————. "Thinking About My Poetry." *Civil Wars.* Boston: Beacon, 1981.

Kaye, Melanie. "On Being a Lesbian-Feminist Artist." *We Speak in Code.* Pittsburgh: Motheroot Publications, 1980.

Leglorn, Lisa, and Katherine Parker. *Woman's Worth: Sexual Economics and the World of Women.* Boston: Routledge & Kegan Paul, 1981.

Lessing, Doris. *Canopus in Argos: Archives Re: Colonized Planet 5 Shikasta Personal, Psychological, Historical Documents Relating to Visit by Johor (George Sherban) Emissary (Grade 9) 87th of the Period of the Last Days.* New York: Alfred A. Knopf, 1979.

LeSueur, Meridel. *Harvest.* Cambridge: West End, 1977.

————. *Rites of Ancient Ripening.* Minneapolis, MN: Vanilla Press, 1975.

————. *Song for My Time.* Cambridge: West End, 1977.

————. *Women on the Breadlines.* Cambridge: West End, 1977.

Lorde, Audre. "A Litany for Survival." *The Black Unicorn.* New York: Norton, 1978.

_____. "Poetry Is Not a Luxury." *Ikon* Second Series 1 (1982).

_____. "School Note." *The Black Unicorn*. New York: Norton, 1978.

_____. "Who Said It Was Simple?" *Chosen Poems: Old and New*. New York: Norton, 1982.

_____. *Zami: A New Spelling of My Name*. Freedom, CA: Crossing Press, 1982.

Macdonald, Barbara. "The Power of the Old Woman." *New Women's Times Feminist Review* 26 (March/April 1983).

Mandelstam, Osip. "Fourth Prose." *The Complete Critical Prose and Letters*. Trans. Jane Gary Harris and Constance Link. Ann Arbor: Ardis, 1979.

_____. *Selected Poems*. Trans. David McDuff. New York: The Noonday Press, 1975.

McAllister, Pam, ed. *Reweaving the Web of Life: Feminism and Non-Violence*. Philadelphia: New Society, 1982.

McDaniel, Judith. Remarks transcribed in "The Transformation of Silence into Language and Action." *Sinister Wisdom* 6 (1978).

_____. *Sanctuary: A Journey*. Ithaca, NY: Firebrand Books, 1987.

Milosz, Czeslaw. *The Captive Mind*. New York: Vintage, 1981.

Moraga, Cherríe. *Giving Up the Ghost*. Los Angeles: West End Press, 1986.

_____. "A Long Line of Vendidas." *Loving in the War Years: lo que nunca pasó por sus labios*. Boston: South End Press, 1983.

Moraga, Cherríe, and Gloria Anzaldúa, eds. *This Bridge Called My Back: Writings by Radical Women of Color*. Foreword by Tony Cade Bambara. Latham, NY: Kitchen Table: Women of Color Press, 1983.

Moirai, Catherine Risingflame, and Merril Mushroom. "White Lies and Common Language: Notes for Lesbian Writers and Readers." *Common Lives/Lesbian Lives* 5 (1982).

Morejón, Nancy. *Where the Island Sleeps Like a Wing*. Bilingual edition with preface by Miguel Barnet and introduction by Kathleen Weaver, translated by Kathleen Weaver. San Francisco: Black Scholar, 1985.

Niedecker, Lorine. *Complete Works: From this Condensery*. Winston-Salem: The Jargon Society, 1985.

_____. *The Granite Pail*. Ed. Cid Corman. Berkeley: North Point Press, 1985.

Paley, Grace, *Leaning Forward*. Penobscot, ME: Granite Press, 1985.

Parks, Adrienne. "The Lesbian Feminist as Writer as Lesbian Feminist" *Margins* 23 (August 1975).

Ram, Kalpana, "Sexual Violence in India: A Critique of Some Feminist Writings on the Third World." *Bitches, Witches, & Dykes*. (New Zealand: May 1981).

Ramos, Juanita, ed. *Compañeras: Latina Lesbians*. New York: Latina Lesbian History Project.

Rich, Adrienne. "Cartographies of Silence." *The Dream of a Common Language*. New York: Norton, 1978.

———. "Natural Resources." *The Dream of a Common Language*.

———. "Phantasia for Elvira Shatayev." *The Dream of a Common Language*.

———. "Power." *The Dream of a Common Language*.

———. "Power and Danger: Works of a Common Woman." *On Lies, Secrets, and Silence*. New York: Norton, 1979.

———. "Transcendental Etude." *The Dream of a Common Language*.

———. "Vesuvius at Home: The Power of Emily Dickinson." *On Lies, Secrets, and Silence*.

———. "When We Dead Awaken: Writing as Re-Vision." *On Lies, Secrets, and Silence*.

Rölvaag, O. E. *Giants in the Earth*. New York: Harper & Row, Perennial Classic edition, undated. First Edition 1927.

Segrest, Mab. *My Mama's Dead Squirrel: Lesbian Essays on Southern Culture*. Ithaca, NY: Firebrand Books, 1986.

Sherman, Susan, "Amerika." *Lesbian Poetry: An Anthology*. Ed. Elly Bulkin. New York: Gay Presses of New York, 1981.

Smith, Barbara, ed. *Home Girls: A Black Feminist Anthology*. Latham, NY: Kitchen Table: Women of Color Press, 1983.

Téllez, Dora María. "La voz del Pueblo es la voz de las pintas." *Nicaráuac* VI 12 (April 1986).

Vance, Carole, ed. *Pleasure and Danger: Exploring Female Sexuality*. Boston: Routledge and Kegan Paul, 1984.

Walker, Alice. *The Color Purple*. Washington Square Press/Pocket Books, 1982.

Walker-Crawford, Vivian. Review of *Narratives* by Cheryl Clarke. *New Women's Times Feminist Review* 30 (November/December 1983).

Warnock, Donna. "Patriarchy Is a Killer: What People Concerned About Peace and Justice Should Know." *Reweaving the Web of Life: Feminism and Non-Violence*. Pam McAllister, ed. Philadelphia: New Society, 1982.

Winant, Fran. "Lesbians Publish Lesbians: My Life and Times with Violet Press." *Margins* 23 (August 1975).

Woodwoman, Libby. Interview. "Pat Parker Talks about Her Life and Her Work." *Margins* 23 (August 1975).

Woolf, Virginia. *A Room of One's Own*. New York: Harcourt, Brace, 1929, 1957.

Wright, Richard. "How 'Bigger' Was Born." *Native Son*. New York: Harper, Perennial Classics Edition, 1966.

Yeats, William Butler. "Leda and the Swan." *The Collected Poems of W. B. Yeats*. New York: MacMillan, Definitive Edition, 1956.

SMALL PRESS ADDRESSES

Because books published by small presses are frequently difficult or impossible to find in bookstores, I've compiled the following address list. Write directly to the presses for current price and ordering information.

- The Black Scholar Press, Box 7106, San Francisco, CA 94120
- The Crossing Press, P.O. Box 1048, Freedom, CA 95019
- Firebrand Books, 141 The Commons, Ithaca, NY 14850
- Gay Presses of New York, Box 294, New York, NY 10014
- Granite Press, Box 7, Penobscot, ME 04476
- Kitchen Table: Women of Color Press, Box 908, Latham, NY 12110
- Latina Lesbian History Project, LLHP c/o Latina Women's Educational Resources, Box 627, Peter Stuyvesant Station, New York, NY 10009
- New Society Publishers, 4527 Springfield Ave., Philadelphia, PA 19143
- North Point Press, 850 Talbot Avenue, Berkeley, CA 94706
- South End Press, 302 Columbus Ave., Boston, MA 02116
- Spinsters/Aunt Lute, P.O. Box 410687, San Francisco, CA 94141
- Thunder's Mouth Press, 93–99 Greene St., New York, NY 10012, Suite 2A
- West End Press, P.O. Box 27334, Albuquerque, NM 87125